Michael Augustine

Complete Bible history

From the creation of the world down to the death of the Apostles

Michael Augustine

Complete Bible history
From the creation of the world down to the death of the Apostles

ISBN/EAN: 9783741112386

Manufactured in Europe, USA, Canada, Australia, Japa

Cover: Foto ©Lupo / pixelio.de

Manufactured and distributed by brebook publishing software (www.brebook.com)

Michael Augustine

Complete Bible history

THE NATIVITY.—(Frontispiece.)

COMPLETE BIBLE HISTORY

FROM

THE CREATION OF THE WORLD

DOWN TO

THE DEATH OF THE APOSTLES.

PREPARED FOR THE USE OF PUPILS IN CATHOLIC
SCHOOLS AND COLLEGES.

BY THE
AUTHOR OF "SHORT SCRIPTURE HISTORY."

*CONTAINING THREE COLORED MAPS, AND
NUMEROUS ILLUSTRATIONS.*

NEW YORK:
D. & J. SADLIER & CO.
73 MURRAY STREET.

IMPRIMATUR:

✠ MICHAEL AUGUSTINE,
Archbishop of New York.

CONTENTS.

Part I.

HISTORY OF THE OLD TESTAMENT.

I.—Era of Creation.

CHAPTER	PAGE
I.—The Creation of the World and of Man	1
II.—The Fall of Man	4
III.—Cain and Abel	7

II.—Era of the Deluge.

I.—Noe Saved From the Deluge	11
II.—The Tower of Babel	16

III.—Era of the Patriarchs.

I.—The Call of Abraham	23
II.—Abraham and Isaac	28
III.—Jacob and Esau	32
IV.—Jacob	36
V.—Joseph	38
VI.—The Meeting of Joseph and his Brethren	43
VII.—The Family of Jacob enter Egypt	48

IV.—Era of the Written Law and the Tabernacle.

I.—Egypt	54
II.—Moses	56
III.—The Ten Plagues of Egypt	60
IV.—The Exodus of Israel	62
V.—The Giving of the Law on Mount Sinai	64
VI.—Israel Becomes the Church of God	68
VII.—The Institution of the Priesthood and the Great Hebrew Feasts	73
VIII.—The Spies—Revolt of Core, Dathan, and Abiron	76

CONTENTS.

CHAPTER	PAGE
X.—Israel Enters the Promised Land	83
XI.—Israel Under the Judges—Barac—Gedeon—Jepthe	85
XII.—The Judges of Israel—Samson—The Story of Ruth.	91
XIII.—Israel Under the Judges—Heli—Samuel	93
XIV.—Israel Under the Kings—Saul	97
XV.—Persecution of David by Saul	100
XVI.—The Reign of David	103
XVII.—The Revolt of Absalom	106

V.—ERA OF THE TEMPLE AND THE PROPHETS.

I.—The Reign of Solomon	112
II.—The Reign of Solomon—(Concluded)	116
III.—Division of the Kingdom of Israel	121
IV.—The Kingdom of Israel—(Continued)	124
V.—The Kingdom of Israel—(Continued)	129
VI.—The Kingdom of Israel—(Continued)	132
VII.—End of the Kingdom of Israel—The Samaritans	135
VIII.—The Story of Tobias	137
IX.—The Kingdom of Juda	142
X.—The Kingdom of Juda—(Continued)	145
XI.—The Kingdom of Juda—(Continued)—Judith	149
XII.—The Prophet Jeremias—Fall of the Kingdom of Juda	154
XIII.—The Jews in Captivity—Ezekiel—Daniel—The Story of Susanna	157
XIV.—Daniel Interprets Nebuchadnezzar's Dream—The God Bel—The Three Young Men in the Fiery Furnace	161
XV.—Capture of Babylon by Cyrus	164
XVI.—Daniel Cast into the Lions' Den—His Prophecies of the Messiah—Return of the Jews to Jerusalem	167
XVII.—Queen Esther	172
XVIII.—Esdras, "The Second Moses"—Nehemias—The Greek Empire Succeeds the Persian	176
XIX.—Evil Influence of Greek Literature and Customs on the Jews—Their Persecution by Antiochus, King of Syria	181
XX.—The Asmoneans—Mathathias—Judas Maccabeus	184
XXI.—Asmonean Priest-Princes	188
XXII.—The Reign of Herod—Last Days Before Christ	192

PART II.

HISTORY OF THE NEW TESTAMENT.

I.—BIRTH AND CHILDHOOD OF JESUS CHRIST.

I.—Annunciation of the Birth of John the Baptist	196
II.—Annunciation of the Birth of Our Lord Jesus Christ	198
III.—Birth of John the Baptist	202

CONTENTS.

CHAPTER	PAGE
IV.—Birth of Our Lord Jesus Christ	203
V.—Adoration of Our Divine Lord by the Magi	207
VI.—Return of the Holy Family to Judea—Jesus in the Temple	212

II.—PUBLIC LIFE OF OUR LORD JESUS CHRIST.

I.—Mission of John the Baptist, the Precursor of Christ	216
II.—Our Lord is Baptized by John the Baptist—Is Tempted by the Devil	220
III.—The First Disciples of Our Lord	223
IV.—The Marriage Feast of Cana—Our Lord Fixes His Dwelling at Capharnaum	227
V.—Our Lord Drives the Hucksters From the Temple—Nicodemus	230
VI.—Imprisonment of John the Baptist—Our Lord and the Samaritan Woman	234
VII.—Our Lord Heals the Nobleman's Son—Preaches in the Synagogue at Nazareth, and is Driven Out—A Sabbath Day at Capharnaum	238
VIII.—The Miraculous Draught of Fishes—The Healing of the Leper—Our Lord goes up to Jerusalem for the Second Pasch—Heals the Paralytic—Declares His Divinity to the Pharisees	242
IX.—Christ Chooses His Apostles—The Sermon on the Mount	248
X.—Christ Heals the Roman Centurion's Servant—Restores the Widow of Naim's Son to Life—Answers John the Baptist's Messengers—Forgives the Sins of Mary Magdalen	255
XI.—Our Lord Restores the Deaf and Dumb Man—Relates the Parables of the Sower and the Cockle	261
XII.—Christ Stills the Storm—Heals the Possessed Man—Attends Matthew's Banquet—Restores to Life the Daughter of Jairus	264
XIII.—The Mission of the Apostles—Martyrdom of John the Baptist—Miracle of the Loaves and Fishes—Christ Walks on the Waters	269
XIV.—Christ Reveals the Mystery of the Eucharist—Heals the Woman of Chanaan's Daughter—Peter Proclaims the Divinity of Christ	274
XV.—Our Lord is Transfigured on Mount Tabor—Pays the Tax by a Miracle—Blesses Little Children—Parable of the Unforgiving Servant	278
XVI.—Our Lord Goes up to Jerusalem—Repulses the Scribe—Calls the Young Man From the House of Mourning—The Sanhedrin Send Guards to Seize Him—Nicodemus Defends Him—Christ Restores Sight to the Man Born Blind	282
XVII.—Our Lord Sends the Seventy-two Disciples—Parable of the Good Samaritan—Mary and Martha	285
XVIII.—Our Lord Teaches His Disciples to Pray—Declares Mary Blessed—Parables of the Foolish Rich Man, and the Barren Fig Tree—Christ Declares His Divinity	289
XIX.—Our Lord Raises Lazarus from the Dead	293
XX.—Christ's Teaching in Regard to Divorce	296
XXI.—Our Lord Calls Zaccheus—Banquet at Bethany, at which Mary Magdalen Anoints Him	300

III.—HOLY WEEK.

I.—Palm Sunday—Our Lord Enters Jerusalem in Triumph	303
II.—The Last Day in the Ministry of Jesus	306
III.—Our Lord Foretells the Destruction of Jerusalem, and of the World	309
IV.—The Last Supper	313

CONTENTS.

CHAPTER	PAGE
V.—The Passion of Our Divine Lord—The Agony in the Garden	319
VI.—The Passion of Our Divine Lord—The Via Dolorosa	323
VII.—The Passion of Our Lord—The Via Dolorosa—(Continued)	327
VIII.—The Passion of Our Lord—The Via Dolorosa—(Concluded)	331

IV.—OUR LORD'S FORTY DAYS' SOJOURN ON EARTH.

I.—Resurrection of Our Divine Lord 339
II.—Our Lord Appears to His Apostles—Institutes the Sacrament of Penance—Makes Peter the Head of His Church—The Ascension 342

V.—ACTS OF THE APOSTLES.

I.—Election of Matthias—Descent of the Holy Ghost—The Apostles Preach the Gospel—Ananias and Saphira 347
II.—The Sanhedrin Arrests the Apostles—The Rabbi Gamaliel's Counsel to the Sanhedrin—St. Stephen, the First Martyr—Philip Baptizes the Officer of Queen Candace—Conversion of Saul 350
III.—St. Peter Cures the Sick Man—Restores Tabitha to Life—Vision of the Upright Pagan, Cornelius—Vision of Peter, Enjoining Him to Preach the Gospel to the Gentiles—Imprisonment and Miraculous Deliverance of Peter—Punishment of Herod 355
IV.—First Mission of St. Paul (A. D. 45 to A. D. 48) 358
V.—Second Mission of St. Paul—Third Mission of St. Paul (A. D. 51 to 54) ... 361
VI.—The Other Apostles 365

PART FIRST.

HISTORY OF THE OLD TESTAMENT.

I.—ERA OF CREATION.

(FROM THE BEGINNING OF TIME TO B. C. 2524.)

CHAPTER I.

CREATION OF THE WORLD AND OF MAN.

1. IN the beginning of time, God created the heavens and the earth. At first the earth was a mere shapeless mass o matter, hanging motionless in space, and surrounded with deep darkness. But during six days, God continued His creative work, until He made it the fair and fruitful earth which we behold.

2. These days, however, were not like our days, for as yet there was no way of measuring time. They were long ages or epochs, comprising thousands of years, during which God prepared the world to be the home of man.

3. The first day, God said, "Let there be light," and there was light. God then called the light, day, and the darkness, night.

4. The second day, God said, "Let there be the firmament." And it was so. The beautiful blue sky arched over the earth, and a part of the waters were changed into clouds, and went up

---

1. How did the earth appear when first created? 2. Were these days of which Scripture speaks, like our day? 3. What did God create the first day? 4. The second?

to their place in the sky, to descend again in the form of rain, dew, frost, hail and snow.

5. The third day, God said, "Let the waters that cover the earth be gathered together in one place, and let the dry land appear."

6. And it was so. The land and the sea were divided; mountains and hills rose up with their valleys; fountains, brooks, and rivers freshened the dry land, and poured themselves into the sea.

7. The fourth day, God said, "Let the earth bring forth grass and herbs, and trees bearing fruit." And it was so. The earth grew green as in spring-time with grass and herbs, and thousands of trees and flowers put forth bright blossoms.

8. On the fifth day, God said, "Let there be lights in the heavens, that they may divide the days and the years, and give light to the earth."

9. And it was so. The golden sun rose to give its light to the day, and the silvery moon shed its soft beams on the night; the countless stars also began to give forth their light.

10. On the sixth day, God said, "Let the water bring forth fish, and the air winged fowl, and the earth living creatures of all kinds."

11. And at once all these came into being. Fishes, great and small, swam in the water, all kinds of birds filled the air, woods and fields were alive with wild beasts and cattle; the grass, flowers and bushes were filled with gay butterflies, bees and other insects.

12. The lovely, blooming earth was now completed, but there was as yet no human eye to delight in its beauty, no human voice to praise its Creator. So God said, "Let us make man in our image and likeness; he shall have dominion over the fishes of the sea, the birds of the air, the beasts of the field, and over the whole earth."

---

5. The third day? 6. Was it so? 7. What did God do on the fourth day? 8. On the fifth? 9. Was it so? 10. What did God do on the sixth day? 11. What followed? 12. Whom did God now resolve to create?

WORK OF THE FIRST DAY.

13. Almighty God then made man out of soft, moist earth, and breathed into him the breath of life. Thus man became a living soul. And God called him Adam, which means, in Hebrew, *man taken from the earth.*

14. And God saw that all which He had made was very good. So on the seventh day He rested from his work, and thus set apart a day for man to devote to the worship of his Maker, and to holy rest from his labor.

CHAPTER II.

THE FALL OF MAN.

1. GOD placed Adam in a lovely garden, called Eden. It was planted with noble trees, which bore the sweetest blossoms and fruits; flowers of every kind and hue filled it with beauty and fragrance, while from a crystal spring that gushed forth in its depths, four rivers flowed in different directions, and kept its verdure green and bright.

2. In the centre of Eden, there were two trees. One was called the TREE OF LIFE; the other the TREE OF KNOWLEDGE. Of this TREE OF KNOWLEDGE, Adam was forbidden to eat under penalty of death, but of all the others he might eat freely.

3. God now made all the animals which He had created pass before Adam, and he gave them their names. But among them all, the first man saw none like himself, who could be a companion to him.

4. And his Creator, seeing this need of Adam's soul, said: "It is not good for man to be alone; let us make him a helpmate like unto himself." And casting Adam into a deep sleep, He took one of his ribs and formed it into a woman.

---

13. Out of what did God form man? 14. To what did God devote the seventh day?
1. Where did God place Adam? 2. What was in the centre of Eden?
3. What did God now do? 4. How did God supply this need?

5. When Adam awoke and beheld his beautiful companion, he was filled with joy, and exclaiming, "This is bone of my bone, and flesh of my flesh," he called her Eve, which means, *the mother of all the living.*

6. It was on the sixth day of the primeval week that God created man, and on the sixth day of the most momentous week in the history of the world—Good Friday—He re-created him by redeeming him.

7. And even as Eve, the mother of man, was formed from the rib taken from Adam's side, so the Church, man's spiritual mother, sprang from the blood of the Sacred Heart of Jesus Christ pierced on the cross.

8. Adam and Eve dwelt in a state of blissful innocence in the lovely vales of Eden. They had no care for their subsistence, for the fair, new, blessed earth gave forth its produce without toil. Mind and body were in full perfection; neither sorrow nor passion troubled the one; the other knew neither pain nor sickness.

9. The angels were their companions; even God Himself deigned to come and converse with them. Thus, filled with pure knowledge and heavenly delights, their days passed in tranquil happiness, upon which death cast no shadow.

10. Before God had created man, He had created another species of beings called angels, with whom He peopled heaven. Many of these rebelled against Him, and God cast them from heaven into hell. The chief of these, Satan, envying the happiness of our first parents, determined to destroy it by inducing them to break the command of God.

11. The better to effect his purpose, he assumed the form of a serpent, and twined himself about the branches of the Tree of Knowledge, and when Eve drew near it, said to her, "Why hath God commanded you that you should not eat of every tree in Paradise?"

---

5. What did Adam do when he awoke? 6. What makes the sixth day remarkable? 7. Continue the analogy. 8. Describe life in Eden. 9. What other joys did they know? 10. Whom had God created before Adam? 11. What did he do in order to effect his purpose?

12. Eve answered, "We are allowed to eat of the fruit of the trees in the garden; only of the fruit of this tree we are forbidden to eat lest we die."

13. "No," replied the serpent, "you will not die, if you eat of the fruit of this tree. But rather your eyes shall be opened and you shall be as gods, knowing good and evil."

14. On hearing this, Eve hesitated, and looked at the fruit, which seemed to her very fair to look upon, and very good to eat. And as she gazed, the command of God not to eat it went out of her mind, and at last she plucked some and began to eat it. She then carried some to Adam, who also ate of it.

15. But no sooner was this, the first sin, committed, than the eyes of our unhappy first parents were opened, and the fact that they were naked, which had not troubled them in their innocence, now filled them with shame.

16. In their confusion they tried to make coverings for themselves out of the leaves of the fig tree. "But in the cool air of the evening they heard the voice of the Lord God walking in paradise." Instead of running to meet Him as before, however, they hid themselves in the trees.

17. But soon they heard the voice of God calling, "Adam, where art thou?" Trembling, Adam went to Him and said, "I heard Thy voice in the garden, and I was afraid, because I was naked, and I hid myself." And God said, "Who told thee thou wast naked? Hast thou eaten of the forbidden fruit?" And Adam answered, "The woman whom Thou gavest me to be my companion gave me of the fruit and I did eat."

18. Then God said to Eve, "Why hast thou done this?" She replied, "The serpent deceived me, and I did eat." So God called the serpent before Him and said, "Because thou hast done this thing thou art cursed above all the beasts of the earth. Upon thy breast thou shalt go, and dust shalt

---

12. What did Eve answer? 13. State the serpent's reply. 14. What effect had his words? 15. What was the consequence of their sin? 16. What did they do? 17. What did they hear? 18. What did God say to Eve?

thou eat all the days of thy life. Of the daughters of Eve, one shall crush thy head, and thou shalt lie in wait for her heel."

19. Then turning to Eve, God said, "In sorrow and pain shalt thou bring forth thy children. Thou shalt be subject to thy husband, and he shall have power over thee."

20. To Adam God said, "Because thou hast listened to the voice of thy wife, and hast eaten of the tree of which I commanded thee not to eat, cursed is the earth for thy sake; with toil shalt thou eat of its fruits all the days of thy life.

21. "Thorns and thistles shall be its produce: and in the sweat of thy brow shalt thou eat bread, until thou dost return to the earth, out of which thou wast made; for dust thou art, and into dust shalt thou return."

22. God then gave Adam and Eve garments of skin to clothe themselves, and sent them out of paradise, at whose entrance he placed an angel with a flaming sword turning every way, to guard the entrance and keep the tree of life.

CHAPTER III.

CAIN AND ABEL.

1. LONELY and wretched, our unhappy first parents turned away from Eden, to take up the burden of life in a world which had been cursed for their sin. Only one hope dwelt with them to lighten their pain—the blessed promise of a Redeemer who should one day undo their fearful work, and triumph over Satan.

2. Almighty God, too, continued His mercy to Adam and Eve. As a comfort amidst their toil He taught them to sanctify the seventh day by resting from their labors, and

---

19. What punishment did He inflict on Eve? 20. What punishment did God inflict upon Adam? 21. Continue. 22. What did God then do?
1. What lightened Adam and Eve's lot? 2. Did Almighty God turn

by offering to Him some part of the produce of the earth or of the increase of their flocks.

3. God had a twofold motive in this. He wished firstly that Adam should make acknowledgment of the fact that all he won from the earth by his labor was the gift of God. Secondly, He desired that these sacrifices should serve as a token that in time the Blood of Jesus Christ, the Son of God, should be shed for the sins of all the guilty children of Adam.

4. Adam and Eve had many children, the first two of whom were Cain and Abel. Cain, who was a tiller of the soil, was filled with a proud and bad spirit; but Abel, who was a shepherd, was just, and found favor in the eyes of God.

5. On the Sabbath Day, both Cain and Abel prepared sacrifices. Cain offered the fruits of the earth, and Abel a spotless lamb. God accepted the sacrifice of Abel, but rejected that of Cain, who consequently grew so jealous of Abel that he resolved to kill him.

6. Soon after, having induced Abel to walk with him in the fields, he slew him. Hardly had his crime been committed, when Almighty God called him, and said, "Where is thy brother?" Cain answered, "I know not," and then added with awful insolence, " Am I my brother's keeper?"

7. The Almighty replied, "What hast thou done?" And then He cursed the impenitent murderer, declaring that he should be a fugitive and a vagabond on the face of the earth.

8. On hearing this terrible doom, Cain was seized with terror and despair, and cried out that his crime was too great for pardon, and that, when cast out by Almighty God, whoever found him would kill him. But God, merciful even to this most guilty creature, assured him that such should not be his fate. And He set a mark on him, accordingly, that whosoever found him should not kill him.

9. And so Cain departed from his kindred and went to the

---

3. Why did God exact this? 4. Who were Adam and Eve's first children? 5. What happened to their sacrifices? 6. Did he do so? 7. What did God answer? 8. What effect had this on Cain? 9. Whither did Cain go?

THE DEATH OF ABEL.

east of Eden, where he built a city, which he called Henoch (hē'nock) after his son. He was the founder of a numerous race, noted for their gigantic stature, as well as for their wickedness.

10. Eve mourned long and bitterly for her son Abel, and at last, in order to console her, God sent her another son, Sĕth. He became a just man, and founded a pious race who were known as the children of God, to distinguish them from the wicked descendants of Cain, who were called the children of men.

Eve weeping over the dead Abel is a type of the Blessed Virgin, weeping over the dead body of her Divine Son, when taken down from the cross. Abel, the just, murdered by his brother, through jealousy, is a type of Our Lord, crucified by the chief priests and people of his own nation, from the same kind of hatred. Cain, an outcast, with the stain of his brother's blood upon him, is a type of the fugitive Jews, who, after the destruction of their city, were scattered throughout all nations.

---

10. How did God console Eve for the death of Abel ?

II.—ERA OF THE DELUGE.

(B. C. 2524—B. C. 2107.)

CHAPTER I.

NOE SAVED FROM THE DELUGE.

Mount Ar'-a-rat is a mountain situated in Armenia, in the W. of Asia between the Black and Caspian Seas, near the spot where the Garden of Eden is supposed to have been situated. It is 17,200 feet high.

1. ADAM lived to be 930 years of age. At the time of his death, the world was well peopled, and as our Saviour has told us, not particularly different from what it is now. There were numbers of famous men who made it ring with their names, while the ordinary mass of mankind were busy planting their vineyards, building their houses, plying their trades, and attending to their family affairs.

2. The race of Cain enjoyed great material prosperity. They built many strong, walled cities, set boundaries about land, and invented weights and measures. One of his descendants, Jū'bal, was the father of harpers and organists, Tu'bal, of warriors, and Tu'balcain, of smiths and artificers.

3. For many generations, the children of Seth and the other children of Adam, held no intercourse with the wicked and infidel race of Cain, who in their turn, entertained the same scorn and contempt for those who believed in God, as the same kind of people do in the present day.

4. But as time went on, the children of God lost their fer-

---

1. Describe mankind before the flood. 2. What attended the race of

vor, began to mingle with the unbelievers, and finally to intermarry with them. Thus, they gradually lost their knowledge of the true God, and fell with them into idolatry.

5. At first, the glory of the sun, the pale beauty of the moon, and the steady lustre of the stars, made them take these objects for gods. But as they fell deeper into wickedness, they set up idols of brass and clay, and bowed down before them in adoration.

6. Amidst this corruption of the human race, only one man kept his faith in God, and brought up his family according to the sacred traditions of his forefathers. This was Noe (No'-ah), and God now resolved to destroy all mankind, save this just man and his family, in order that the earth might be re-peopled by his virtuous race.

7. God, therefore, told Noe that if in one hundred and twenty years men did not repent, He would destroy them by a deluge, and commanded him to build an ark in which he and his family might find refuge.

8. Thus adjured, Noe at once commenced the work of building the ark. It was a great ship, three hundred cubits (about 450 feet) in length, fifty cubits wide, and thirty cubits high. It was built of cedar wood, covered within and without with pitch, in order to make it water tight, and was three stories in height, with a window in the top, and a door in the side.

9. The allotted period of one hundred and twenty years went by, while the ark was taking shape under Noe's busy hands, and his warning voice uttered awful prophecies of the divine wrath, and urged repentance on the people. But, as Holy Scripture tells us, men went on eating, and drinking, and marrying and giving in marriage, and paid no heed; save, no doubt, to utter many a scoff and sneer at the folly of building a ship far from any water.

10. At last the ark was finished, and God said to Noe, "Go

---

5. To what objects did they pay divine worship? 6. Were all unfaithful to God? 7. What did God tell Noe? 8. Did Noe obey? 9. Did men repent? 10. What did God command Noe, when the ark was finished?

NOE ENTERS THE ARK.

in, thou and all thy house into the ark, for thee I have seen just before me in this generation. For yet awhile, after seven days, I will rain upon the earth forty days and forty nights; and I will destroy every substance that I have made from the face of the earth."

11. Noe and his family obeyed; and then God caused to enter also, seven and seven, male and female, of all clean beasts and fowls of the air; and of all unclean beasts, two and two, male and female. Seven days were employed in doing this, after which, God closed the door of the ark.

12. Then in the six hundredth year of the life of Noe (B.C. 2524) all the fountains of the great deep were broken up, the flood-gates of heaven were opened, and the rain fell for forty days and forty nights. Gradually, the green earth with its great mass of guilty, terrified, human beings, disappeared from view, until at length the tops of the highest mountains were fifteen cubits beneath the flood.

13. Whether or not the deluge covered the whole earth is not positively known. As God's only object was to destroy mankind, He may not have permitted it to extend to those parts of the world which were yet unpeopled. All we do know is that every human being on the earth perished, save those within the ark.

14. As the flood rose, the ark rose with it, and floated securely on its raging waters. After the rain had ceased, the flood remained at its full for one hundred and fifty days. Then God sent a strong wind which caused it to abate so rapidly that in the seventh month of the Deluge the Ark rested on Mount Ararat. Forty days after this, Noe sent forth a raven which did not return. He then sent forth a dove, which finding no place to rest returned to the Ark.

15. Seven more days went by and then Noe sent forth a dove again. In the evening it returned to him bearing a green olive

---

11. What else did God cause to enter? 12. Describe the flood. 13. Did the deluge cover the whole world? 14. What happened to the ark? 14. What birds did Noe send forth? 15. How did he find that the waters had subsided?

branch in its mouth. After some time had passed, Noe sent out the dove the third time. It did not return, so he understood that the waters had entirely subsided.

16. It was not until he had been a year in the ark, that Noe received God's command to come forth. His first act, on doing so, was to build an altar, on which he sacrificed all the clean animals and fowls that had been saved, in witness of God's sovereignty over all things, and in gratitude for his preservation.

17. God accepted the holy man's offering, and blessed him and his family, saying, "Increase and multiply, and fill the earth." He also promised never more to destroy the earth by water, saying, "Henceforward, seed-time and harvest, cold and heat, summer and winter, night and day, shall no more cease." And in confirmation of His words, He set the rainbow in the clouds that it might serve to all future ages as a memorial of His solemn promise.

18. Before the deluge, man had lived on fruit and vegetables, but God now confirmed his dominion over the creatures of the earth, and gave him permission to use them as food. At the same time He decreed that human life should be held sacred, and pronounced the doom of the murderer in the following awful words: "Whosoever shall shed man's blood, his blood shall be shed, for man was made in the image of God."

19. Noe began his new life as a husbandman. He and his three sons, Sĕm, Cham (kăm) and Japheth (jā'-fĕth), tilled the ground, and planted a vineyard. When the time of the vintage came, Noe drank freely of the wine, not knowing its power, and becoming intoxicated, fell asleep, uncovered, in his tent.

20. His son Cham was the first to behold him thus, but instead of covering him he ran off to his brothers, and jested of it. But Sem and Japheth, filled with reverence for their father in his humiliation, took a cloak and going backwards towards him where he lay, covered him with it.

21. When Noe awoke, and heard what had taken place, he

---

16. When did God permit him to come forth? 17. Did God accept it? 18. What did God decree? 19. How did Noe begin his new life? 20. Relate the conduct of his three sons. 21. What did Noe do on awaking?

cursed Cham in the person of his son Chanaan (kā'năn) who, it is thought, had shared in his father's sin, declaring that he should be the servant of servants to his brethren. In the general slavery of the African race we see Noe's curse fulfilled.

22. But Sem and Japheth he blessed. Filled with the spirit of God, he announced that from the race of Sem should spring the Redeemer, saying "Blessed be the Lord God of Sem, be Chanaan his servant."

23. To Japheth he said, "May God enlarge Japheth and may he dwell in the tents of Sem." This meant that the children of Japheth were to be blessed in listening to the heavenly doctrine which was to come into the world through the family of Sem.

In the saving of Noe and his family in the ark, we have a type of the Sacrament of Baptism: the deluge is a type of the General Judgment. The story of Noe is a foreshadowing of the Passion of our Lord. The vine which he had himself planted gave him only the cup of affliction. This humiliation and weakness roused the scorn of unbelievers, but only deepened the reverence of those who truly loved him.

CHAPTER II.

THE TOWER OF BABEL

Mes-o-po-ta-mi-a, is from 600 to 700 miles in length and lies between the Tigris and Euphrates rivers. It is now part of the Turkish Empire, whose seat of government is at Constantinople. Ti'-gris river is 1,150 miles long, rises in the eastern part of Asiatic Turkey, and flows S. E. into the Euphrates river.

Eu-phrates (u-fra'tez) river 1,780 miles long, rises in the N. E. of Asiatic Turkey, and flows into the Persian gulf.

1. As time went on the descendants of Noe grew very numerous, and at length many families were forced to move forward from the Highlands of Armenia, in the neighborhood of Ararat, into the Great Plain of Shi'nar, that is the southern part of Mesopotamia.

---

22. How did he reward his other sons? 23. What did he say to Japheth?
1. Whither did Noe's descendants move?

THE TOWER OF BABEL.

2. In this extremely fertile land, they prospered greatly, but soon forgot God's mercy in having saved their ancestors from the deluge, and fell into wickedness. At length they grew so numerous again that a number of families or tribes determined to seek homes in lands yet unpeopled.

3. Such a plan was easily carried into effect at that time, because kingdoms did not exist. The people lived more like the existing Tartar or Mongol tribes of northern Asia, than like any nation on the earth to-day. Each family or tribe was governed by patriarchs or old men. Wealth consisted of vast flocks and herds and it was the difficulty of finding sufficient pasture for these that led to the removal of certain tribes.

4. Before separating, however, they began to build a city and a tower which should reach even to heaven. The city was intended as a monument of their greatness; the tower was to serve as a place of refuge in case of another deluge.

5. Their pride and impious distrust of God's solemn promise to Noe, to never destroy the earth again by water, met with speedy punishment. Up to this time all mankind had spoken only one and the same language. But now even as they were toiling at their colossal work, God confounded their speech, so that each workman began to speak in a language that his neighbor could not understand.

6. The dreadful confusion which followed, put a stop to the work. The ruins of the tower which was named Babel, which means confusion, remain to this day, a memorial of human pride and folly, while its builders were scattered abroad on the face of the earth, never to meet again.

7. Thus divided by space, as well as by language, each tribe carried away into its new settlement the clear knowledge of a Supreme Being and the remembrance of a Deluge, great truths which in some form or other, however distorted, have been preserved in the traditions of all races, no matter to what depths of ignorance and superstition they may have sunk.

---

2. How did they prosper? 3. What aided such a plan? 4. What great project did they conceive? 5. Did they carry it out? 6. What ensued? 7. What did each tribe possess?

8. At the time of this great dispersion of the human family, the race of Sem—called from him the Se-mit'-ic race—remained in Asia. One of his sons, As'-sur, settled on the banks of the Tigris, and founded the kingdom of Assyria, whose capital was Nin-i-veh.

9. Another of Sem's sons, named E'-lam, settled eastward of the Tigris on the Persian Gulf, and founded a kingdom whose capital was Sü'sa. Another branch established itself in a fertile district on the western coast of Asia, and became the Phœnician (fe-nish'-an) nation, the greatest mercantile people of antiquity. From the Semitic race, also sprang the Israelites.

10. The family of Japheth, which is also called the Ar'-y-an race, because it first dwelt in the vast districts of Ar-i-an'-a in Asia, is divided into two great branches; the eastern and the western, which together are thought to comprise more than one half of the human race.

11. From the eastern branch sprang the Hindu races of India, and the Medes and the Pérsians, who conquered the Semitic people of E'-lam, and developed the great empires of Media and Persia. The western branch peopled Europe, and from it sprang the Grecian, Celtic, Italian, Teutonic, and Slavonic nations.

12. The race of Japheth was the last to attain greatness. It was not until the greatness of the descendants of his brethren had passed, that many of the western branches began to emerge from obscurity. On the other hand, they developed a civilization far superior to any ever known in the East, and for centuries have occupied the foremost place in history.

13. The family of Cham settled principally in Africa. One of his sons Mesraim (mes'-ra-im) founded Egypt, one of the great kingdoms of antiquity. Some branches of it, however, remained in Asia. Nimrod, the grandson of Cham, through his son Cush (kŭsh), founded a kingdom on the Euphrates (u-

---

8. Where did the race of Sem remain? 9. Name some of the principal nations descended from Sem. 10. What is the race of Japheth called? 11. Name the principal descendants of the eastern branch of the Aryan race. 12. What of the race of Japheth? 13. Where did the family of Cham settle?

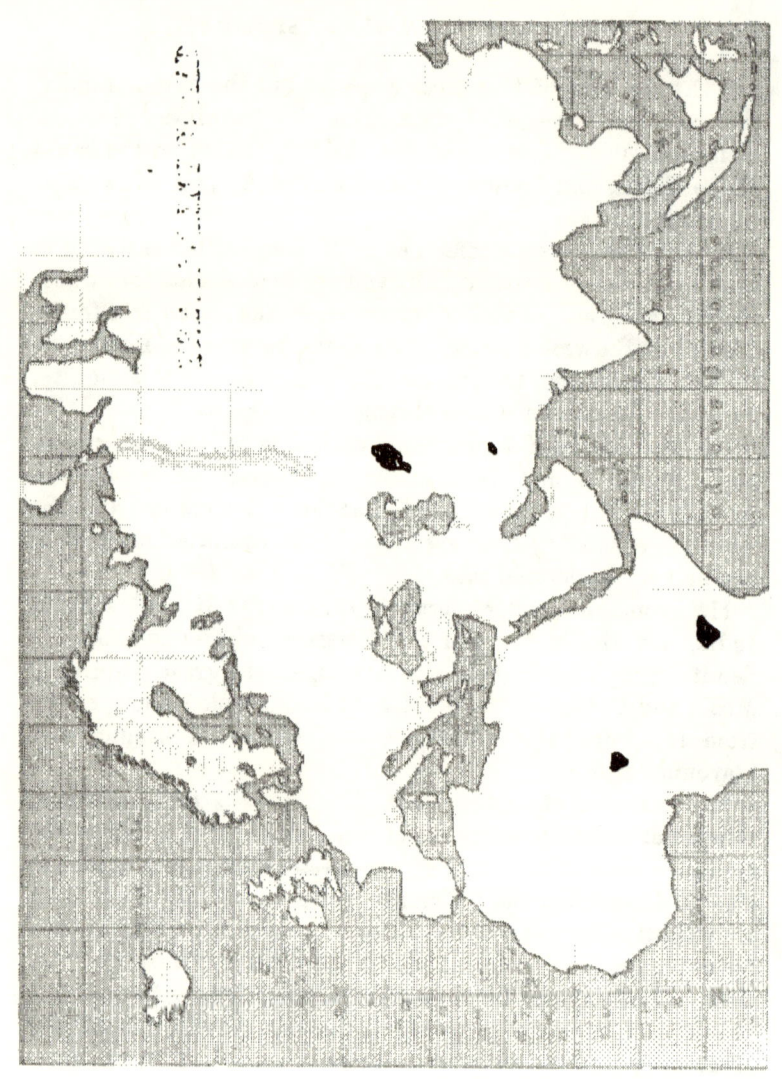

frā'-tez) river in Lower Mesopotamia which was known as Chaldea (kal-de'-a) or Babylonia.

14. Under Nimrod and his successors primeval civilization developed rapidly in this fertile plain of Shinar, which was covered with forests of the date palm—that wonderful tree which furnished the people with bread, wine, honey, porridge, vinegar and ropes—and where wheat, barley, and many kinds of shelled fruit grew wild.

15. This once famed region is now a wilderness, covered thickly with huge mounds. During the present century these were excavated, with the result of bringing to light the ruins of great cities, with gorgeous palaces, stately temples, magnificent public buildings, and splendid statues and monuments bearing inscriptions in curious wedge-shaped characters which no man living could read.

15. When, after patient endeavor, men learned how to decipher the inscriptions on these unearthed monuments of the once great Chaldean empire, they learned that its records extended back beyond that of Egypt, which, up to that time, was thought to be historically, the oldest country in the world.

16. From these records we learn that at some unknown period, a branch of the descendants of Sem conquered Babylonia. This conquest may have been but the peaceable yielding of the inferior race of Cham to the superior Semitic race, but, at all events, it was a lasting one.

17. Under the Semitic rule, Babylonian civilization reached its highest point. The flat land was intersected by fine roads, and drained by a system of canals. Vast buildings erected of bricks, cemented with bitumen instead of lime, and on which buttresses, columns, and arched drains appear, bear witness to their skill in architecture.

18. They were skilled in terracotta and bronze work, and were famous for their manufacture of textile fabrics, and embroideries, and their arts of dyeing these. They also understood

---

14. Did they prosper? 15. What proves this? 15. Were these ever understood? 16. What do we learn from these records? 17. What happened under the Semitic rule? 18. What else attests their civilization?

how to carve gems, make pottery, and work in gold; and were acquainted with porcelain and glass.

19. From the first, the Babylonians had possessed a cuneiform (ku-nē'-i-form) system of writing, and under the Semitic ascendency, this reached its full development. Libraries, stocked with clay books, were open to the public in all the towns, and every one knew how to read and write.

20. They were also highly skilled in astronomy, and every temple had its observatory, from which the priests noted the movements of the heavenly bodies. The capital of the empire was Babylon, a great and beautiful city on the Euphrates river, near the site of the Tower of Babel.

21. While thus advancing in civilization, however, the Babylonians were falling away from the knowledge of the true God. They began to worship, first the moon, and then the sun, as their chief god, and sunk into extreme wickedness.

22. The Egyptians, the other civilized nation of this time, had also lost all knowledge of their Creator. Some great spiritual truths still remained with them, but shrouded in myths, and mingled with debasing animal worship. The rest of mankind consisted of nomad tribes who were equally sunk in wickedness and idolatry.

---

19. What of their writing? 20. In what science were they skilled? 21. What was their religion? 22. Was the true God now worshipped by any nation?

III.—ERA OF THE PATRIARCHS.

B. C. 2107—B. C. 1490.)

CHAPTER I.

THE CALL OF ABRAHAM.

Pal'-es-tine is situated in the S. E. of Syria, a country which lies in the S. E. of Asia, and is a division of Turkey in Asia.

Jordan River is 120 miles long, and flows from the Ante-Libanus Mountains, southward through the Holy Land to the Dead Sea.

1. In the midst of the almost universal corruption which now prevailed among mankind, there were a few faithful ones who, like Noe before the Flood, remained faithful to God, and preserved His worship in their families. Of these was A'bram, the Sem'-ite, who dwelt in Ur, a great city of the Chaldean Empire, dedicated to the Moon-God.

2. God, therefore, resolved to make this just man the founder of a nation who should be His chosen people, and preserve on the earth the knowledge and worship of Him, and the hope of the promised Redeemer.

3. While Abram's father was still living, the family removed to Hā-ran, another city of Chaldea, and there they remained till Abram had attained his seventy-fifth year. Then God told him to arise and leave his friends and his kindred, and go to dwell in a strange land which He would show him.

4. God had two reasons for giving this command to Abram; the first was, that having chosen him to be the forefather of

---

1. Did none now remain faithful to God? 2. What did God resolve to make of Abram? 3. To what city had Abram's family removed? 4. Why did God give this command to Abram?

ABRAHAM LEAVES MESOPOTAMIA.

the Redeemer, He required a proof on the part of Abram that he loved God more than father and mother, and kindred, and country, by obeying His call to go forth and dwell as a stranger in a strange land.

5. The second reason was that God also intended to preserve him by this means from further contact with the idolatry of the Chaldeans, as well as from the influence of the equally idolatrous nations among whom he was to fix his abode.

6. Abram at once went forth as the Lord had commanded, taking with him only his wife Sā′rāi, and his nephew Lot, along with his servants and his flocks and herds, and moved in a southwesterly direction till he came to the land of Cha′naan (kā′nan), his future home. As soon as he arrived there God appeared to him and promised to give the land to his descendants.

7. The beautiful land of Chanaan (kā-nan), now known as Palestine or the Holy Land, was so rich and fertile that it was called a land flowing with milk and honey. Though it is not much larger than the state of Massachusetts, it exhibits great contrasts of scenery.

8. In the north the uplands are clothed with cedars, and the valleys are filled with the vegetation of northern latitudes, while in the south there are found groves of palm and forests of olive trees. In Abraham's day, no doubt, rich vineyards clothed the sunny slopes, and vast tracts waved with corn.

9. After a time the number of Abraham's flocks and herds increased so greatly that the pasture land became insufficient to support both. Abraham saw that they would be compelled to separate, and besought Lot to choose his abode in some other part of the land.

10. Lot chose the country about the Jørdan for his abode, and dwelt in Sod′-om, one of the five cities of the plain of the Lower Jordan. These were subject to the king of E′lam, but

---

5. What was the other reason? 6. Did Abram obey the call of God? 7. Describe the Land of Chanaan. 8. Continue. 9. What happened in time? 10. What part of the land did Lot choose?

shortly after Lot had gone to dwell in Sodom, they revolted, and declared themselves free.

11. The king of Elam at once marched against the rebels and defeated them in the vale now covered by the waters of the Dead Sea. He and his allies then advanced, plundered the cities, and carried off, with an immense number of other captives, Lot and his family, with all his flocks and herds.

12. Meanwhile, Abram had fixed his tents beneath the oaks of Hē'bron, where he had raised an altar to God. Here, where there was abundant pasture ground for his vast herds, he was dwelling in peace and prosperity, when he heard that Lot had been carried off by the Elamites.

13. He at once armed his servants, three hundred and eighteen in number, and placing himself at the head of this little force, he set off in pursuit of the invaders, and came up with them at Dan, where he surprised them at night, and rescued Lot with all the spoils.

14. On his return homeward from this victory, Abram was met by the king of Sodom and Melchisedek (mel-kis'-e-dek) the king of Salem.

15. Melchisedek, who was a priest of the Most High, offered to the Lord a sacrifice of bread and wine, and said, "Blessed be Abram by the Most High God who created heaven and earth; and blessed be the Most High God, by whose protection the enemies are in thy hands." Abram then gave him the tithes or tenth part of the spoils.

16. The king of Sodom then said to Abram, "Give me the persons, and the rest take to thyself." But Abram, mindful of the wickedness of the men of Sodom, would have nothing to do with them, and refusing all reward, returned homeward. In Melchisedek we have a figure of the eternal High Priest, Jesus Christ, and in his sacrifice a figure of the Mass.

17. In the midst of his great prosperity, Abram was troubled

---

11. What was the consequence? 12. Where was Abram dwelling? 13. What did he do? 14. Who met him as he returned homeward? 15. What did Melchisedek do? 16. What did the king of Sodom say to Abram? 17. What troubled Abram?

by the fact that he was childless. At last he complained of it to God, who brought him abroad one night and told him to look up to heaven and number the stars, if he could, for his descendants should be as numerous as they.

18. When Abram was ninety-nine years of age, God appeared to him again, and said to him, "I am the Almighty God. Walk before me and be perfect. Neither shall thy name be called any more Abram, a high father, but Abraham, father of the multitude, because I have made thee a father of many nations.

19. I will establish my covenant between me and thee: all the male kind of you shall be circumcised. Sarai, thy wife, shall be called Sara, and she shall bear thee a son whose name thou shalt call Isaac (i-zak)."

20. Not long after this, as Abraham was sitting at the door of his tent in the heat of the day, he saw three strangers approaching. He hastened to meet them, bowed down before them, and begged them to rest in his tent. Then he told Sara to bake some cakes of the finest flour, and having caused the finest young calf in the herd to be boiled, he placed this food, with milk and butter and honey, before his guests.

21. Abraham himself waited on his guests at their meal, and when they had finished, and were about to depart, one of the strangers said to Abraham that in a year he would return, and that then Sara his wife should have a son. Then Abraham knew that the Lord God himself, accompanied by his angels, was his guest.

22. Abraham went a part of the way with his guests towards Sodom, and the Lord told him that He was about to destroy the cities of Sodom and Go-mor'-rah, on account of their wickedness. But the holy man, filled with charity for his sinful neighbors, begged the Lord to spare them if fifty just men could be found therein, and won from Him a promise that He would do so.

---

18. When did God again appear to him? 19. Continue. 20. What happened not long after? 21. What took place after the meal? 22. Did Abraham accompany his guests?

23. Then Abraham besought Him to spare them if five and forty just persons could be found within the precincts; and so kept on pleading till at last he obtained the promise of God to spare them if ten just persons could be found within them. Then the Lord disappeared, and Abraham returned home.

24. So wicked were the cities of the plain, that even ten just men were not found within their limits; and two angels were sent to destroy them. They entered Sodom in the evening, and sought the house of Lot. They told him that the city was to be destroyed, and early next morning led him with his wife and family, out into the open country.

25. Then, turning them with their faces from the doomed city, they admonished them to go on their way without looking back, lest they be included in the destruction. Scarcely had the sun risen, when fire and brimstone rained upon the wicked cities, and utterly destroyed them. Lot's wife, unable to restrain her curiosity, looked back, and was changed into a pillar of salt.

26. The site of these cities is now covered by a sulphurous lake whose sickening odor infects the air and causes it to be shunned by man and beast. This fearful memorial of God's judgment and man's depravity, is called the Dead Sea.

CHAPTER II.

ABRAHAM AND ISAAC.

1. As the Lord had promised, Sara gave birth to a son. He was called Isaac, which means *laughter*, and circumcised on the eighth day. While he was still young, God, who wished to see whether Abraham loved his child more than his God, resolved to subject him to a supreme test.

---

23. What did Abraham then plead for? 24. Were the required number of just men found? 25. Continue. 26. What now occupies their site?

1. Did Sarah have a son?

2. He therefore appeared to him and said, "Take thy only begotten son Isaac, whom thou lovest, and go into the land of vision, and there thou shalt offer him for a holocaust upon one of the mountains which I will show thee."

3. Abraham at once rose up in the night, saddled his ass, and taking with him only two servants and Isaac, cut wood for the holocaust, and set off for the appointed place. And on the third day, lifting up his eyes, he saw the place afar off.

4. At length they reached the spot—Mount Mor-i-a, and Abraham bade his servants remain at the foot. Then placing the wood for the holocaust on Isaac's shoulders, while he himself bore the fire and sword, they began the steep ascent.

5. As they thus toiled up Moria's rugged slopes, Isaac said, "My father?" "What wilt thou, my son," answered the holy patriarch. "Behold," replied Isaac, "the fire and the sword; where is the victim for the holocaust?"

6. Abraham answered that God would provide the victim, and they went on till they reached the top of the mountain. Then Abraham erected an altar, placed the wood on it, and having bound his son, placed him on the wood.

7. The supreme moment had now come. The holy patriarch had taken his sword and raised his hand to slay his only son, when the voice of an angel cried out, "Abraham! Abraham!" "Here I am," answered Abraham. Then the angel said, "Lay not thy hand on the boy. Now I know that thou fearest God and hast not spared thy only-begotten son for My sake."

8. Then lifting up his eyes, Abraham saw near by a ram entangled in the thicket, and he took this animal and offered it in place of his son. Then the angel spoke again and told him that in reward for his faith and courage in obeying the divine command, God would multiply his descendants like the stars of heaven, or the sands on the seashore. Then Abraham returned home with his son.

---

2. What did God command? 3. Did Abraham obey? 4. Continue. 5. What did Isaac say? 6. What did Abraham answer? 7. Did Abra-

9. Isaac willingly bearing the wood which was to kindle the fire intended to consume him, up the mountain, is a type of Our Divine Lord bearing his cross.

10. When Abraham was stricken in years and felt the time of his death drawing near, he became anxious to have his son married to a daughter of his kindred, and a worshipper of the true God. So he charged his faithful servant, Eliezer (ĕ-le-ā′-zur) to go to Haran in Chaldea, where his brother Nachor (na′-kor) dwelt, and bring from thence a wife for Isaac.

11. Eliezer took ten camels of his master's herd, and loaded them with rich presents for Abraham's kindred. Then he set out and in due time arrived at Haran. It was evening; the time when it is the custom of the women of Asia to come and draw water at the public wells.

12. So Eliezer let his camels lie down to rest near one of these wells, outside the city, and prayed to God to grant that the maiden whom he should ask for a drink, and who should answer, "Drink, and I will give thy camels drink also," might be the wife he destined for Isaac.

13. Scarcely had he finished his prayer, when a modest, lovely maiden drew near the well with her water-jar. Eliezer went to her and asked her for a drink. She answered, "Drink, and I will also draw water for thy camels."

14. Eliezer then eagerly inquired her name and parentage, and was overjoyed to find that she was Rebecca, the daughter of Ba-thu′el, the son of Nachor. He then told her who he was and gave her gold ear-rings and bracelets, and she hastened home to tell her people that a messenger had come from their kinsman Abraham.

15. At the joyful tidings, her brother La′ban went out and conducted Eliezer to Bathuel's house. Then the faithful servant told the family of Abraham's prosperity in the distant land to which God had conducted him, and how he desired to

---

9. Of whom is Isaac a type? 10. Of what did Abraham become desirous? 11. Did Eliezer go? 12. What did he do? 13. What followed? 14. What did he inquire? 15. Who came to Eliezer?

THE SACRIFICE OF ABRAHAM.

see his son Isaac wedded to one of his own kindred before he died.

16. He then asked for permission to conduct Rebecca to Chanaan to become the wife of Isaac. They consented, and the following day, a great feast was given to celebrate the betrothal, after which, Rebecca and her maidens set out with Eliezer for the land of Canaan.

17. As they drew near the abode of Abraham, Isaac chanced to be walking in the fields. When Rebecca saw him, and learned who he was, she veiled herself. Isaac was deeply pleased by her modesty, and taking her by the hand, led her into his mother's tent.

18. Soon after the marriage of Isaac and Rebecca, Sarah died and was buried in the double cave of Mambre which Abraham had bought for a tomb from the children of Hĕth. Abraham dwelt with his children till he had reached the age of one hundred and seventy-five years. Then he too, was gathered to his fathers, and they laid him by the side of Sarah.

Abraham is the model of believers. His unhesitating obedience, and trust in God, joined to his self-sacrifice, as shown in rising up and going into exile; his piety, in raising altars to God; his peacefulness, in separating from Lot; his courage, in his pursuit and defeat of the king of Elam and his allies; his sublime faith, in the intended sacrifice of Isaac, and his holiness, which God rewarded by manifesting Himself to him more intimately than to any other mortal save Adam, all combine to make him worthy of the glorious title of the Father of the Faithful, for all time, and merited that the place of their repose in eternity, before the opening of Heaven by Jesus Christ, should be known as his bosom.

CHAPTER III.

JACOB AND ESAU.

1. For a long time, Isaac and Rebecca remained childless. But at length, when Isaac was sixty years of age, Rebecca

---

16. What did he ask? 17. How did Isaac and Rebecca meet? 18. What took place soon after the marriage of Isaac and Rebecca?
1. Had Isaac and Rebecca children?

had twin sons, Esau and Jacob, but Esau was the first-born.

2. The two brothers were unlike in every respect; Esau was red and hairy, and a great hunter; Jacob was smooth-skinned and gentle, and loved to dwell quietly in his tent. Esau was dear to Isaac, because of his strength and fearless spirit; but Rebecca loved Jacob.

3. One day Jacob was boiling some pottage, when Esau came in from hunting. He was faint and tired, and said to Jacob, "Give me of this pottage." Jacob replied that he would, on condition that Esau gave him his birthright in exchange.

4. So great was Esau's weakness and hunger, that he accepted Jacob's conditions, and gave up his sacred right of eldest son which made him the head of the family, for the mess of pottage. Having confirmed the sale with an oath, he ate and went his way, thinking little of what he had cast away.

5. But when Rebecca heard what had taken place, she resolved that Jacob should enjoy all the privileges of the birthright which the reckless Esau had so lightly yielded to him.

6. Time passed, and Isaac grew very old and blind. At length he felt that death was drawing near, so he one day summoned Esau to his bedside, and bade him go forth with his bow and quiver, and kill some game, and make of it a savory dish, such as he liked to eat, and then he would give him his blessing before he died.

7. In those days the blessing of a father to his son was a very solemn ceremony, and made the eldest son the chief, and priest of his family. So when Rebecca heard Isaac's command, she resolved that Jacob should receive the blessing, instead of Esau, for such, she knew, was the will of God. Esau had no sooner gone, than she called Jacob, and bade him fetch a kid,

---

2. Describe them. 3. What happened one day? 4. Did Esau accept? 5. What did Rebecca resolve? 6. What did Isaac say to Esau? 7. Con-

and of this animal's flesh she quickly made a savory dish, such as Isaac loved.

8. Then she clothed Jacob in Esau's finest garments, and having covered his hands and the smooth part of his neck with the skin of the kid, so as to make him rough and hairy to the touch, like Esau, she sent him to his blind father with the dish she had prepared.

9. Jacob bore it to the bedside and said, "My father?" "Who art thou, my son?" answered Isaac. "I am Esau, thy first-born," answered Jacob. "I have done as thou didst command me; arise and eat of my venison, that thy soul may bless me."

10. But Isaac, who thought he recognized the voice of Jacob, replied, "Come hither, that I may feel thee, my son, and prove whether thou be my son Esau or not." Jacob drew near, and when the blind patriarch had felt his hands, he said: "The voice is the voice of Jacob, but the hands are the hands of Esau." Then he gave him his blessing.

11. Scarcely had Jacob left his father, when Esau returned with the game. Quickly preparing it, he presented himself at his father's bedside and asked for the promised blessing. "Who art thou?" asked Isaac in surprise. "I am Esau, thy first-born," he answered. Then Isaac saw how he had been deceived.

12. But when he told Esau how he had been betrayed into giving Jacob his blessing, Esau gave an exceeding bitter cry, saying, "Rightly his name is called Jacob (supplanter); he hath already robbed me of my birthright, and now he hath robbed me of my father's blessing!"

13. Then he besought his father to bless him too. And Isaac, filled with compassion, said to him: "In the fat of the earth, and in the dew of heaven from above, shall thy blessing be. Thou shalt live by the sword, and shalt serve thy brother, and

---

8. What else did she do? 9. What did Jacob do? 10. Did Isaac suspect? 11. What of Esau? 12. How did Esau take this? 13. What did he beseech his father?

the time shall come when thou shalt shake off his yoke from thy neck."

14. The idea of the dependence on his brother foretold by the prophetic voice of Isaac, made so intense a hatred for Jacob spring up in Esau's heart, that he waited only for a favorable moment to kill him.

15. Rebecca was quick to perceive this, and induced Isaac to send Jacob to her former home Haran, where her brother Laban dwelt, that he might choose a wife among his kindred.

16. Jacob set out on his long journey, more like a poor fugitive, than the son of the rich patriarch Isaac. When night came he took his repose on the ground, with a stone for a pillow.

17. But in his sleep he had a marvellous vision—he saw a great ladder, reaching from earth to heaven. Throngs of angels were ascending and descending it, and at the top was the Lord Himself. And He said to Jacob, "I am the God of Abraham, and the God of Isaac. The land wherein thou sleepest, I will give to thy descendants, and they shall be as the dust of the earth.

18. Thou shalt spread abroad to the east and to the west, to the north and to the south, and in thee and thy seed shall all the nations of the earth be blest. And I will be thy keeper whithersoever thou goest, and will bring thee back into this land ; neither will I leave thee till I shall have accomplished all that I have said."

19. When Jacob awoke, his soul was filled with awe. "Indeed," he said, "the Lord is in this place, and I did not know it." Then he took the stone which he had used as a pillow, and pouring oil on it, made an altar of it, and called the place Běth'-el, which means, the house of God.

Esau prefigures the rejection of the Jews who desired only earthly goods, as Jacob does the election of the church, which like David, sought of God only one thing—His benediction. The ladder of Jacob's dream is

---

14. What effect had this prophecy on Esau ? 15. What did Rebecca do ? 16. How did he travel ? 17. What had he in his sleep ? 18. Continue. 19. How was Jacob affected ?

a figure of christian churches in which angels constantly bear the prayers of the faithful to heaven, and return to earth laden with blessings. The seed in whom all nations shall be blessed is the Savior who was first promised in Paradise, then to Abraham, then to Isaac, and now to Jacob.

CHAPTER IV.

JACOB.

1. JACOB continued his journey, and in due time arrived in Chaldea. As he drew near the city of Haran, he saw some flocks of sheep, and said to the shepherds who were tending them, "Brethren, whence are you?" They answered "From Haran."

2. Then he asked if they knew his Uncle La'-ban. "We know him," they answered "and behold, his daughter Rachel cometh with his flock." Turning, Jacob saw his cousin and running to her weeping for joy, he told her who he was.

3. Rachel hurried home and told her father that Jacob, his sister Rebecca's son, was come. And Laban came to meet Jacob, embraced him, and conducted him home.

4. After Jacob had told his story, it was agreed that Jacob should serve Laban for seven years, and as a recompense receive Rachel, Laban's second daughter, as his wife. And so great was Jacob's love for Rachel that the time seemed to pass quickly.

5. But when the time for the marriage arrived, Laban deceived Jacob, and gave him instead of Rachel, Lia, his older daughter. Jacob was angry at this deception, but finally obtained Rachel as his wife, on condition of serving Laban for another seven years.

6. During these seven years, Lia gave birth to six sons. But Rachel remained childless for several years. Then God heard

---

1. Did Jacob arrive safe? 2. What did he then ask? 3. What did Rachel do? 4. What was agreed? 5. Was this done? 6. Had Lia and Rachel children?

her fervent prayers and sent her a son, who was called Joseph.

7. After the birth of this son, Jacob, who had prospered greatly in his exile, begged Laban for leave to return to his own land. The fourteen years agreed upon, he urged, had gone by, and he had served Laban faithfully, and it was now time for him to think of his own family.

8. But Laban besought him to remain with him a little longer, and Jacob yielded and stayed six more years with him. Then, seeing how hopeless it was to obtain Laban's permission to depart, he set out secretly with his family, and servants, and herds, and camels.

9. But he was soon overtaken by Laban. He had set out in pursuit with hostile intentions towards Jacob, but God had warned him in a dream not to injure his son-in-law. So they met and parted in peace.

10. As Jacob drew near the river Jordan, the boundary of the land of Cha-naan, he began to dread the meeting with his brother Esau. Remembering his former violence, he sent on messengers ahead with presents of herds of cattle, for him.

11. But these had no effect on Esau, who advanced to attack his brother with a force of four hundred men. But during the night an angel appeared to Jacob, who wrestled with the heavenly visitant till morning, saying, "I will not let thee go except thou bless me." Then the angel told him that thenceforth his name should be Israel, that is, one who has wrestled with God.

12. In the morning Jacob divided his family and servants into companies, and putting himself at the head of one of them, advanced to meet his brother, and when they met, bowed down seven times before him.

13. Esau was touched by this humility, and embraced Jacob warmly and welcomed his children. Then Jacob besought him to accept some of his flocks, and after much pleading on

---

7. What did Jacob now do? 8. Did Laban consent? 9. What happened? 10. Did Jacob fear Esau? 11. Did this means succeed? 12. What did Jacob do? 13. How was Esau affected?

Jacob's part, Esau did so. They then parted, and Jacob continued his journey to the home of his father.

14. But on the way thither, his wife Rachel died, soon after the birth of her son Benjamin, and was buried by the wayside, where her tomb is still pointed out. Jacob's grief was increased on his arrival home by finding that his mother Rebecca had also passed away.

15. But the holy patriarch Isaac, was still living to welcome his son after his long exile, and console him in his double bereavement. And they dwelt together until Isaac reached the age of one hundred and eighty years. Then he died, and Esau and Jacob laid him beside his father Abraham.

CHAPTER V.

JOSEPH.

1. JACOB continued to dwell in the land of Chanaan. He had twelve sons, of whom Joseph and Benjamin, Rachel's children, were the dearest to his heart. For Joseph, in particular, he had so deep an affection, that it aroused the envy and hatred of his brethren.

2. This feeling on their part was increased when Joseph discovered some evil conduct on their part, and informed his father of it. It was still further deepened when he chanced to relate to them some remarkable dreams which foretold his dominion over them. And so they only waited an opportunity to wreak their anger on him.

3. This soon came to pass. One time when they had gone with their flocks some distance from home, Jacob sent Joseph to see if all things went well with them. And when they saw him drawing near, they said, "Here comes the dreamer. Let us kill him and cast him into some old pit, and we will say some evil beast hath devoured him."

---

14. What sorrow came to Jacob? 15. Who was living?
1. How many sons had Jacob? 2. What increased this? 3. Did they get this opportunity?

4. So when Joseph reached them, they tore off his coat of divers colors which his father had given him, and cast him into a dry pit. Then they sat down to eat. But while they were at their meal, some merchants passed by carrying spices, balm and myrrh to Egypt. And Juda proposed that instead of killing Joseph, they sell him to these merchants.

5. The others agreed to this; so Joseph was drawn out of the pit, and in spite of his entreaties, sold to the merchants for twenty pieces of silver. Then they killed a kid and dipping Joseph's coat in it, sent it to their father, saying: "This we have found; see if it be thy son's coat or not."

6. The wretched father was quick to recognize his own gift to his beloved Joseph, and cried out: "It's my son's coat; a wild beast has devoured Joseph." Then Jacob rent his garments and put on sackcloth, and mourned long and deeply for his son's death.

7. While his poor father was grieving, Joseph was being carried into bondage in a strange land. On arriving in Egypt, the merchants sold him to Putiphar (pu'-ti-far), the captain of the royal guard, who soon learned to apprecate his worth, and made him steward of his household.

8. The Lord blessed Joseph's stewardship, and the household of the Egyptian prospered. But there were new trials in store for Joseph. The wife of Putiphar urged him to commit a grievous sin. And when she found she could not move his virtue, she grew to hate him, and resolved to ruin him.

9. So she told her husband that Joseph had sought to induce her to commit a horrible sin, and he, placing too much confidence in her story, caused Joseph to be thrown into prison, amongst the vilest criminals.

10. But God did not desert Joseph. He soon found such favor with the chief keeper that he was placed over the other prisoners. Among these were the butler and chief baker of Pharao (fā'-ro), the Egyptian king, who were charged with treason.

---

4. Continue. 5. Did they agree? 6. Did Jacob recognize it? 7. What became of Joseph? 8. What happened? 9. How did she do this? 10. Did God favor him here?

11. One night both of these men had each a dream which perplexed and saddened them because they knew not how to interpret them. Joseph, seeing that they were troubled, asked them the reason. They told him and he answered: "Does not interpretation belong to God? Tell me what you have dreamed."

12. Then the chief butler told how he had dreamed that he saw before him a vine with three branches, which little by little, put forth buds, which in turn put forth ripe grapes. He squeezed these grapes into the cup of Pharao, and gave the cup to Pharao to drink.

13. Joseph told him that the dream signified that after three days he should be restored to his place, and present Pharao the cup as he had been used to do. And he besought the butler, when he should thus be reinstated, to remember him and try to obtain his pardon.

14. The butler promised, and then the chief baker told his dream. He thought he had three baskets of meal on his head, and that in the uppermost basket there were all kinds of pastry, which the birds came and ate of.

15. Then Joseph interpreted this dream as follows: The three baskets were three days, and after they had gone by, Pharao would have the chief baker beheaded, and hung on a cross, and the birds would eat his flesh.

16. All happened according to his prediction. The third day following was Pharao's birthday, and on it he had the chief baker beheaded, but restored the chief butler to his place. But in the restored favor of his master the butler forgot his promise and gave no thought to Joseph.

17. Two years went by, and then Pharao had two dreams which sorely troubled him. He thought he saw seven fat cows come up out of the river Nile, and feed in rich meadows. Then seven lean ones followed, and devoured the fat ones.

---

11. What happened to these men? 12. What did the chief butler relate? 13. How did Joseph interpret it? 14. What did the chief baker relate? 15. How did Joseph interpret this dream? 16. Did it so happen? 17. What troubled Pharao?

18. The king then awoke, but fell asleep again and had another dream. He saw seven full, fair ears of corn growing on one stalk, and then seven other ears sprang up. But these were thin and withered and ate up the fine, full ears.

19. The following morning Pharao sent for all the wise men and soothsayers of Egypt, and related these remarkable dreams to them. But he found that none could interpret them.

20. Then the chief butler remembered Joseph, and told Pharao how he had interpreted the dreams in prison. So the king sent for him, and, after he had related to him his visions, Joseph told him that both dreams had the same meaning, and by them God had revealed to the king what He was about to do.

21. The seven fat kine and the seven fair ears of corn both signified seven years of plenty; and the seven lean kine and seven withered ears of corn, seven years of famine which should follow them, and be felt in the surrounding lands as well as in Egypt.

22. Joseph, therefore, advised the king to select some wise and prudent man to take charge of the surplus crops during the years of plenty, and store them in granaries for food in the years of famine.

23. Deeply pleased with the modesty and wisdom of Joseph, Pharao concluded that he could find no one who would perform such a duty better than Joseph himself. So he had him clothed in a silk robe, a gold chain was placed on his neck, and a gold ring from the king's own finger on his hand; and then, mounted in one of Pharao's state chariots, he was driven through the streets, while a herald went before and proclaimed him governor of Egypt.

24. Pharao also changed his name to one signifying "Saviour of the world." At the time of Joseph's elevation to one of the highest positions in a great kingdom, which was the

---

18. Relate his second dream. 19. For whom did he send? 20. Whom did the chief butler recommend? 21. How did he interpret the dreams? 22. What did he advise Pharao? 23. What did Pharao conclude, and how did he honor him? 24. What did Pharao also do?

only rival of the Chaldean Empire, he was only thirty years of age.

25. Time went on, and everything happened exactly as Joseph had foretold. Seven fruitful years, during which the harvests were so great that wheat was as plentiful as the sand on the seashore, came and went. During this time of plenty Joseph had vast quantities of the surplus grain stored in granaries in every city, and appointed overseers to see that it was kept in safety.

26. Seven years of scarcity followed, during which Egypt's fields lay barren, and there was no ploughing nor reaping in the land. But, thanks to Joseph, there was plenty of corn, and the people did not want for bread.

The life of Joseph shows us in what wonderful ways the designs of God are accomplished. Hated, because of his virtue, by his wicked brethren, he is consigned by them to a life of bondage in a distant land. But their hatred proves the root of his greatness, which he attains by the road of ignominy and disgrace. But, through all his misfortunes his faith in God remains unshaken, and he meekly endures his exile, and separation from his loving father, as well as his imprisonment among criminals, without repining, and thus earns a glorious reward, even before men.

Sold by his brethren for twenty pieces of silver, Joseph prefigures Our Saviour sold to the high-priests by Judas; as in prison, promising reward to one servant of Pharao, and punishment to another, he prefigures Him on the Cross, promising Paradise to the penitent thief, while the other dies blaspheming.

---

25. Was Joseph's prophecy fulfilled?   26. What followed?

CHAPTER VI.

THE MEETING OF JOSEPH AND HIS BRETHREN.

The River Nile, the chief river of Egypt, is 4,100 miles long. It rises in Victoria Ny-an-za lake, and flows northward to the Mediterranean Sea.

There is no rain in Egypt, and it would be a desert save for the annual overflow of the Nile. It was held sacred by the ancient Egyptians.

1. THE prevailing famine was felt even in the land of Chanaan, and Jacob, having heard that there was wheat for sale in Egypt, sent ten of his sons thither, with money to buy some. But he kept Benjamin, his youngest son, with him, for he was fearful lest some accident might rob him of the child who was the light of his old age.

2. So the ten brothers set out on their long journey across the desert, and at last, when no doubt, the camels were growing weak from the scant fare, a dark, low line appeared on the horizon, and presently they came into sight of the fields and gardens, and obelisks and palaces of Egypt, by the broad flood of the Nile.

3. On stating their mission they were referred to the governor. When they entered his presence they were far from recognizing in this mighty potentate, clad in the rich robes of his rank, the simple shepherd whom they had sold on the uplands of Palestine. But Joseph knew them again, and the dreams he had dreamed in youth, in which they had bowed down before him, at once came back to his mind.

4. He did not betray himself, however, but, putting on a stern countenance, asked, through his interpreter, whence they came. They answered, from the land of Chanaan, to buy food. But Joseph pretended to disbelieve their story, and declared that they were spies, sent by Egypt's enemies to find out the weak parts of the land.

5. In vain they protested their innocence; Joseph had them

1. Was the famine felt in Chanaan? 2. Describe their journey. 3.

cast into prison, and kept them there three days. Then he had them brought before him again, and told them that they must leave one of their number in prison as a hostage, while the rest went home and brought back Benjamin, as a proof of the truth of their story.

6. In the anguish which seized them on hearing this stern decree, the memory of their crime returned to them. And they said to one another that they were justly punished for their sin against Joseph. When he heard them thus reproaching themselves, Joseph was so deeply moved, that he had to leave the audience chamber in order to hide his emotion.

7. As soon as he had succeeded in mastering his feelings, he returned, and ordered Simeon to be bound before their eyes. Then he gave the rest the provisions they had requested, and dismissed them. But he privately ordered his servants to place each man's money in his sack.

8. The nine brothers loaded their camels with the sacks of wheat and sorrowfully departed on their homeward journey. When they reached Chanaan, and opened their sacks they were astonished to find their money. But when they told their father all, he mourned deeply for Simeon.

9. "Joseph is not living," he cried, "Simeon is in bonds, and Benjamin ye will take away. But my son shall not go down into Egypt, for if any evil befall him, you will bring my gray hairs in sorrow to the grave."

10. But the famine increased, and at last Jacob saw they must all starve if he did not send again to Egypt to buy wheat. But when he commanded his sons to go, they reminded him that the governor had forbidden them to return into the land of Egypt without Benjamin.

11. The aged patriarch hesitated, divided between his sore need, and his dread of losing Benjamin. Then Juda, to induce him to consent, swore to bring Benjamin back safe to him. So Jacob yielded, and bade them carry presents of balm,

---

6. What good effect had this treatment? 7. Did he carry it out? 8. Continue. 9. What did Jacob exclaim? 10. Did the famine increase? 11. What made him yield?

honey, incense, myrrh, dates and almonds, to Joseph, along with the money which they had found in their sacks.

12. Once more the little caravan set off across the desert. On arriving in Egypt, the brothers applied to Joseph for provisions, declaring that they had brought Benjamin with them, according to his command. At the news he ordered his steward to prepare a great feast, to which he bade the strangers at noon.

13. When the brothers found themselves in the governor's house, along with Simeon, who had been set free, they were filled with fear, and said to one another that he meant to make slaves of them, on account of the money which they had carried away in their sacks. So they told the steward about the money, and how they had brought it back. The steward answered, "Peace be with you; fear not."

14. At the hour of noon Joseph arrived, and with their gifts in their hands they bowed down before him. He received them graciously, and asked for their father. But when Benjamin was presented to him, he said, "God be gracious to thee, my son;" and then hastily left the room, to hide his tears, for the sight of the youth touched him deeply.

15. When he returned, the banquet was served. Joseph sat at a table apart from the others, according to the custom of the Egyptians, who considered it unlawful to eat with the Hebrews, because they were shepherds. But he sent meat to each of them, during the feast, and the share of Benjamin was five times larger than that of the others.

16. When they were ready to depart, Joseph resolved to subject them to a final test to see if their repentance was sincere for their sin against him, or if the favor he had shown Benjamin would arouse their old jealousy which had led to their crime. So he bade his steward fill their sacks with wheat, and put each man's money in his own sack, but to put in Benjamin's sack his own silver drinking cup.

---

12. Describe their journey and reception. 13. What emotion filled them? 14. How did they act towards Joseph? 15. What took place when he returned? 16. What did Joseph resolve?

17. The steward did so; and in the morning the brothers departed on their camels. But they had gone only a short distance, when they were overtaken by the steward, who, instructed by Joseph, had pursued them, and charged by him with having stolen his master's drinking cup.

18. Of course they indignantly denied the theft, and declared that if the cup were found in any of their sacks, the owner of it should die, and the others would become slaves to the governor.

19. But what was their consternation, when the steward, after searching every other sack, finally found the stolen cup in Benjamin's! Rending their garments, they remounted their camels and returned to the city, and, falling at Joseph's feet, offered themselves as his slaves.

20. But Joseph answered that none should be his slave, save him who stole the cup. Then Juda told him how much it had cost Jacob to part with Benjamin, and how they would all sooner die than return to their aged father without the young son whom he had confided to their care.

21. Juda ended by imploring Joseph to keep him a slave till his death, and let Benjamin return home. When Joseph heard this offer, he knew that their repentance was sincere; and resolved to disclose his identity.

22. He hastily dismissed his attendants, for he did not wish any stranger to be present when he made himself known to them. Then, giving vent to his long repressed emotion, he lifted up his voice and wept so loud that all who were in the house of Pharao, heard him. Then at last he said, "I am Joseph."

23. At the sight of the governor's grief, and the sound of his voice, declaring in their own tongue that he was their injured brother, the sons of Jacob were struck dumb with fear.

24. But Joseph said to them mildly: "Come nearer to me.

---

17. What happened in consequence? 18. How did they act? 19. Did the steward find the cup? 20. What did Joseph say? 21. What did Juda implore? 22. How did he reveal himself? 23. How were the brothers affected? 24. Did Joseph reassure them?

JOSEPH MAKES HIMSELF KNOWN TO HIS BRETHREN.

I am Joseph, your brother, whom you sold into Egypt. Fear nothing, for God sent me before you into Egypt for your preservation. You shall tell my father of all my glory, and all the things you have seen in Egypt; make haste and bring him to me."

25. Then he fell upon his brother Benjamin's neck and kissed him, and wept; and Benjamin, in like manner, wept upon his neck. And then Joseph embraced all the rest of his brethren, and wept with them, and afterwards they got courage to speak with him.

CHAPTER VII.

THE FAMILY OF JACOB ENTER EGYPT.

1. WHEN Pharao heard Joseph's story, he told him to tell his father to come down and settle in Egypt with his family. So Joseph gave his brothers chariots, and other rich presents, and, after warning them not to quarrel on the way, sent them home with Pharao's invitation.

2. When they arrived and told Jacob that his son Joseph was still living, and ruler of Egypt, he would not credit it till they showed him all the rich presents he had bestowed on them. Then, filled with joy, he cried out, "It is enough for me if Joseph, my son, be yet living. I will go and see him before I die."

3. He at once set out for Egypt, with his family and all his possessions. When he reached the southern boundary of Chanaan he offered sacrifice to God. And he had a vision in the night. God spoke to him and told him to fear not, but go down into Egypt where He would make a great nation of him, and bring him back to Chanaan.

4. Strengthened and consoled, Jacob continued his journey

---

25. What did he then do?
1. What did Pharao say to Joseph's story? 2. Did Jacob believe the glad news at first? 3. Did he go? 4. Describe his meeting with Joseph.

and sent on Juda to inform Joseph of his approach. Joseph at once mounted his chariot and went to meet his father. And when they met, he fell upon his neck and wept, while the patriarch cried out, "Now I shall die with joy, for I have seen thy face and leave thee alive."

5. Joseph then presented his father to Pharao, and Jacob blessed the king. Pharao asked him, "How many are the days of the years of thy life?" Jacob answered, "The days of the years of my pilgrimage are a hundred and thirty years, few and evil, and they are not come up to the days of the pilgrimage of my fathers."

6. As the Egyptians held all shepherds in abomination, Pharao decided to give the colony of Hebrews a part of the land for themselves. So he settled them in Ges-sen, or Go'shen, one of the most beautiful and fertile parts of lower Egypt. And here Jacob dwelt for seventeen years in peace and prosperity.

7. When the time of his father's death drew near, Joseph visited him with his two sons, Eph-raim and Man-as-ses. The holy patriarch embraced and blessed the boys, and prayed that the angel who had delivered him from evil during life might also protect them. To Joseph he said, "Behold I die, and God will be with you, and will bring you back into the land of your fathers."

8. Then he solemnly blessed his children and grandchildren, who were all assembled about his bed. But to Juda he gave a special blessing, and the promise of being the forefather of the Messias. "*The sceptre shall not be taken away from Juda, till He come that is to be sent; and He shall be the expectation of the nations.*"

9. Then he died. And, according to Pharao's command, all Egypt mourned for him for seventy days. After that, Joseph, who had his father's body embalmed, conveyed it, as he had

---

5. What did Pharao ask Joseph? 6. What did he decide? 7. What happened before his death? 8. Who was specially blessed among Jacob's sons? 9. What did Pharao command?

promised his father he would do, back to Chanaan, and buried it in the tomb of Abraham at Hebron.

10. The principal nobles of the court of Pharao and the elders of Egypt accompanied the families of Jacob and of Joseph on their journey. When the long funeral train had crossed the Jordan, seven days were spent in lamentation, so that the Chananites said, "This is a great mourning to the Egyptians." And from that day, the place was called the Mourning of Egypt.

11. When they returned to Egypt, Joseph's brethren grew fearful lest, now that their father was dead, Joseph might take vengeance for the wrong they had done him. So they came to him and begged his forgiveness anew. Joseph received them kindly, and assured them of his good will, saying, "You thought evil against me, but God turned it into good."

12. Joseph lived to the age of one hundred and ten years, and saw his children's children to the third generation. When he was about to die, he told his people that God would one day bring them out of Egypt into Chanaan, and made them promise to take his body with them when they went. After his death, his body was embalmed according to the custom of the Egyptians, and laid in a stone coffin.

13. HISTORY OF JOB.—Although God had revealed Himself in a special manner to Abraham, Isaac and Jacob, and given them the special promises that from them should descend the Messias, His holy name was still known and feared by some holy persons who were not of their people.

14. Of these few faithful ones was a holy and upright man named Job who lived in Arabia, some time between the death of Joseph, and the birth of Moses. He was very rich in sheep, camels and oxen, the wealth of Arabia, and was looked upon as a prince by the people of the East.

15. But one day the Lord said to Satan, "Hast thou consid-

---

10. Who accompanied them? 11. What did Joseph's brethren fear? 12. How long did Joseph live? 13. Did any, save the Hebrews, still retain the worship of the true God? 14. Who was Job? 15. Relate what Our Lord said to Satan.

ered my servant, Job, that there is none like him in the earth, a simple and upright man, fearing God and avoiding evil?"

16. But Satan, answering, said, "Doth Job fear God in vain? Thou hast blessed the work of his hands, and increased his possessions on the earth. But stretch forth thy hand and take away his possessions, then thou shalt see that he will murmur against thee!" The Lord answered, "Behold, all that he hath is in thy hand, only touch not thou his life."

17. Satan lost no time in availing himself of the Divine permission to afflict the holy man. A few days after, a messenger rushed into Job's presence with the news that the Sā-be-ans, a hostile tribe, had fallen upon his servants and slain them, and carried off all his asses and oxen.

18. While the servant was still speaking, a second one arrived to tell how that his flocks of sheep and his shepherds had been killed by lightning. The second messenger had not finished his story, when a third arrived with the news that the Chaldeans had taken his camels, and slain all the servants, save the speaker.

19. Then came a fourth messenger to tell him that while his sons and daughters were seated at a feast in the house of their eldest brother, a violent wind had suddenly swept up from the desert and blown the house down on his children and killed them.

20. Then Job rose up and rent his garments, and having shaved his head, fell down on the ground and worshipped, saying, "The Lord gave, and the Lord hath taken away. Blessed be the name of the Lord!"

21. But Job's trials were not yet over, for when the Lord commended Job's fortitude, Satan said that though it had enabled him to endure the loss of his possessions, it would surely give way if he was afflicted in body.

22. So God permitted Satan to strike Job's whole body with

---

16. What did Satan answer? 17. How did Satan act? 18. What new disaster befell him? 19. What did the fourth messenger tell? 20. What did Job do? 21. Was Job still further afflicted? 22. What did God now permit Satan to do?

JOB IN HIS AFFLICTION.

a putrid ulcer. And, in his poverty and misery, the holy man sat on a dunghill, and scraped the ulcerated matter from his skin, with a pot-sherd, or fragment of a broken pot. And his wife said to him, "Curse God and die!" But Job reproved her, saying, "If we have received good things at the hand of God, why should we not receive evil?"

23. Three friends of Job, hearing of his misfortunes, came to visit him. When they saw him from afar off, they knew him not, and crying out they wept, and rent their garments, and sprinkled dust on their heads. And they sat on the ground beside him seven days and seven nights, and none of them spoke a word, for they saw that his grief was very great.

24. But when, at length, Job began to bewail his misery, they answered only by reproaching him for the secret sins which had deserved so terrible a punishment. But Job firmly asserted his innocence, and insisted that he had lived a just, upright and charitable life, and finished by declaring his hope in the resurrection of the body.

25. Their dispute was ended by God's revealing Himself in a whirlwind to Job. He gently reproved Job for not being more perfectly resigned to His will, but his wrath was great against the three friends, and He commanded them to offer a holocaust for themselves, while Job prayed to obtain forgiveness for them.

26. Job meekly acknowledged his fault, and in reward of his humility the Lord cured him, and restored him his possessions double-fold. New children were born to him, and he lived to the age of one hundred and forty years, and saw his children's children to the fourth generation.

Job prefigures Our Lord in the power which was given to Satan to afflict him, and in the reproaches of his own people. From Job we learn that the highest virtue is to suffer wrongs patiently, for the devil who had not feared him in his just and prosperous life, trembled before him in his sinless misery and affliction. We also learn from his life how powerful with God is the intercession of the saints.

---

23. Who came to visit him? 24. How did they answer Job's complaints? 25. How was their dispute ended ? 26. How did God reward Job ?

IV.—ERA OF THE WRITTEN LAW, AND THE TABERNACLE.

(B. C. 1570—B. C. 1010.)

CHAPTER I.

EGYPT.

Hi-e-ro-glyph'-ics. Picture writing in which symbols are employed instead of words or syllables of words.

Pa-py'-rus. A material resembling paper obtained by the Egyptians from reeds, by taking the layer between the flesh and thick bark of the plant and uniting the strips with a gelatinous substance.

Ob-e-lisk. A tall, four-sided pillar, made of one entire stone, gradually tapering as it rises, and cut off at the top in the form of a flat pyramid.

Thebes was situated in upper Egypt on the Nile. It is now in ruins.

Memphis was situated in lower Egypt on the Nile, 10 miles south of Cairo. Like Thebes, it is now a ruin.

1. In Egypt, as in Chaldea, we are surprised by meeting at the dawn of history, a people who surpassed in many arts of civilized life, the enlightened nineteenth century. Egypt was the only rival of Chaldea, and these two great empires, divided by the desert, flourished for centuries, and laid the material basis for all later civilization.

2. It is in their architecture that the greatness of the Egyptians especially revealed itself. Unlike the brick edifices of Chaldea, which crumbled away, the stupendous stone monuments beside the Nile have remained throughout the ages, tell-

---

1. What surprises us in Egypt's early history ? 2. In what does the greatness of the Egyptians reveal itself ?

ing in their mutilated grandeur, of a time when the land, now silent and desolate, was covered with 20,000 prosperous cities, and Egypt was the mistress of the world.

3. But while thus testifying by their very existence, to the genius and greatness of the nation which erected them, the monuments bore another message from antiquity, in the mysterious carvings which covered them.

4. As in the case of the Chaldean inscriptions, it was reserved for the nineteenth century to decipher these hieroglyphics, or sacred carvings, and the knowledge thus gained was supplemented by the rolls of papyrus, covered with the same signs, which were found in the coffins with the mummies.

5. From these sources we learn that the pyramids are the earliest monuments of Egypt. They were erected to serve as the tombs of the kings of what is known as the Old Empire, which began at some unknown period, and lasted until 2000 years B. C. The seat of government of the Old Empire was at Memphis.

6. The Pyramids are sixty in number. Three of these are most wonderful in size; the largest covering thirteen acres of ground—twice the area of the largest building in the world, St. Peter's at Rome,—and reaching 480 feet in height. This Pyramid contained but two tomb chambers, one for the king, and one for the queen.

7. The Old Empire was overthrown by an invasion of wandering tribes from Asia, who established in its stead what is known as the Middle Empire. These foreign conquerors were called shepherds by the Egyptians on account of the pastoral life which they had led on the plains of Asia.

8. It was during the reign of one of the shepherd dynasty of kings, that Joseph was brought into Egypt (about 1750, B. C.) And it was no doubt the fact that he came from Asia and was a shepherd, like the king's forefathers, that caused Pharao to

---

3. Did they bear any other message? 4. When were these deciphered ? 5. What do we learn from these sources ? 6. What of the pyramids? 7. Who overthrew the Old Empire ? 8. When did Joseph come into Egypt ?

regard him with favor, and invite his family to settle in the country.

9. As time went on, the Egyptians made efforts to overthrow the shepherd power, and at length succeeded in doing so completely under Thŏth-mes III. Under this monarch begins what is known as the New Empire (about 1600 B. C.) during which Egypt reached the zenith of her glory.

10. Thothmes was a great warrior, and made Egypt the great military power of the age. Thebes, the city of the hundred gates, was the seat of his government, and became the capital of the world. From it he issued every year at the head of his armies, to make descents on Asia, and cause Egypt's great rival, Chaldea, to tremble.

11. He would return from these expeditions laden with the products of the country, goodly stores of gold and silver, and accompanied by long trains of captives to toil at the colossal monuments which he delighted in erecting.

12. Rome possesses an obelisk of Thothmes—the grandest ever built by him. But two companion ones erected by him have lately been transported—one to London, and the other to New York, where it stands in the Central Park.

13. While these changes had been taking place in Egypt, the family of Jacob had multiplied in Gessen, and become a great and prosperous people. There is no reason for believing that they were treated otherwise than kindly by Thothmes and the succeeding kings of his dynasty for almost three hundred years.

CHAPTER II.

MOSES.

1. AT length a king of the same dynasty, Ram-ses II., came to the throne. He found that the several of the nations of Asia

---

9. Did the Egyptians ever throw off the shepherd yoke ? 10. What was Thothmes ? 11. How would he return ? 12. Where are three of his obelisks ? 13. What of the Israelites during this time ? 1. Who began to oppress the Israelites ?

were about to unite in a war against him, and became fearful lest the vast body of Israelites who were kindred to his enemies, should unite with them against him.

2. So he resolved to try and reduce their number by harsh treatment and oppression, and to this end ordered them to be put at work constructing the Great Wall which he was building to guard the country from approach by way of Asia.

3. Others of the children of Israel toiled at the construction of his strong treasure cities, while more labored at the erection of the huge and solemn temples which rose in such numbers during this Pharao's reign.

4. But though watched by cruel overseers, who made them furnish mortar, bricks, and all manner of service in the field, the Israelites continued to multiply. So Ramses ordered that every male child thenceforth born among them should at once be cast into the river, and drowned.

5. Soon after the issue of this barbarous royal decree an Israelite woman of the tribe of Levi bore a son, and seeing that he was a goodly child, hid him for three months. Then finding that she could conceal him no longer, she laid the babe in a basket of bulrushes, which she placed in the sedge by the river's brink.

6. Presently the daughter of Pharao came down to bathe in the river. And when she saw the basket, she told one of her maids to bring it to her. When it was opened and the princess saw the lovely infant, her heart was touched, the more so as it began to cry.

7. "This is one of the Hebrew babes," said the princess. Then the child's sister, Mary, who was watching near by, came forward and said, "Shall I go and call to thee a Hebrew woman to nurse the babe?" The princess answered, "Go," and the maid went and brought her mother.

8. When the mother came, the princess said, "Take this

---

2. What did he resolve? 3. What did others toil at? 4. Did this treatment reduce them? 5. What did one mother do? 6. What happened? 7. What did the princess say? 8. What did the princess say to the mother?

child and nurse him for me, and I will give thee thy wages."
Joyfully the mother took back her child and nursed him, and when he had grown up, delivered him to the princess, who called him Moses (drawn out) because she said, "I drew him out of the water."

9. The youth thus strangely saved, had a far different fate from his people. While they toiled as slaves, he was brought up as a prince at the magnificent court of Pharao, and was instructed in all the wisdom of the Egyptians. He remained there till he was forty years of age, and then becoming desirous of knowing something of his own people, he left the court and dwelt among them.

10. One day, he happened to see an Egyptian overseer cruelly beating a Hebrew, and in his anger, slew the Egyptian. For this offence the king ordered him to be put to death. But Moses fled away into Ma-di-an or Me-di-a, a province of Asia, which bordered on Egypt.

11. While on his journey, he one day sat down by a well, and presently seven maidens came thither to draw water for their flocks. But just as the sheep were about to drink, some shepherds rushed up and drove them away. Moses at once arose, drove off the shepherds, and watered the maidens' flocks.

12. These maidens were the daughters of Jeth-ro, a priest of Me-di-a. When he heard what had taken place, he came and welcomed Moses to his home. And Moses married his daughter Sephora, and remained with him for forty years.

13. One day Moses drove the flocks of his father-in-law into the desert as far as Mount Horeb. And there the Lord appeared to him in the midst of a burning bush, and spoke to him, telling him to put the shoes from his feet, for he stood on holy ground, and the God of Abraham, Isaac, and Jacob, was speaking to him.

14. Filled with holy fear, Moses hid his face. And the Lord said, "I have seen the affliction of my people in Egypt, and I

---

9. What was Moses' fate? 10. What did he do one day? 11. What took place on his journey? 12. Who were these maidens? 13. Relate the vision of God to Moses? 14. How did Moses act?

am come to deliver them out of the hands of the Egyptians, and to bring them out of that land into a land flowing with milk and honey."

15. "And I will send thee to Pharao, then thou mayest bring forth my people, the children of Israel, out of Egypt." But Moses answered, "Who am I that I should go to Pharao, and bring forth the children of Israel out of Egypt?"

16. The Lord, to give him confidence, answered, "I will be with thee." But Moses declared that the people would ask who sent him. The Lord answered "I AM WHO AM. Thus shalt thou say to the children of Israel, 'HE WHO IS hath sent me to you.'"

17. Still Moses was not convinced. Then God made him cast his staff on the ground, when it became a serpent. Then God bade him take it by the tail, when it became once more a rod. And He told him to work this sign before the Israelites, and they would be convinced of the truth of his mission.

18. But Moses still objected, saying that he was slow and hesitating in his speech. But the Lord said that Aaron (ah-ron), his brother, who had the gift of eloquence, should speak, only Moses must tell him what to say.

19. So at last Moses yielded, and returning home, took leave of his father-in-law, and set out with his wife and children for Egypt. And on the way he met Aaron whom God had inspired to come forth and meet him.

20. Together they entered Egypt, and before the assembled children of Israel, Aaron spoke and told that the Lord had willed their deliverance. And Moses wrought the sign of the rod, and other miracles, and the people believed, and falling prostrate, adored the Lord.

---

15. Continue. 16. What did the Lord answer? 17. Was Moses convinced? 18. What last objection did Moses make? 19. Did he yield? 20. How did they convince Israel?

CHAPTER III.

THE TEN PLAGUES OF EGYPT.

1. RAM-SES, the Pharao who had decreed Moses' death, was now dead, and his son Me-neph'-tah, reigned in his stead. So Moses one day presented himself at his court, and demanded permission in the name of God, to conduct the Israelites out of Egypt into the desert, to sacrifice to the Lord.

2. The haughty monarch answered, "Who is the Lord that I should hear his voice, and let Israel go? I know not the Lord, neither will I let Israel go." And from that day he oppressed Israel more then ever.

3. The Lord bade Moses and Aaron appear again before Pharao. They did so, and Aaron cast his rod before Pharao and it was changed into a serpent. Pharao summoned magicians, who also turned their rods into serpents, but Aaron's rod devoured their rods. But Pharao refused to hear Moses' prayer.

4. The Lord now sent ten plagues on Egypt. The following morning Aaron went to the Nile and struck it with his rod, and at once it was turned into blood, and the fish in it died. Still Pharao's heart remained hard.

5. Moses now stretched forth his rod over the streams, the rivers and the pools of Egypt, and there came up an innumerable multitude of frogs, which covered the land, and came into the palace of the king, and filled all the rooms and even the beds, ovens and cisterns.

6. Filled with consternation, Pharao promised to let Israel depart, if the plague were removed; but as soon as the frogs had vanished, he refused once more. So Moses brought a third plague, myriads of gnats, which tormented both man and beast, so that they had no peace.

7. But even under this torment, Pharao remained obstinate.

---

1. Was Ram-ses dead? 2. What did he answer? 3. What did the Lord command Moses and Aaron? 4. How did God punish Pharao? 5. What did Moses do now? 6. Did Pharao relent? 7. Did he yield?

THE TEN PLAGUES OF EGYPT. 61

Then God sent a fourth plague, a grievous swarm of flies that filled the houses of all the Egyptians, so that the whole land was corrupted by them. Pharao then gave way, and he said, "I will let you go to sacrifice to the Lord your God in the wilderness, but go no further. Pray for me."

8. Moses went out and prayed for Pharao that the flies might be removed, but no sooner were they gone than he again refused. Then God sent a fifth plague which attacked the cattle, and destroyed the best part of the flocks and herds of the Egyptians, but spared those of the Israelites. Still Pharao would not yield.

9. God then sent in succession on the land, a plague of boils and swelling blains on man and beast, a hail storm that destroyed all the crops that were above ground, and a swarm of beasts that ate up every blade of grass and green herb in the land. And on the occasion of each plague, Pharao promised to let Israel go, but broke his word as soon as they were removed.

10. At last God sent a horrible darkness, which covered the land for three days. It was so thick that it could be felt, and while it lasted no Egyptian could see another, or durst move from the spot where he was. But with the children of Israel, there was light.

11. In terror Pharao summoned Moses, and offered to let the Israelites go, if they would leave their flocks and herds in Egypt. Moses answered, "All the flocks shall go with us."

12. Pharao then revoked his permission, and said to Moses, "Get thee from me. And beware thou see not my face any more, for in what day soever thou shalt come into my sight, thou shalt die."

13. Moses answered, "So shall it be as thou hast spoken, I will not see thy face any more." And filled with wrath at the duplicity of the wicked king, he quitted the court, little dreaming how soon, and under what circumstances, he and Pharao were to meet again.

---

8. Did Moses pray for Pharao? 9. What plagues did God then send in succession? 10. What did God send at last? 11. What effect had

CHAPTER IV.

THE EXODUS OF ISRAEL.

Red Sea. An inland sea, 1450 miles in length, lying between Egypt and Arabia. It is connected by Bab-el-Mandeb Strait, with the Gulf of Aden, which opens into the Indian Ocean.

1. THE Lord now told Moses that He would send one more plague on Egypt which would cause Pharao to yield, and gave him certain instructions to impart to the children of Israel. So Moses told the people that the Lord would pass through Egypt at midnight, and kill every first-born of the Egyptians from the child of Pharao, to the child of the peasant.

2. He then went on to tell them that the Lord commanded them to kill in every family, on the fourteenth day of the month, a lamb without blemish, and to sprinkle the door-posts with its blood.

3. The Lord also commanded that on the night of that day they should eat the flesh of the lamb, with unleavened bread and wild lettuce. They were to eat in haste, with their loins girt, their shoes on their feet, their staves in their hands : for it was the passage of the Lord, whose angel would that night slay every first-born of the Egyptians.

4. Thus was the feast of the Pasch (pask), or Passage, instituted. The children of Israel did as Moses had commanded, and while within their dwellings, marked by the saving blood of the lamb, they celebrated the solemn feast, the Angel of the Lord passed through the land and slew every first-born of the Egyptians.

5. And at midnight a cry of woe rose throughout Egypt, for there was death in every dwelling from the king's palace to the peasant's hut. And Pharao's pride was broken at last, and while it was still night, he sent for Moses and Aaron, and

---

1. What did the Lord say to Moses? 2. What else did he tell them?
3. What more did God command? 4. What Feast was thus instituted?

bade them depart at once with all their people, and possessions.

6. The Egyptian people also besought them to depart, and in return, the Israelites asked for vessels of gold and silver, and rich garments, as some compensation for the unpaid labor of their long slavery. Having obtained these, they departed in such haste, that they took the unleavened dough, mixed for their bread, tied in their cloaks which they slung over their shoulders.

7. Dawn saw the long train of Israelites, numbering six hundred thousand, moving out of Egypt, four hundred and thirty years after the time that Jacob had entered it with his family. They bore with them the bones of Joseph, according to the promise made him by the Israelites on his deathbed.

8. And Moses said to them, "Remember this day, on which with a strong hand, the Lord brought you forth out of this place, that you eat none but unleavened bread." He also bade them sanctify every first-born to the Lord, because the Lord had slain every first-born of the Egyptians for them.

9. God Himself conducted the Israelites in their march, going before them as a pillar of cloud by day, and a pillar of fire by night. At first they kept on the beaten track towards Palestine, but then received the Divine command to turn aside into the wilderness, and to encamp on the shore of the Red Sea.

10. Meanwhile Pharao's anguish and terror had abated, and he began to repent of having let his vast and useful slave population depart. So he made ready his chariots and came in pursuit of them at the head of his army.

11. When the Israelites beheld their oppressor coming down upon them, they feared exceedingly and said to Moses, "Were there no graves in Egypt, that thou hast brought us out to die in the wilderness?" But Moses said, "Fear not; the Lord will fight for you."

12. It was night by the time the Egyptians came up to the

---

6. What did the Egyptian people do? 7. What did the dawn see? 8. What did Moses say to them? 9. How were they conducted? 10. What of Pharao? 11. Were the Israelites terrified? 12. What mir-

encampment of Israel, and the pillar of cloud that was before Israel, changed its place, and stood between the two hosts, so that they could not come near each other. And it gave light to Israel, but enveloped their enemy in so deep a darkness that they dared not stir.

13. Then Moses, at God's command, stretched his rod over the broad sea that lay before him, and at once the waters divided and rose like a great wall on each side, leaving a dry road on which the children of Israel passed over to the opposite shore.

14. At the dawn of day, the Egyptians dashed into the sea in pursuit of them. But the hour was now at hand when the cruel and impenitent king was to feel God's vengeance. At the command of God, Moses stretched his hand over the riven waters, and they rushed together again and engulfed Pharao and all his host: while all Israel, in thankfulness for this splendid miracle, burst into a song of triumph on the shore.

The Paschal lamb was a figure of Jesus slain for the sins of men. Its blood, sprinkled on the door posts, prevented the Destroying Angel from entering in. So the blood of the Lamb of God prevents the devil harming those who receive it worthily in Holy Communion.

The Passage of the Red Sea is a figure of the sacrament of Baptism. As there was no other way for Israel to escape Pharao, so there is no other way to escape from the power of Satan, save by Baptism.

CHAPTER V.

THE GIVING OF THE LAW ON MOUNT SINAI.

Mount Sinai (si'nā) is situated in the north-western part of Arabia near the Red Sea. It is 8,593 feet in height.

1. SCARCELY had the echoes of the song of triumph died away when murmuring and discontent were heard amongst the Israelites. For three days they could find no water in the desert, and then when they found a well, its waters proved to be bitter.

---

13. What did Moses do? 14. Did the Egyptians pursue them, and

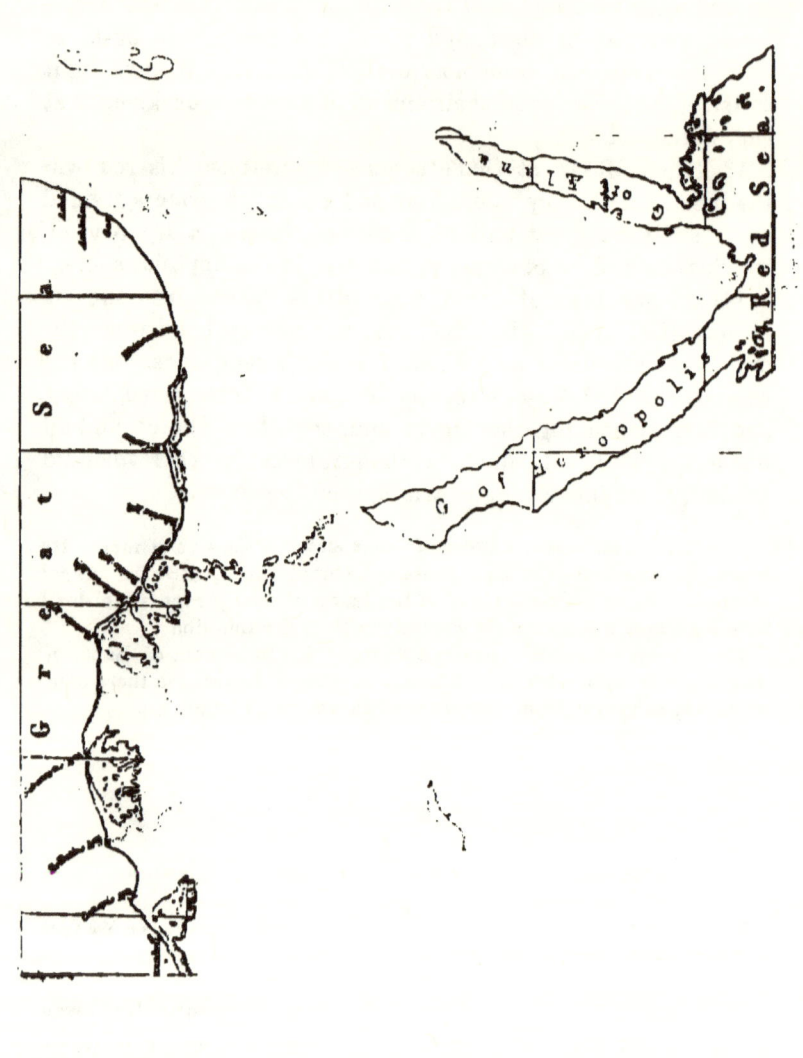

THE ROCK OF HOREB.

But Moses quieted them by casting a tree into the well at God's command, which rendered it sweet.

2. They moved on further into the wilderness, but at their next encampment, the bread which they had brought from Egypt began to fail. So they began to murmur again, and regret the bondage of Egypt, with its flesh-pots. But God instead of punishing them for their want of confidence, promised them food in abundance.

3. That evening He caused the camp to be covered with quails, and in the morning, a dew like hoar-frost, lay on the ground around it. And when the Israelites saw this glistening substance, they exclaimed " Manhu?" which means in Hebrew, What is this?

4. Then Moses told them that it was bread which the Lord had sent them, and bade every one gather as much as he needed. They did so and found it pleasant to the taste, like flour mixed with honey. And Moses told them to gather a double portion on the eve of the Sabbath, as none would fall on that day.

5. This heavenly bread continued to fall during the forty years of Israel's wandering in the desert, and they called it Manna. It is a type of the sacrament of the Holy Eucharist, which is given to nourish our souls for everlasting life.

6. As they moved on through the desert they reached another place where there was no water, and their murmurings against Moses began again. Moses rebuked them for their want of confidence in God, and prayed for guidance. And God bade him strike a rock on the side of Mount Hōreb. He did so and an abundant stream of water gushed forth at his blow.

7. About this time a fierce and war-like nation named the Am'-al-ek-ites attacked the Israelites. Moses sent Josue (Josh-u-ă) at the head of a chosen band of Israelites to meet them, while he went up on to a mountain near by to pray.

8. And as long as Moses' hands remained uplifted in prayer, the Israelites overcame, but when through fatigue they fell, even

---

2. Did they murmur again? 3. How did He provide for their wants?
4. What did Moses tell them? 5. Did the supply of bread continue? 6. What caused them to murmur again? 7. What nation attacked them?
8. What happened in consequence?

a little, Israel lost. So Aaron and Hur held up his hands till the enemy was put to flight.

9. The prayer of Moses is a figure of the prayers of the church; and especially of the contemplative religious orders. The active work of the church for the conversion of nations, and the relief of suffering, can never prosper unless it is aided by the prayers of those who have retired like Moses to pray, while the battle goes on in the plain below.

10. In the third month after their departure from Egypt, the Israelites reached to Mount Sinai, where they pitched their tents. Moses was summoned to the top of the mountain, where God appeared to him, and bade him remind the people of all the miracles He had wrought in their behalf, and tell them that if they would keep His law, they should continue to be His chosen people.

11. Moses went down from the mountain and told the people all that the Lord had said. And they cried as with one voice, "All that the Lord hath spoken we will do." Then Moses ascended the mountain again and received God's instructions as to how Israel should prepare for the reception of the Law.

12. They were to purify themselves from all defilement, and sanctify themselves so as to be fit to appear in His presence. Then on the third day, they were to come to the mountain, around which barriers were to be placed, lest they should approach too near and die.

13. These instructions were obeyed, and on the third morning, the mountain began to be covered with a thick cloud, thunder was heard, and the lightning began to flash. The mountain began to tremble, while smoke and fire ascended from it, as from a furnace.

14. In the midst of these fearful signs, the sound of a mighty trumpet was heard, and then, from the midst of the cloud that covered the mountain, the Voice of the Lord delivered

---

9. Of what is the prayer of Moses a figure? 10. Where did the Israelites go in the third month of their departure from Egypt? 11. Did Moses tell them? 12. Repeat his instructions. 13. Was this done? 14. What was heard?

the Ten Commandments, to serve as mankind's moral guide till the end of time.

15. When the Voice had ceased, the terrified people cried out to Moses, "Speak thou to us, and we will hear; let not the Lord speak to us, lest we die." And they fell back from the mountain, but Moses went into the cloud, and received other laws from the Lord, which he wrote down.

16. Then he came forth and explained them to the people who cried out, "We will do all the words of the Lord which he hath spoken." Moses then built an altar at the foot of the mountain, and offered victims on it, and he took half their blood, and poured it into bowls, and half he poured upon the altar.

17. And when he had read the words of the Covenant or Agreement, to the people, and they had agreed to observe it, he took the blood and sprinkled it on the people, and said, "This is the blood of the Covenant which the Lord hath made with you, concerning all these words."

18. Thus was the first Covenant completed on Mount Sinai, and solemnly sealed with the blood of animals, to hold good till the New Covenant, sealed in the blood of Our Lord on Mount Calvary, should take its place.

CHAPTER VI.

ISRAEL BECOMES THE CHURCH OF GOD.

1. ALTHOUGH the people of Israel held the Covenant of circumcision by inheritance from their great forefather, Abraham, and though they had just concluded a still more solemn Covenant sealed with blood, yet for want of a priesthood, an altar, and a sacrifice, they were not as yet the Church of God.

2. The Lord was now about to raise them to the dignity of

Repeat the Ten Commandments. 15. What did the people do? 16. What did Moses do? 17. Continue. 18. How long was the Covenant to hold?

1. What did Israel still lack? 2. What was the Lord about to do?

ISRAEL BECOMES THE CHURCH OF GOD.

being His Church, and for this purpose He commanded Moses to set about erecting the Sacred Tabernacle. And Moses was desirous that the people should show their sense of the blessing, by freely offering their most precious and beautiful possessions to aid in its adornment.

3. The people obeyed the call with great joy, and offerings of gold, silver, precious stones, and fine linen, were so numerous that at length Moses was forced to make a proclamation that no more was needed.

4. Then God inspired the workmen, and in the barren desert, the Tabernacle rose in beauty before the eyes of Israel. It was a portable church, a shrine that could be taken apart and carried from place to place, as suited the wandering life of Israel.

5. It was built of the precious and imperishable sētim wood, and was thirty cubits in length, ten cubits in height, and ten also in breadth. The boards were overlaid with plates of gold, and the sockets for the supports, were of silver.

6. It was divided into two parts: the outer court which held the Altar of Holocausts, and the laver, a large brass basin for the priest to cleanse his hands and feet in before and during the sacrifice; and the Holy Tabernacle.

7. The Tabernacle itself was again divided into two compartments. The outer or larger part was called the Sanctuary, and was draped with rich hangings of fine linen, with embroideries of cherubim and palms and flowers, in blue and crimson, and gold and purple.

8. In this Sanctuary stood the Altar of Incense, a Golden Altar, from which clouds of incense rose perpetually from the people's offering of rich spices that burned upon it. On the left of this altar stood the seven-branched candlestick of gold, holding seven lamps, which burned continually; fed with the purest oil.

---

3. Did they respond? 4. Did the Sanctuary take shape? 5. Of what was it built? 6. How was it divided? 7. How was the Tabernacle itself divided? 8. What stood in this sanctuary?

THE TABERNACLE.

LOAVES OF PROPOSITION.

ISRAEL BECOMES THE CHURCH OF GOD. 71

9. To the right of the altar was a table of setim wood covered with gold, which contained twelve loaves of bread, made of the finest flour, and unleavened, and a gold cup, filled with wine.

10. These loaves, which were called the Loaves of Proposition, were kept in their places by a golden frame, while three small golden tubes were placed between each loaf to prevent mouldiness. They were renewed before each Sabbath, and the ones that were removed were eaten by the priests only.

11. The second or inner chamber of the Sanctuary was called the Holy of Holies. It too was draped with richly embroidered linen, and contained the Ark of the Covenant which was covered with gold, within and without.

12. The ark was a coffer of imperishable wood, about three feet, nine inches in width, by two feet, nine inches in height. By the time it was completed, Moses had received from God stone tables with the Ten Commandments engraved on them, and these were placed within it, and a vase filled with manna.

13. Over the Ark was placed a plate of gold which served as a cover to it, and was known as the Mercy Seat. Two cherubims, one on either side, bent in adoration over it, with their wings overshadowing it.

14. Over this Mercy Seat, the shadow of the Divine Presence rested, day and night, and alone lighted the Holy of Holies. Into this place none but the High Priest alone might enter, and he only on one day in the year, the day of solemn annual atonement.

15. The whole frame of the Tabernacle was enclosed by a tent of goats' hair, then by one of rams' skins, dyed red, and finally, one of fine furs. A regular body of Levites or priests were set apart, to carry the different parts of the Tabernacle when it was taken down or removed.

---

9. What stood at the right of this altar? 10. How were these loaves arranged? 11. Describe the Holy of Holies. 12. Describe the Ark. 13. What was the Mercy Seat? 14. What rested over the Mercy Seat? 15. What enclosed the whole frame of the Tabernacle?

16. Sad to relate, while this work of glory and beauty was going forward, the Israelites exhibited the blackest ingratitude to the God who had brought them from slavery to freedom and happiness.

17. Moses had again been summoned into the Presence of God on the mountain, and remained there forty days, and forty nights, conversing with God. And at the end of that time God gave him two tables of stone on which were written the ten commandments.

18. Meanwhile the people, thinking from his long absence that he was dead, forgot God and begged Aaron to make them a god whom they could see. Afraid to resist, Aaron took the gold ornaments which they brought him, and fashioned them into the form of a molten calf.

19. When it was finished, he set it up, and the people were delighted, and cried out, "These are thy gods, O Israel, that brought thee out of the land of Egypt." And they built an altar and offered sacrifice to it, and began to feast and dance before it, after the custom of the Egyptians.

20. The sound of their impious rejoicing reached the ears of Moses as he descended the mountain, and when he reached the camp and saw them adoring the idol, he was filled with just wrath, and dashed the tables of stone which God had given him to the ground, and broke them into pieces. Then he melted the calf and ground it to powder.

21. He sternly rebuked Aaron for yielding to the wicked desires of the people, and ordered all who were on the Lord's side to join him. The sons of Levi at once gathered about him, and Moses ordered them to take their swords and go through the camp, and slay all whom they found practicing idolatry.

22. They did as they were commanded, and almost twenty-three thousand men were put to death. Then Moses once more ascended the mountain, and interceded with the Lord for the

---

16. What took place at this time ? 17. Where was Moses ? 18. What did the people demand of Aaron ? 19. Continue. 20. What effect had their sin on Moses ? 21. What did he say to Aaron ? 22. What was the result ?

INSTITUTION OF THE PRIESTHOOD, HEBREW FEASTS. 73

ungrateful people, and after earnest pleading, obtained forgiveness for their crime.

23. Then the Lord told him to prepare two other tables of stone, and when he had done so, the Lord once more wrote the ten commandments.

24. Moses then descended the mountain with the precious burden in his arms, and his face was so radiant with glory from his communing with the Lord, that the people were afraid to approach him, and from that time he had to veil his face whenever he spoke to them.

<small>Moses, the mediator of the Old Covenant, prefigures Jesus Christ, the mediator of the New Testament. The prayer of Moses shows us how powerful is the intercession of the saints to avert the chastisement of God.</small>

CHAPTER VII.

THE INSTITUTION OF THE PRIESTHOOD AND THE GREAT HEBREW FEASTS.

1. THE work of the Holy Sanctuary, which had been interrupted by the sin of the Golden Calf, was now resumed, and when all was completed, according to God's command, Moses poured sacred oil on the Tabernacle and all that it contained.

2. And thenceforth a cloud covered the Ark of the Covenant, and the Glory of God filled the tabernacle, and rested on the Mercy Seat between the two cherubim. And wherever the children of Israel removed, the Lord was present over the Tabernacle in a pillar of cloud by day, and a pillar of fire by night.

3. A priesthood had now to be instituted. Aaron was chosen High Priest, and Moses proceeded to consecrate him. Before the assembled people, he presented Aaron and his sons before the

---

<small>23. What did God then command him to do? 24. What happened when he descended?

1. What was now resumed? 2. What was thenceforth seen? 3. What had now to be instituted?</small>

Lord, and then after purifying Aaron with water, he clothed him with the sacred vestments.

4. First he placed on him a short linen garment, and over it a violet tunic, and then the eph'od. This was a kind of girdle which was brought from behind the neck over the shoulder, then crossed on the breast and finally carried under the arms, so as to serve as a girdle to the tunic. All priests wore ephods, but theirs were of simple linen, while the high priest's was richly embroidered in purple and gold.

5. Moses than suspended from his neck the rational, on which were twelve stones, each bearing the name of one of the twelve tribes of Israel, and placed on his head the mitre, in the middle of the front of which was a gold plate with the inscription, "The Holy of the Lord." Then he poured oil on his head and consecrated him.

6. After his sons and the Levites had been consecrated, Aaron advanced to the altar, and having offered a victim, stretched forth his hands over the people, and blessed them, saying, "The Lord bless thee, and keep thee, the Lord show his face to thee, and have mercy on thee, the Lord turn his countenance to thee, and give thee peace."

7. This threefold blessing contains an indication of the mystery of the Most Holy Trinity. Hardly had the sound of it died on Aaron's lips, when fire came forth from the pillar of cloud, and consumed the holocaust. And the people fell prostrate, and adored the Lord.

8. After the institution of the priesthood, Moses prescribed by God's command the sacrifices which were to be offered him, and the manner in which they were to be offered. Some of these were bloody sacrifices, and consisted of sheep, goats, and oxen; others were unbloody and consisted of flour, fruit, oil, and wine.

9. When the thing offered was wholly consumed, it was called

---

4. Describe these. 5. What else did he place on Aaron? 6. What blessing did Aaron then give to the people? 7. What does this blessing contain and what miracle followed? 8. What else did Moses prescribe?

a holocaust, or whole burnt offering, and constituted the highest act of adoration. But when only the fat, as the most delicate portion, was consumed by fire, and the rest was eaten, it was called either a sacrifice of thanksgiving or of expiation.

10. Moses also instituted the Feasts of the Lord, according to His command. The first of these was the Festival of the Pasch or Passover, in memory of the Paschal Lamb eaten by them on the night of their deliverance from Egyptian bondage. During the seven days of its observance, they ate unleavened bread.

11. The Feast of the Passover prefigured the Christian Feast of Easter and of our delivery from the power of Satan by the Resurrection of Christ.

12. The next great Feast was the Feast of weeks, fifty days, or seven weeks after the Passover, corresponding to the Christian Feast of Pentecost. It was observed in remembrance of the law given them on Mount Sinai, and on it they offered the first fruits of the harvest to the Lord.

13. Their third great festival was the Feast of Tabernacles in the autumn, when the vintage was over. In later years, when the Israelites had entered the Promised Land, and dwelt in houses, they left them at the time of this feast, and abode in tents built of the branches of the trees, in memory of their wandering in the wilderness, and of their being fed with manna in the desert.

14. Though it was a season of joy, the Feast of Tabernacles had the same object in view as the Christian Lent, to remind the people that life was short, and that heaven, not earth, was their home. On these three feasts, the men of Israel had to appear before the Lord in the Tabernacle.

15. There was also a Day of Atonement, kept as a most solemn fast, when the high priest sacrificed a calf for his own sins, and a he-goat for the sins of the people.

16. This Day of Atonement was the only time he was permitted

---

10. What did Moses also institute? 11. What did this feast prefigure? 12. What was the next great feast? 13. What was the third? 14. What was its object? 15. What else was observed by Israel? 16. What pri-

to draw aside the veil which hung before the Holy of Holies, and enter it. He took with him the blood of the victim, and the golden censer; and after having incensed the Mercy Seat, he sprinkled it and the front of the ark with the blood.

The unbloody sacrifices prefigured the unbloody sacrifice of the Mass, by which the fruit of the sacrifice of the Cross is constantly applied to us. The High Priest is a figure of Jesus Christ, who offered Himself to His Father on the Cross in a bloody manner, and who daily at Mass, repeats the sacrifice in an unbloody manner.

CHAPTER VIII.

THE SPIES—REVOLT OF CORE, DATHAN, AND ABIRON.

1. IN the second year after their departure from Egypt, the silver trumpets sounded the warning of departure, and the great host of Israel began to move from Sinai towards the borders of the Land of Chanaan. And when they came to the desert of Phar'an on its southern borders, Moses sent forth twelve men, one of every tribe, to explore the Promised Land.

2. These twelve spies crossed the Jordan, and entering Chanaan from the south, came to Hebron, where Abraham had once dwelt. After some further exploration they returned to the camp, having been absent forty days.

3. They brought with them bunches of grapes, so huge that they had to be carried, hung from poles, borne on the shoulders of two men, along with figs and other rich fruits, which confirmed the truth of Chanaan's being a land flowing with milk and honey.

4. But all save two of them, Caleb and Josue, united in declaring that it would be utterly impossible to conquer it. They described the men as giants, in comparison with whom

---

1. When did they remove from Sinai? 2. How did these spies proceed? 3. What did they bring with them? 4. What did ten of them declare?

they seemed as locusts,, and the cities as surrounded with strong walls, before which they would be powerless.

5. And when the people heard them, they began to murmur, and say, "Would to God we had died in Egypt, and would to God we might die in this wilderness; is it not better to return to Egypt?" And when Moses and Aaron heard them, they were so filled with sorrow and regret, that they fell prostrate on the ground.

6. In vain Caleb and Josue implored Israel to remen.ber that the Lord was all powerful, and would enable them to prevail against the enemy. In their fury they would have stoned them to death, had not the glory of the Lord manifested itself over the Covenant to all the children of Israel.

7. And the Lord said to Moses, "How long will this people not believe me for the signs I have wrought before them? I will strike them with pestilence, but thee I will make a ruler over a nation mightier than this is."

8. But Moses interceded for the guilty people, and the Lord at length consented to spare their lives, but declared that not one of those over twenty years of age, who had murmured against Him, should enter the land. They should die in the wilderness, but the children, whom in their wickedness, they had declared would be the prey of their enemies, should enter in, and conquer it.

9. The messengers who had encouraged the fears of the people, were struck dead. And when Moses told the people the doom which God had pronounced on them, they mourned bitterly.

10. A new evil now broke out in the camp. Moses had ordered a certain man to be stoned to death, for breaking the Sabbath, and about two hundred and fifty of the leading men of the congregation, joined with Core (kō're) a prominent Levite, in resenting this action on the part of Moses.

---

5. What effect had their tale on the people? 6. What did Caleb and Josue do? 7. What did the Lord say to Moses? 8. Did Moses succeed in saving them? 9. What of the messengers? 10. What broke out in the camp?

11. And Core said to Moses, "All the people are holy; why do you raise yourself above the people of God?" On hearing his words Moses knew they only masked his feelings of rebellion against God, and fell prostrate in grief.

12. Afterwards he reproved the rebellious Levites. "Is it," he asked, "because God has desired you to serve near the Tabernacle, that you desire to usurp the dignity of the priesthood also? To-morrow the Lord will make known who they are that belong to him. Prepare then, and stand, each with his censer, on one side, and Aaron will stand on the other."

13. But on the following day, when the two hundred and fifty were to appear before the Lord, Dā'than and A-bī'ron, of the tribe of Reuben, who with Core, led the revolt, refused to come forth from their tents.

14. So Moses went to them, and told the people to separate themselves from these wicked men, lest they perish with them. Then he said, "If these men die the common death of men, the Lord did not send me, but if the earth opens her mouth and swallows them, and they go down alive into hell, you shall know they have blasphemed the Lord."

15. Scarcely had he finished speaking, than the earth opened and swallowed Core, Dathan, and Abiron, with their tents and all that belonged to them. At the same time, fire descended from heaven, and destroyed the two hundred and fifty who had taken sides with them.

16. After this the Lord bade Moses take a rod from a prince of every one of the twelve tribes of Israel, and after writing the name of each man on his rod, lay them in the Tabernacle of the Covenant. "And whomsoever of these I will choose," said the Lord, "his rod shall blossom."

17. Moses did as the Lord commanded, and when he entered the Tabernacle on the following day, he found that the rod of Aaron had blossomed. He then brought out the rods and

---

11. What did Core say to Moses? 12. What did he do afterwards? 13. What took place on the next day? 14. What did Moses do? 15. What happened? 16. What did the Lord bid Moses? 17. What was the

THE ROD OF AARON BLOSSOM-BLOOMING.

showed them to Israel, but afterwards by God's command, replaced Aaron's rod in the Tabernacle, where it remained as a memorial of the rebellion and punishment of the wicked children of Israel.

CHAPTER IX.

CLOSE OF ISRAEL'S WANDERINGS—DEATH OF MOSES.

1. THE years went by, and the Israelites who had murmured against God, gradually died, until at last, when the fortieth year of their wandering dawned, there was not one left. It was their children whom Moses was now conducting, but the murmuring and discontented spirit of their parents was present in them.

2. So when they came to a place where they suffered for want of water they began to complain and ask Moses why he had brought them out of Egypt. Then the Lord commanded Moses to strike a certain rock and it would yield water.

3. So Moses assembled the people, and raising his rod, struck the rock, but as the water did not instantly flow, he doubted, and struck a second time. The water gushed forth, but the Lord was so displeased with the sin of Moses in doubting him, that He told him he should not lead his people into the Promised Land.

4. The Lord then gave the place the name of the Waters of Contradiction, because the children of Israel had there striven with words against the Lord, and He was sanctified in them.

5. The next encampment of the Israelites was at Mount Hor. Here Aaron, who had shared in the sin of Moses, died, and E-le-ä-zar, his son, was made high priest in his place.

6. Some time later, the Israelites, weary of their long wandering and the daily manna, began to murmur against the Lord

---

1. What changes did the years make? 2. What roused this anew? 3. Did Moses do so? 4. What name did the Lord give the place? 5. Where did they next encamp? 6. Did they murmur again?

and Moses. And God sent fiery serpents among them, by whose deadly bite, a great multitude perished. And knowing that the serpents had been sent in punishment of their sins they besought Moses to intercede for them, that they might be taken away.

7. The Lord heard the prayer of Moses, and bade him make a brazen serpent, and set it up in the sight of all. He did so and all who looked at it were healed.

8. The brazen serpent is a figure of the Redeemer as He himself afterwards declared, "As Moses lifted up the serpent in the desert, so must the Son of Man be lifted up, that whosoever believeth in Him should not perish, but have life everlasting."—(John iii, 14.)

9. The term of the wanderings of Israel was now drawing to a close, and they drew near to the Promised Land. They had now prevailed over so many of the hostile nations about them, that when they came to the borders of the territory of Bä′lac, the king of Mō-ab, he was filled with fear.

10. So he sent the elders and nobles of his kingdom with rich presents to Bū-laam, a noted soothsayer of the Am-mon-ites, a neighboring nation, to ask him to come and curse the Israelites for him. And Balaam told them to pass the night at his dwelling, and he would see what the Lord would command.

11. Now Balaam was a believer in the true God, though he had dealings with a familiar spirit. So when God forbade him in the night, he told them the next morning that he would not go. But the king sent again, and this time, God told Balaam to go.

12. So Balaam arose and went to the king of Moab, who took him to three different mountains in turn, whence he could behold the Israelites in the valley. Then he told him to curse them, but Balaam, constrained by God, burst forth into blessings instead.

---

7. Did the Lord hear his prayer? 8. Of what is the brazen serpent a figure? 9. What king grew fearful of the Israelites? 10. What did Balac do? 11. Did Balaam believe in God? 12. Did Balaam go?

13. "How beautiful are thy tabernacles, O Jacob," he exclaimed, "and thy tents, O Israel! He that blesseth thee, shall also himself be blessed, and he that curseth thee shall be reckoned accursed."

14. Balac grew angry, and dismissed him in disgrace to his home. Thereupon the eyes of Balaam were opened, and he saw a vision, and his lips were opened and he uttered the following prophecy:

15. "I shall see him, but not now; I shall behold him, but not near. A star shall arise out of Jacob, and a sceptre shall spring up from Israel and shall strike the chiefs of Moab, and shall smite the children of Seth."

16. This striking and beautiful prophecy refers to the Saviour, and the star mentioned is the star which appeared to the three Eastern sages at the birth of Christ.

17. The time of Moses on earth was now drawing to a close. According to God's command, he laid his hands on Josue in the presence of all Israel and presented him to them as their future ruler.

18. The great law-giver, faithful to his mission to the last, then charged the assembled people to remain true to God, and to avoid consulting soothsayers, or placing belief in dreams or omens. He also told them that God would send them a prophet like himself, whom they should hear.

19. He reminded them of all the wonders God had wrought for them, and assured them that if they kept His commandments, they should be blessed in their houses, blessed in their fields, blessed in the fruits of the land, blessed in their cattle, blessed when they came in and when they went out.

20. He then warned them of the judgments with which the Lord would visit them if they failed to keep His commandments. He then gave a book in which he had written all the

---

13. Repeat his words. 14. What was the result? 15. Repeat this prophecy. 16. To whom does this refer? 17. What did Moses do before his death? 18. What did he charge Israel? 19. What else did he say? 20. What warning did he give them?

words of His law, to the Levites, with a charge to put it inside of the Ark of the Covenant.

21. Then having blessed, the tribes of Israel, he went up from the plains of Moab to Mount Nebo. He was now one hundred and twenty years old, " yet his teeth were not loosed, neither were his eyes dim."

22. From the summit of the mountain, God showed him the fair and smiling Land of Chanaan, which He had promised to his fathers, Abraham, Isaac and Jacob, but which he was not to enter. And there the great leader died, and angels buried him, so that no man ever knew the place of his sepulchre.

Moses was a figure of Jesus Christ. Like Him, he proclaimed the Law of God, and confirmed his teaching by miracles, prophecies and a holy life. The prophet of whom Moses spoke was the Saviour, who was to establish a new law, more perfect than that of Moses.

CHAPTER X.

ISRAEL ENTERS THE PROMISED LAND.

Jericho is situated in the south of the Holy Land, and is famous for its roses. It is still more interesting, however, as the scene of many of our Lord's miracles. In His time it was a rich and prosperous city.

1. ISRAEL mourned Moses for thirty days. At the end of that time, the Lord commanded Josue to lead the people past the Jordan, into the Promised Land. And He promised him that He would deliver to him every spot that the sole of his foot should tread on.

2. Secure of victory, Josue led the host of Israel to the Jordan. When they reached its banks, he ordered the priests to take the Ark of the Lord, and go before the people. They did so, and as soon as their feet touched the waters they rolled back on either side, and left a dry channel through which the people crossed to the opposite shore.

---

21. Whither did he go? 22. What did he see?
1. What did God command Josue? 2. Did Josue obey?

3. They now pitched their tents before the strongly fortified city of Jericho. On the following day they celebrated the Pasch, and ate of the fruits of the earth. After this the manna ceased to fall.

4. When they saw how strong Jericho was, they began to despair of taking it. The Lord therefore ordered Josue to make all the fighting men of Israel march around it in utter silence, once a day for six days.

5. Then, on the seventh day they were to march in silence around it six times, but at the last time, when the priests sounded the trumpets, they were to give a great shout. These commands were carried out, and when, on the seventh day, the great shout of the people mingled with the sound of the trumpets, the walls of Jericho fell, and the Israelites took the city.

6. Josue pursued his victorious career, though his enemies were strong and numerous. Once five kings of the Am-or-rhites attacked him. It was late in the day before the tide of victory turned in favor of the Israelites, and Josue grew fearful lest the enemy should escape in the darkness and gain reinforcements.

7. So Josue spoke to the Lord in the sight of the people and said, "Move not, O Sun, towards Gab'-a-on, nor thou, O Moon, towards the valley of Aj'-a-lon." And the Lord heard the voice of man, and fought for Israel, and the day did not fade till Josue had utterly defeated the enemy.

8. When the land of Chanaan was conquered Josue proceeded to divide it among the tribes of Israel. The tribe of Levi alone received no portion, being supported by tithes and sacrifices, but they received forty-eight cities in different parts of the country.

9. The tribes of Reuben and Gad and half the tribe of Manasses had obtained permission from Moses to remain in possession

---

3. Where did they pitch their tents? 4. Did they lose heart? 5. What was to be done on the seventh day? 6. Did Josue continue to prevail? 7. What miracle did he obtain from God? 8. What did he proceed to do when Chanaan was conquered? 9. What tribes remained east of the Jordan?

of the meadow and pasture lands to the east of the Jordan, from the territory of Moab, northward to the borders of Damascus.

10. Of the other eight tribes and a half, those of Juda, Simeon, and Benjamin, settled in the south of Chanaan, adjacent to the cities of the Philistines on the sea-coast; while those of Asser, Dan, and Nephtali (Nef-tā-ly) held the north adjoining the great merchant cities of Tyre and Sidon, and Mount Lebanon.

11. The remaining tribes of Ephraim (Ef-ram) Zab'u-lon and Issachar (Is'-sa-kar), and the half tribe of Manasses, settled in the middle of Chanaan, the part of the country most fruitful for the purposes of agriculture.

12. Josue governed Israel until he was one hundred and ten years of age. When about to die, he summoned the people before him, and admonished them to observe the law of God, and avoid marriage with the heathens. Then he passed away, and they buried him on his own land in Mount Ephraim.

The Promised Land is a figure of Heaven. As the Israelites did not obtain it without toil and suffering and contention, so only shall Heaven be won, by bravely contending with the enemies of salvation.

CHAPTER XI.

ISRAEL UNDER THE JUDGES—BARAC—GEDEON—JEPHTE.

Mount Thabor (tā'bor), is situated in Palestine, eight miles east of Nazareth. It is 1000 feet in height. It was the spot where Our Lord was afterward transfigured. On its summit there now stands a church.

1. So long as these Israelites lived who had wandered in the desert, and eaten the heavenly manna, the nation remained faithful to God, but after they had departed, their children began to

---

10. What of the remaining tribes? 11. Who settled in the middle of Chanaan? 12. How long did Josue govern Israel?
1. Did Israel remain faithful to God?

contract marriages with the heathen nations around them, and in consequence fell into idolatry.

2. This brought heavy judgments on them which caused them to repent and turn once more to God, who would then raise up a deliverer, who would free them from their enemies, and restore the faith and worship of the God of Israel.

3. These men were called Judges. The first of them was called Ba'-rac. Israel had fallen under the power of Ja'lin, the king of the Chanaanites, when Deb'bor-a, a holy prophetess, sent word to Barac to raise an army and free Israel.

4. So Barac went forth and met the Chanaanites at Mount Thabor. They were mounted in chariots, and armed with scythes, but the Lord struck them with such terror at the sight of Barac that they fled in complete disorder.

5. Sis'a ra, their general, leaped from his chariot, and took refuge in the dwelling of Ja-el, a woman who belonged to a tribe that was friendly to his own nation. But when he was asleep, Jael drove a nail through his temple and killed him, and when Barac arrived in pursuit of him, she showed him the dead body.

6. When the news of this great victory reached Debbora, she sang a song of triumph before all Israel. And the land had rest for forty years, until, as the memory of the victory died away, Israel again did evil in the sight of God.

7. The Lord punished them by delivering them into the hands of their old enemies, the Ma'-di-an-ites, who swept through the land and laid it waste, so that there was nothing left to support life, and the Israelites were forced to take refuge in dens and caves in the mountains.

8. In their humiliation, they cried to the Lord for help against their nation's enemy, and He heard them and sent an angel to a youth named Ged'eon, the youngest son of a hum-

---

2. How did God punish them? 3. What were these men called? 4. Did he go? 5. What befell Sisara? 6. What did Debbora do on hearing the glad news? 7. How did God punish them now? 8. What did they do?

JAEL AND SISARA.

ble Israelite of the tribe of Manasses, to tell him that he was chosen to deliver Israel.

9. From that day the spirit of the Lord came on Gedeon, so when the army of the Madianites crossed the Jordan again, he sounded the trumpet, and sent messengers to the tribes of Israel to follow him, and soon had an army of thirty-two thousand men.

10. Before leading them to battle, Gedeon sought a sign from God as to whether or not he was to really be the savior of Israel. He put his fleece of wool on the ground, and begged that it might be wet with dew, while all the ground remained dry, if he was the destined deliverer. And the next morning he found it so wet that he filled a vessel with the dew which he wrung out of it.

11. On the next night he requested a further sign of his mission, that the ground might be wet but the fleece remain dry, and God granted him what he asked. So Gedeon hesitated no longer, but led his troops to meet the enemy.

12. But on the way, God commanded him to reduce his army, lest Israel should think they had conquered by their own strength. So Gedeon ordered all who felt timorous to return home, and twenty-two thousand departed, leaving only ten thousand to meet the enemy.

13. But God bade him reduce their numbers still further. "Bring them to the waters," he commanded, "and then I will try them." He then told Gedeon to observe how they drank, and to dismiss all who knelt down to drink at their ease, but to keep those who lifted the water to their mouths in the hollow of their hands, in order to save time.

14. Only three hundred men stood this test, and this little force Gedeon divided into three companies. Then he gave each man a trumpet and a pitcher with a lamp within it, and told them to do exactly as he did.

---

9. What happened to Gedeon? 10. What sign did he seek? 11. Was he satisfied? 12. What did God command on the way? 13. Was his army small enough now? 14. How many men were left to him?

15. At the midnight watch, he led his little force to the camp of the enemy. As they entered it they blew their trumpets, and dashed the pitchers against one another, while they cried with a loud voice, "The sword of the Lord and of Gedeon."

16. The terrific noise and the dazzling light, whose source they could not see, filled the Madianites with the wildest panic, and in the confusion, they turned their swords against one another, and fled in all directions. And Israel went in pursuit of them, and slew almost their whole army.

17. Gedeon ruled Israel for forty years, and during that time the nation enjoyed peace and prosperity. But after his death they fell again into idolatry, and were punished by being delivered into the hands of the Ammonites. And when they repented God raised up a valiant warrior, named Jephte (Jef'tĕ) to deliver them.

18. When about to lead the armies of Israel against the Ammonites, Jephte promised that if the Lord would grant him the victory, he would in return offer to the Lord, whatever should meet him first on his way home.

19. The Lord heard him; victory perched on his banners, and he was returning in joy and peace to his home, when he met his daughter coming with a band of maidens, with their timbrels, to do him honor.

20. And when he saw her, he rent his garments in sorrow, for she was his only child, but he kept his vow, and the maiden lived a solitary life, retired from the world, till her death.

---

15. What did he do? 16. How were the Madianites affected? 17. How long did Gedeon rule Israel? 18. What vow did Jephte make? 19. Was he victorious? 20. What did he do when he saw her?

SAMSON KILLS THE LION.

CHAPTER XII.

THE JUDGES OF ISRAEL—SAMSON—THE STORY OF RUTH.

Ga'za. The strongest city of the Philistines. It was regarded as the key to Syria. It was situated in the southern part of Palestine on the Mediterranean Sea. It is now known as Ghuzzah.

1. While Jephte was leading the tribes of Israel in the valley of the Jordan, God raised up another deliverer for His people in the south of Israel, which was menaced by the Philistines. This was Samson, of the tribe of Dan, and the strongest man that ever lived.

2. On one occasion, he met a young lion, and moved by the spirit of the Lord, tore it into pieces, as if it had been a young kid. Another time, when the Philistines had captured him, he burst his bonds, and snatching up the jaw bone of an ass, slew a thousand of them with it.

3. On another occasion he went to the city of Gaza. His presence was discovered, and they locked the gates to prevent his departure during the night, intending to kill him in the morning. But in the night Samson rose, and carried off the gates of Gaza with him to the top of a neighboring hill.

4. But though Samson was the chosen instrument of God, his conduct was often very bad, and resulted in his ruin. He became infatuated with a Philistine woman named Dalila, and after long pleading on her part, confided to her that the secret of his strength lay in the fact that his hair had never been cut, for he was a Nazarite, that is, one consecrated to God.

5. One day, when he was asleep, the treacherous Dalila cut off his hair, and then the Philistines rushed in, and after putting out his eyes, cast him into prison. And there he languished, till one day, when they held a great feast in honor of

---

1. What was taking place at this time in the south of Israel? 2. Relate some of his feats. 3. What happened in Gaza? 4. What must be said of Samson? 5. What did Dalila do?

their god Dagon, they had him brought out to amuse themselves with the sight of their great foe's humiliation.

6. His hair had now grown again, and his strength had returned to him. So after he had amused them by some wonderful feats, he asked the boy who led him, to place him where he could touch the pillars that supported the whole house. And when the boy did so, he prayed, "O Lord God, remember me, and restore to me my former strength."

7. Then, grasping the pillars, he shook them violently, exclaiming, "Let me die with the Philistines." And the building rocked and fell, and killed all who were in it, so that in his death, Samson slew more of the enemies of God than he had done in his whole life.

8. THE STORY OF RUTH.—During the time of the rule of Judges in Israel, there was a famine in the land, so that a certain man who dwelt in Bethlehem, named E-lim'-e-lech, went with his wife No'-e-mī, and his two sons, to live in the land of Moab.

9. There his two sons married, and died. Their father died, also, and Noemi, being left a poor widow, desired to return to Israel. She told her two daughters-in-law of her resolve, and advised them to return to their families.

10. One of them, Orpha, obeyed, but Ruth, the other, refused to stay in her own land without Noemi. "Whithersoever thou shalt go, I will go," said the young Moabitess, "where thou shalt dwell, I will dwell also. Thy people shall be my people, and thy God, my God."

11. So the two women journeyed back to Bethlehem. It was the beginning of the barley harvest, when they reached there, and Ruth said to her mother-in-law that she would go into the fields, and glean the ears that escaped the reapers. And Noemi answered "Go, my daughter."

12. So Ruth went into the fields. And when the owner of

---

6. What took place? 7. What terrible vengeance did he inflict? 8. What caused Elimelech to leave Israel? 9. What took place there? 10. Did they obey? 11. Did they go back to Israel? 12. What happened in the fields?

the land, who was named Bō'az, saw her, he asked the gleaners who she was. And when he had heard her story, he spoke to her graciously and ordered the men to let fall some handfuls of barley, "that she might gather them without shame."

13. And when evening came, Ruth found that she had three bushels of barley. When she carried it home, Noemi was surprised, and said, " Where hast thou gleaned to-day, and where hast thou wrought?" and Ruth told her that she had been in the fields of Boaz.

14. Day after day she gleaned there till the barley harvest was over. And some time after, Boaz said to her, "My daughter, all the people that dwell within the gates of my city, know that thou art a virtuous woman." And he wedded her.

15. Then the elders of the city witnessed the marriage, and said, "The Lord make this woman like Rachel and Lia who built up the house of Israel, that she may be an example of virtue, in Eph'ra-tă, and have a famous name in Bethlehem."

16. The Lord blessed the union of this virtuous pair, and gave them a son, whom they named O'bed. Noemi, full of joy, fulfilled the duties of nurse to the child, who was the father of I'sai, whose son was David, of whose race Christ was born.

CHAPTER XIII.

ISRAEL UNDER THE JUDGES—HELI—SAMUEL.

1. The next Judge of Israel after Samson, was He'-lĭ, who was also the High-Priest. He had two sons, Ophni (of'-nĭ) and Phinees (fin'-e-es) who were a scandal to Israel on account of their wicked conduct. When the people came to offer sacrifice, this pair would carry away the flesh of the victims by force.

---

13. Was Noemi surprised? 14. Did she continue to glean? 15. What blessing did the elders wish her? 16. Who sprang from this union?

2. Heli knew this, but instead of taking the stern measures which their wicked conduct called for, he contented himself with mildly rebuking them, saying, "It is no good report I hear, that you make the people of the Lord to transgress." And so they continued in their evil courses.

3. About this time, there dwelt in Mount Ephraim a virtuous pair named Elkanah and Anna. Now Anna had no children, which was a heavy trial to her. So she went up to the Tabernacle, which was at Si'lo, and besought God to grant her the blessing of a son, vowing that if He did so, she would dedicate him to God all the days of his life.

4. God heard her prayer, and sent her a son, whom she named Samuel, which means, the gift of God. And when he had reached the age of three years, Anna took him to Si-lo, and gave him to Heli, who consecrated him to the service of God.

5. Heli was now an old man, and his eyes were dim, so every night Samuel reposed near his couch, which stood near the Tabernacle, in order to watch the lamp of God in the sanctuary. And one night a Voice called Samuel. The child answered "Here am I," and went to Heli, and asked, "Why hast thou called me?"

6. Heli answered, "I did not call thee, my son, return and sleep." So the child went back to his couch. But the Voice called again, and Samuel rose once more and went to Heli, who told him as before that he had not called, and bade him return to his bed and sleep.

7. But when the Voice called the third time, and Samuel once more rose and went to Heli, the high-priest understood that it was the Lord who had called the child. So he told him to return to his couch, and if the Voice called again, to answer, "Speak, Lord, for thy servant heareth."

8. The Voice did call once more, and Samuel answered as

---

2. Was Heli to blame? 3. Who dwelt at this time in Mount Ephraim? 4. Did God hear her prayer? 5. What happened to Samuel one night? 6. What did Heli answer? 7. Did the voice call again? 8. Did it call the fourth time?

he had been instructed. And the Lord said, "Behold, I will do a thing in Israel, and whoever shall hear it, both his ears shall tingle. In that day I will raise up against Heli all the things that I have spoken. I will begin, and I will make an end, because he knew his sons did wickedly, and did not chastise them."

9. Samuel feared to make this revelation known to Heli, but Heli insisted upon knowing. And when Samuel told him, he answered humbly, "It is the Lord. Let him do what is just in his sight."

10. Israel was then at war with the Philistines, and suffered a defeat. So the elders of Israel sent to Silo for the Ark of the Covenant, in the hope that its presence would make them victorious in the next battle.

11. But the two wicked sons of Heli accompanied the Ark. And, in consequence, Israel was overthrown. Ophni and Phinees were slain, and the Ark itself captured by the Philistines.

12. When the news of this terrible misfortune was brought to Heli, he was seated on a stool in the gate of Silo, for he was deeply concerned for the fate of the Ark. When the messenger told him that both his sons were dead, he was silent, for he knew it was the chastisement of the Lord; but when he heard that the Ark of the Lord was taken, he fell backwards off his stool, and broke his neck and died.

13. Meanwhile, the Philistines carried the Ark to their own land, and placed it in the temple of Dagon, their god. But the next morning they found the idol broken on the ground. And, as time went on, a great number of plagues broke out in the country.

14. Therefore, after holding the Ark for seven months, they resolved to rid themselves of it. And so they took a cart, and harnessed to it two cows which had calves; then placing the Ark on the cart, they let the cows go with it whither they would.

---

9. Did Samuel tell Heli? 10. With whom was Israel then at war? 11. What happened? 12. How did Heli receive the news? 13. Where did the Philistines take the Ark? 14. What did they resolve?

15. Instead of going to where their calves were, the cows dashed off in the direction of the country of the Israelites, and finally arrived at a town of Israel, called Beth-sā'mĕs. The men who were reaping in the fields beheld it with astonishment, and when the wonderful news spread, there was great and solemn rejoicing throughout Israel.

16. When Samuel reached manhood, he became Judge in Israel. During his administration, Israel returned with fervor to the service of God, and in consequence, enjoyed the blessings of peace and prosperity. The Philistines sustained so terrible a defeat, that for many years after, they dared not approach the frontiers of Israel.

17. When Samuel grew to be old, he appointed his two sons as Judges over Israel. But, unlike their upright father, they took bribes, and caused the people so much misery by their wicked conduct, that the elders of Israel came to Samuel, and demanded a king to reign over them.

18. Samuel was displeased, but he prayed and consulted the Lord, who instructed him to acquaint them with the rights a king would have over them. He did so, and when they persisted in their request, God bade him give them a king as they desired, for their punishment.

19. God then said to Samuel, "To-morrow I will send to thee a man whom thou wilt anoint as king over my people Israel. The next day, accordingly, a young man of the tribe of Benjamin, Saul, the son of Cis, came to the city where Samuel dwelt, to consult him in regard to some of his father's asses, which were lost.

20. Samuel met Saul in the city, and took him home with them. And the next morning, at dawn, he anointed him with oil, and kissed him, and said, "Behold, the Lord hath anointed thee to be prince over His inheritance, and thou shalt deliver His people out of the hands of their enemies that are round about them."

---

15. Whither did the cows go? 16. Was Samuel Judge? 17. What did he do in his old age? 18. Was Samuel displeased? 19. What did

21. Saul then returned to his house, and Samuel assembled all Israel, and held an election for king, and the lot fell on Saul. So Samuel summoned him, and presented him to Israel. His majestic height and comely countenance won their favor, and they cried out, "God save the King." And so Saul was crowned king of Israel.

CHAPTER XIV.

ISRAEL UNDER THE KINGS.—SAUL.

1. ONE of the first acts of Saul's reign was to lead Israel against the Am'al-ek-ites, a nation which had opposed Israel when they were wandering in the desert, after coming out of Egypt. Instead of chastising them then for that offence, God had waited till the measure of their iniquity was full.

2. That time had now come, so God sent Samuel to instruct Saul to exterminate the nation, and destroy their possessions. Saul therefore gave them battle, and utterly defeated them.

3. He then put the entire nation to death, and slew all the flocks and herds, save a few of the finest which he reserved. He also spared the life of Agag their king. Then, flushed with the pride of victory, and forgetting that he owed it solely to God, he erected an arch of triumph, and held a great feast.

4. Samuel came to the camp of Israel to meet Saul. The victorious king said to him, "I have fulfilled the word of the Lord." Samuel answered, "What meaneth these, the bleating of the flocks, and the lowing of the herds, which I hear?"

5. Saul tried to excuse himself by saying that the people had spared the best flocks and herds to sacrifice them to the Lord.

---

21. Continue.
1. What was one of the first acts of Saul's reign? 2. Had the time now come? 3. Did he put the nation to death? 4. What did Saul say to Samuel? 5. How did Saul explain this?

But Samuel sternly answered that obedience was better than sacrifice, and that inasmuch as Saul had rejected the word of the Lord, the Lord had rejected him from being king over Israel.

6. Samuel then put A′gag to death, and departed, and beheld Saul no more till the day of his death. But the holy man loved the unhappy king whom the Lord had rejected, and did not cease to mourn for him.

7. At length the Lord said to him, "How long wilt thou mourn for Saul? Fill thy horn with oil, and come, that I may send thee to I′sāi, the Bethlehemite; for I have provided me a king among his sons."

8. So Samuel went to Bethlehem, and offered sacrifice in the presence of Isai and his seven sons. And when he saw E-li′ab, the eldest, he said, "Is the Lord's anointed before him?" But the Lord told him not to look on the countenance, or the height of the stature, for He did not judge according to the look of man.

9. Isai brought each of the seven then in turn, before Samuel but he rejected them all, and asked if Isai had no other son? Isai said he had one more, who kept the sheep, and Samuel told him to send for him at once. And when the beautiful, ruddy shepherd boy came in, the Lord said to Samuel, "Arise and anoint him, for this is he."

10. And from that day, the spirit of God departed from Saul, and came upon David, and an evil spirit came upon Saul, and troubled him. So his servants sought for one skilled in playing on the harp, that their master's wretchedness might be assuaged with music.

11. Now David was well skilled in playing on the harp, and one of Saul's servants happened to learn of the fact. So he was sent for to come to the court, and whenever the evil spirit was on the wretched king, David would soothe him with sweet music until it departed.

---

6. What did Samuel do? 7. What did the Lord say to him? 8. Did he go? 9. What did Isai do? 10. What came upon David? 11. Was David a musician?

12. David remained at the court of Saul, until the Philistines again attacked Israel, and Saul took the field against them, when he returned home. But three of his brothers were in the army, and Isai sent him to the camp with food.

13. The two armies were encamped opposite each other on two hills, with a valley between them. And while David was conversing with his brothers, a huge Philistine named Go-li′ath, came out of his people's camp, and descended into this valley, whence he challenged Israel to send forth a champion to meet him in single combat.

14. Great was David's surprise to learn that this giant had repeated this challenge for forty days, without any Israelite responding to it. And he said to the soldiers, "What shall be given to the man that slayeth this Philistine, who defieth the army of the living God?" But when his brother Eliab heard his words, he rebuked him for his pride in presuming to think of mating Goliath.

15. But his words were nevertheless reported to the king, who sent for David, and said to him, "Thou art not able to withstand this Philistine, for thou art but a boy, and he is a warrior!" But David answered, "Let no man be dismayed, I, thy servant, will go and fight the Philistine."

16. Then he told Saul how, once when he was tending his sheep, a lion and a bear carried off a ram out of the flock, and how he pursued them, and took the ram from them, and strangled them.

17. "The Lord," he continued, "who delivered me out of the power of the lion and the bear, will deliver me out of the hands of this Philistine." So Saul answered, "Go, and the Lord be with thee." And he would have clothed David with his own armor, but the youth declared he could not move under its weight, and laid it aside.

18. So David took only his staff, and chose five smooth stones from a brook near by, and put them into his shepherd's

---

12. How long did he remain? 13. Who was Goliath? 14. What surprised David? 15. Did Saul hear of David's words? 16. What proof did he give of strength? 17. What did he add? 18. What did he take?

scrip; then, taking a sling in his hand, he went forth to meet the Philistine, who stood waiting in the valley.

19. Goliath was clad in armor from head to foot. He wore a brazen helmet on his head, and greaves of brass on his legs, and bore a brazen shield, while the staff of his spear was like a weaver's beam.

20. When he beheld David drawing near, he cried, "Am I a dog that thou comest to me with a staff?" Then, cursing him by his gods, he added, "Come to me, and I will give thy flesh to the birds of the air, and to the beasts of the earth."

21. But David answered, "I come to thee in the name of the Lord of Hosts whom thou hast defied. I will slay thee, and take thy head from thee, that all may know that there is a God in Israel."

22. The huge Philistine rushed forward to meet David; but he put his hand into his scrip, and took a stone, and fetching it about a few times, struck Goliath so violent a blow in the forehead, that he fell senseless to the earth. Then David drew the sword of his foe from its sheath, and cut off his head.

23. When the Philistines saw the defeat and death of their champion, they were seized with fear and fled. But the Israelites pursued them, and after slaying a great number, took possession of their camp.

CHAPTER XV.

PERSECUTION OF DAVID BY SAUL.

1. WHEN David returned to the camp, after slaying Goliath, Saul questioned him concerning his family, and while David was answering, Jonathan, the son of Saul, began to love him as his own soul. So, according to a Hebrew custom of those

---

19. How was Goliath clad? 20. How did he greet David? 21. Narrate David's reply. 22. Describe the combat. 23. What effect had this on the enemy?

1. What did Saul question David about?

PERSECUTION OF DAVID BY SAUL.

days, he gave his new friend his coat, his sword, and his bow and his girdle.

2. As the army passed homeward, the women of Israel came out from every city, with flutes and cymbals, and sang, "Saul slew his thousands, but David his tens of thousands." This praise roused Saul's jealousy, and shortly after, while David was playing on the harp before him, he threw a spear at him.

3. David then fled from the court. Saul sent messengers to kill him, but Mi'-chol, David's wife, and Saul's daughter, contrived his escape. David was obliged to conceal himself, and complained bitterly to Jonathan of his father's injustice and cruelty.

4. So Jonathan tried to plead his friend's cause with his father, and one day, when the king seemed in a milder mood than usual, he said to him, "Sin not, O king, against thy servant David, because he hath not sinned against thee, and his works are very good towards thee. Why, therefore, wilt thou sin against innocent blood?"

5. Saul was appeased by these words, and received David again at court. But shortly after, David met with new success against the Philistines, and the old evil spirit then returned again in Saul, and he tried once more to pierce David with his spear.

6. Jonathan strove to win back his father's favor for David, but in vain. The envious king reproached his son with his affection for the son of Isai, who was supplanting him with the people, and told him that he need have no hope of ascending the throne so long as David lived. He ended by desiring his son to bring David to him, in order that he might put him to death.

7. But the loyal Jonathan asked, "Why shall he die? What hath he done?" Saul grew so enraged at this, that he caught up a spear to strike his son, but Jonathan fled, and warned

---

2. How did the nation show their pride in David? 3. What was David obliged to do? 4. What did Jonathan endeavor to do? 5. Was Saul appeased? 6. What did Jonathan again strive to do? 7. What did Jonathan answer?

David of his danger. Then, with many tears, the friends parted, and David fled to the mountains of Juda.

8. For some time after this, his life was that of a fugitive on the earth. A little band of followers joined him, and at the head of these, he was hunted from place to place by Saul. Even while constantly running the risk of being betrayed or taken prisoner, however, David never lost his belief that in His own time, God would bring him to the throne.

9. Once, when Saul was returning from battle, he heard that David was in the desert of Engaddi. So he went thither, with a force of three thousand, and scaled its rocky heights in search of David. At length, worn out with fatigue, he entered a cave and fell asleep.

10. Word was brought to David of the fact, and along with a faithful follower, he went to the cave, and found Saul asleep. A-bis'a-i would have killed the defenceless king, but David forbade him to harm the Lord's anointed. He contented himself with taking the spear and the cup of water which stood at the king's head, and stole away.

11. But when he reached a hill, some distance away, he called aloud to Abner, the captain of Saul's army, reproaching him for his negligence, and asking where was the king's spear and cup of water?

12. Then Saul awoke and cried out, "Is this thy voice, my son David?" David answered, "It is my voice, my lord, the king. Wherefore doth my lord persecute his servant? What have I done?"

13. Then Saul felt his own injustice, and cried out, "I have sinned. Return, my son David, for I will no more do thee harm, because my life has been precious in thy eyes this day. Blessed art thou, my son David." Then they parted in peace.

14. Shortly after this, Saul led the hosts of Israel against the Philistines once more. The Israelites were defeated, and

---

8. What was his life afterwards? 9. Where did Saul go in pursuit of him? 10. What did David do? 11. Did he let Saul know? 12. Did Saul learn how near David had been to him? 13. Was he touched? 14. What was Saul's fate?

Saul's three sons were slain. The enemy then hemmed Saul in, hoping to take him alive, and in order to avoid this fate, he slew himself with his own sword.

15. David was thus delivered from his enemy, but far from rejoicing, he wept bitterly at the news of Saul and Jonathan's death, and composed a dirge for them. "How are the valiant fallen! They were swifter than eagles, stronger than lions. I grieve for thee, my brother Jonathan, exceeding amiable. As the mother loveth her only son, so did I love thee!"

16. Thus did the great poet-king of Israel bewail the dead, in the hour of his triumph, not only forgiving the king who had persecuted him so cruelly, but grieving with tender love over his loss.

CHAPTER XVI.

THE REIGN OF DAVID.

Jerusalem is situated in the northern part of Judea, 33 miles east of the Mediterranean Sea. The modern city is far from recalling the beautiful city of David and of our Saviour, which stood on the four hills of Ak'ra, Sion, Bĕ'zeth-a, and Moriah, but is now a heap of ashes and ruins. It has been held by the Turks 700 years.

1. AFTER the death of Saul, David was chosen as king by the tribe of Juda, but seven years and a half went by before he was fully recognized as king of all Israel.

2. His first act, after his power was firmly established, was to attack Jerusalem, the strong city of the Jeb'-us-ites, which Israel had never been able to conquer.

3. Jerusalem consisted of an upper and a lower town. The lower town was soon taken, but the upper, which stood on Mount Si'on, and was guarded by a strong fortress, held out stubbornly against Israel. But at last the generalship of David prevailed, and the fastness of Sion was captured.

---

15. Did David grieve? 16. What can be said of David in this respect? 1. Who chose David as king? 2. What was his first act after he had

4. King David then removed the seat of government to Jerusalem, destined to become the most celebrated city in the world. He erected a palace on Mount Sion, with the aid of workmen sent him by Hiram, king of Tyre, and embellished the city with many other new buildings.

5. He also erected on Mount Sion a new and splendid Tabernacle for the Ark of the Covenant, which was then borne thither by the Levites, in a grand, triumphal procession, amid the solemn rejoicings of Israel. David himself went before the Ark, playing on the harp, and singing, "Lord, who shall dwell in thy Tabernacle, or who shall rest on thy holy hill?"

6. On this occasion, King David made a complete arrangement of the religious musical service; and thenceforth made it his special care that the whole order of divine worship should be carried out according to the law of Moses.

7. His own kingdom, and the service of God's sanctuary being thus established, David proceeded to the final conquest of the enemies of Israel. The Philistines, the Moabites, the Syrians, and the Edomites, were in turn subdued, and the boundaries of his kingdom extended, until at length they reached to the great river Euphrates on the east, and to the borders of Egypt on the west.

8. The limits of the Promised Land were now reached, and the kingdom of Israel had become one of the great Oriental monarchies. The Hebrew power only remained at this height, however, for about sixty years, during the reign of David and that of his son, Solomon.

9. Amid all his toils as a statesman and a warrior, David retained his simplicity and religious fervor, and found his chief joy in composing psalms and canticles, in honor of the Most High. And the Lord blessed him, and prospered him in all his undertakings, and promised him that one of his descend-

---

4. What change did he then make? 5. What else did he erect? 6. What proof of zeal in God's service did he also give? 7. To what did he next give his attention? 8. Describe the condition of Israel at this time. 9. What was King David's chief joy?

ants should rule the whole world, and sit on a throne more lasting than the heavens.

10. God, moreover, endowed him with the gift of prophecy. And in the canticles which he chants to the strains of his harp in his palace on the cliffs of Sion, the Mysterious Figure, the Redeemer, promised first in Paradise to our wretched first parents, then to Abraham, and then to Jacob, the Prophet of whom Moses spoke, stands forth clearly revealed.

11. His very name is discovered to the Psalmist. This King of Kings, the Anointed of God, is to be called the Christ, the Messiah. The scenes of His earthly mission are no less fully revealed; His rejection by the City of David, His crucifixion, with its smallest attendant circumstances, are fully foretold. "They have pierced my hands and feet; they have numbered all my bones."

12. Then the inspired lips of the prophet-king tell of the Resurrection; of the glory of the Ascension, when the Eternal gates shall be lifted up, and the Conqueror of Sin and Death shall enter into Heaven to take possession of His everlasting throne.

13. He also foretells the triumph of Christ over His enemies, and describes the nations of the earth meekly bending to take on themselves the yoke of the Prince of Peace, whom His own people had rejected and despised.

14. Unhappily, this great king, who furnishes us an example worthy of imitation in so many respects, also affords a wonderful proof that eternal vigilance is the only means of guarding against temptation.

15. He conceived a love for Beth-sa'-be-ē, the wife of Uri'as, one of his captains, and took her from her husband; then, in order to conceal his crime, caused the death of Urias by exposing him in the front of the battle

16. Nearly a year after the commission of these two terrible

---

10. With what other gift did God endow David? 11. Mention some of the revelations made to David. 12. Of what other mysteries did he tell? 13. What else does he foretell? 14. What does David also afford us? 15. Relate his double crime. 16. Whom did God send to rebuke him?

sins, God sent the prophet Na'than to rebuke King David for them. In stern words the holy man showed his king the depth of his guilt, and told him that in punishment for it, the sword should never depart from his house.

17. Filled with contrition, David humbled himself most deeply for his sin, and composed the penitential psalms which, since his time, have been used by so many contrite and devout souls. The Fiftieth Psalm, especially, breathes the spirit of the very deepest repentance and humiliation.

18. In consequence of David's sincere repentance, God forgave him the guilt of his sin, but the child which Bethsabee soon afterwards bore him, died, and the sword, as the prophet had foretold, never departed from his house.

CHAPTER XVII.

THE REVOLT OF ABSALOM.

1. DAVID's cherished son, Absalom, a youth of rare and perfect beauty, was the instrument chosen by God for the punishment of his sin. David had given him a body-guard, and a princely retinue of chariots and horsemen, but this was far from satisfying the ambition of the young prince who aimed at supplanting his father, and seizing the crown.

2. In order to effect his purpose, he was accustomed to rise early in the morning, and stand at the gate of the palace, and when any man came on business to the king, he would inquire into the case, and when he had heard it, answer, "Thy words seem just and good to me, but there is no one appointed by the king to hear thy cause."

3. He would also exclaim frequently in the hearing of the people, "O that they would make me judge over the land, that all who have business might come to me that I might do

---

17. How did David act? 18. Did God forgive him?
1. How did God chastise David? 2. What did he do in order to effect his purpose? 3. What would he exclaim?

THE REVOLT OF ABSALOM. 107

them justice." And when any man came to salute him, he took him by the hand and kissed him.

4. Thus the prince enticed the hearts of all Israel from their allegiance to his father, until at last, when he thought the time was ripe for revolt, he asked the king for leave to repair to Mount Hebron in fulfilment of a vow.

5. The unsuspecting king at once accorded it, but as soon as Absalom reached Hebron he sent messengers to all the tribes of Israel to inform them that as soon as they heard the sound of a trumpet, they should say, "Absalom reigneth in Hebron." A great multitude were thus drawn to the standard of the treacherous prince.

6. When the news of Absalom's revolt was brought to King David, he at once quitted Jerusalem lest its citizens should suffer during the impending conflict between himself and his rebellious son.

7. In the garb of a penitent, with bare feet and veiled head, the unhappy king crossed the gloomy chasm through which flowed the brook of Ke'-dron, at the very spot where Our Savior was to cross it on the night of His betrayal, and ascended the Mount of Olives.

8. On the way he was met by a man named Sem'e-i, of the family of Saul, who threw stones and earth at David, and cursed him, saying, "Come out, come out, thou man of blood!" This filled A-bis'-a-I, one of David's captains, with wrath, and he would have slain Semei, had not David restrained him.

9. "Behold, my own son seeketh my life," the king declared sorrowfully, "how much more one of the family of Saul. Perhaps the Lord may look on my affliction, and render me good for the cursing of this day."

10. As Absalom was in close pursuit, David resolved to give him battle. But his counsellors would not permit him to lead

---

4. What was the consequence? 5. Was it granted? 6. What did David do when the news was brought to him? 7. How did he go? 8. Who met him? 9. What did the king exclaim? 10. What did David resolve?

the forces, declaring that it were better for ten thousand of his soldiers to fall, than for him to risk his life, for that if he perished, all was lost.

11. David, therefore, yielded to their entreaties, and remained in the city of Ma'-ha-ra'im, but gave strict orders to Jo'ab, the commander of the forces, and the other officers, to spare the life of Absalom. The battle was fought in the forest of Ephraim, and Absalom's army suffered total defeat.

12. As soon as he saw that the field was lost, Absalom fled. But he could not escape divine justice. As he rode through the forest, mounted on a mule, his long hair became entangled in the branches of an oak tree, and he remained suspended in the air, while the animal ran away.

13. In this situation Joab found him, and pierced his body with three lances. The wretched prince was still breathing, however, when some soldiers also discovered him and dispatched him with their swords. They then flung his body into a deep pit in the forest and piled over it a large heap of stones.

14. The tomb of Absalom is still to be seen near the brook of Kedron, and to this day each passer-by hurls an avenging stone at this memorial of filial ingratitude and rebellion.

15. When the herald reached the king with the news of Absalom's defeat, he asked eagerly if the prince were safe. And when he heard that he was dead, he would not be comforted, but retired into a chamber over the gate of the house, and mourned long and bitterly for his wretched son. "Absalom, my son Absalom," he cried, "would that I might die for thee, my son Absalom!"

16. After some time King David returned to Jerusalem which he entered in triumph, amid the rejoicings of the people. But David was to be purified from his sins by still further trials; a new rebellion broke out, led by Si-ba, of the tribe of Benjamin.

---

11. Did he yield? 12. Did Absalom flee? 13. Who found him thus? 14. What is still to be seen? 15. How did David receive the news of his son's death? 16. Did he return to Jerusalem and enjoy peace?

THE DEATH OF ABSALOM.

110   HISTORY OF THE OLD TESTAMENT.

17. Scarcely had this been suppressed and peace restored to Israel, when David, yielding to a motive of vanity, became desirous to know the exact number of his people, and issued orders for a general census. So displeased was God at this act of David's, that he punished it by a plague which killed seventy thousand in three days.

18. Deeply penitent, David clothed himself in sackcloth and ashes, and humbly prostrating himself before God, besought Him to punish him alone, and spare his innocent people. God heard his prayer and the plague ceased.

19. David reigned forty years. When the time of his death drew near, he summoned the princes of Israel, and told them that it had been his dearest wish to build a temple to the Lord, and that he had gathered together much of the necessary material.

20. But God, he continued, had not suffered him to do the great work because he had been a soldier and shed human blood, but had reserved it for his son Solomon, under whose rule the whole kingdom should continue great and powerful, if he remained faithful to God.

21. Then, turning to his son, David exhorted him to observe God's commandments, and serve Him faithfully. "If thou seek Him" said the aged and holy king, "thou shalt find Him, but if thou forsake Him, He will cast thee off forever." David then gave his son gold for the vessels of the sanctuary, along with the plan of the temple and its precincts.

22. Then he said to him, "All these things came to me written by the hand of the Lord. Act like a man; take courage and fear not; for the Lord, my God, will be with thee, nor forsake thee till thou hast finished the house of the Lord."

---

17. What new fault did David commit? 18. What did David do? 19. How long did King David reign, and what did he do when the time of death was drawing near? 20. What had prevented him? 21. What did he exhort his son to do? 22. What did he then say to Solomon?

23. Then, addressing the assembled princes of Israel, King David said, "The work is great, for a house is prepared, not for man, but for God." Now, if any man is willing to offer, let him fill his hand to-day, and offer what he pleaseth to the Lord." The princes and the people responded joyfully to this appeal, by sending rich and numerous gifts for the temple.

24. David was rejoiced at this proof of faith and devotion, and cried out, "Blessed art Thou, O Lord, the God of Israel, Our Father from eternity to eternity. All things are thine, and we have given Thee what we receive of Thy hand.

25. O Lord, keep forever this will of their heart, and let this mind remain always for the worship of Thee; and give to my son Solomon, a perfect heart, that he may keep Thy commandments." David then passed peacefully away, and was buried on Mount Sion.

In many phases of his life David presents a very striking figure of Christ, who is called the Son of David. The forefather of the Redeemer, like Him, he is born in Bethlehem, and passes his youth in obscurity and loneliness; like Him, too, he is at once a King and a Prophet. In his sorrow and tribulation, crossing the brook of Ke-dron, he prefigures Christ close upon His Passion ; as his triumphal entry into Jerusalem prefigures Our Lord's triumphal entrance into the city of David on Palm Sunday. The meekness and forbearance with his enemies, of Israel's greatest king, also add to his resemblance to Our Savior.

---

23. What did he say to the princes of Israel? 24. How did David receive them? 25. Continue the prayer of David and relate the manner of his dath.

V.—ERA OF THE TEMPLE AND THE PROPHETS.

CHAPTER I.

THE REIGN OF SOLOMON.

Tyre, (tire) was the great merchant city of the ancient world, just as London is in our day. It was situated on the Mediterranean Sea, in Phœnicia, a narrow country lying between Galilee and the Mediterranean Sea. Tyre was renowned for its beauty and wisdom, until its pursuit of wealth led to injustice. Its ruin was foretold in consequence by the prophet Ez'-e'-chi'-el, and its site is now desolate; a few fishing huts alone marking it.

1. SOLOMON now ascended the throne of Israel. He is thought to have been not more than fourteen years of age at the time, but he soon gave proof that he had inherited the mental gifts of his great father, in whose precepts, he strove to walk.

2. Solomon loved the Lord, who looked on him with so much favor that He appeared to him one night in a dream, and said to him, "Ask what thou wilt that I should give thee."

3. Solomon answered "O, Lord God, thou hast made thy servant king instead of David, his father, and I am but a child. Give therefore to thy servant an understanding heart to judge thy people and discern between good and evil."

4. And the Lord replied, "Because thou hast asked this thing, and had not asked for thyself long life, nor riches, nor the lives of thy enemies, but hast asked for thyself wisdom to discern judgment, behold, I have done for thee according to

---

1. Did Solomon now become king? 2. Did Solomon love God? 3. What did Solomon answer? 4. What did the Lord reply?

THE REIGN OF SOLOMON.

thy words, and have given thee a wise and understanding heart, insomuch that there hath been no one like thee, before thee, nor shall rise after thee."

5. Yea, and the things, also, which thou did not ask, I have given thee, riches and glory, so that no one hath been like thee among the kings in all days heretofore. And if thou wilt walk in my ways as thy father walked, I will lengthen thy days."

6. The youthful king soon gave a signal proof of the heavenly wisdom with which God had inspired him. As he sat one day in his accustomed place, hearing the complaints of the people, and dispensing justice, two women appeared before him with a child whom each claimed as her own.

7. The two women had been dwelling in a house by themselves, when each had given birth to a child. The first woman declared that the second had overlaid her child in the night, and having awakened and discovered that it was dead, had risen and stolen her living child, and placed the dead one in its place.

8. In the morning, the first woman continued, she thought her child had died in the night, but after examining it more closely in the daylight, she discovered that the dead child was not hers. The second woman declared that she had not exchanged the children, and that the living child was hers.

9. After the king had heard these conflicting statements, he ordered the executioner to be summoned, and bade him cut the living child in two, and give half of it to one woman and half to the other.

10. At this decree, the first woman beseeched the king to spare the life of the child, and let the second woman take it for her own. But the second woman said, "Let it be neither mine nor thine, but divide it."

11. No sooner had the king heard the second woman's words

---

5. What else did God promise him? 6. What did the youthful king soon give? 7. Relate the circumstances of the case. '8. What took place in the morning? 9. What did the king do? 10. How did the women receive this decree? 11. What decision did the king arrive at?

then he ordered the child to be given to the first woman, rightly judging that only the child's mother could have pleaded for its life, even at the cost of giving it up forever. And when the report of this judgment spread through the land, all Israel feared the king, and knew that the wisdom of God was with him.

12. In the fourth year of his reign, Solomon began to build the Temple of the Lord, (1010 B. C.) The site chosen was Mount Moriah, where, centuries before, Abraham had brought his only son, Isaac, to sacrifice him at the Lord's command.

13. A large part of the material for its construction had already been collected, and in return for the corn, oil and wine, which fertile Palestine produced so abundantly, Solomon obtained from Hiram, King of Tyre, more material, and skilled workmen.

14. Ten thousand men were employed cutting cedars in Mount Lebanon, and seventy thousand in carrying materials to the site of the building. Eighty thousand were engaged in hewing stone, while three thousand acted as overseers of the work.

15. This wonderful building was constructed of stone, each block of which was hewn and fitted to its intended place at a distance, so that no sound of hammers was heard, and the beautiful structure rose in silence before the reverent eyes of the dwellers in Jerusalem.

16. In general plan, the temple of Solomon was an enlarged form of the Tabernacle of Moses, enclosed within a vast citadel, secured with the usual military defences of the time. The utmost height of the temple itself was two hundred feet, built up from deep foundations with colossal masonry, and great beams of cedar from Lebanon.

17. Mount Moriah consists of three rocky terraces. On the lowest of these was erected the first court of the temple, which

---

12. What great work did Solomon now undertake? 13. Whence did he obtain workmen and materials? 14. How were those workmen employed? 15. Of what was it constructed? 16. Describe the temple

was called the Porch of the Gentiles, because pagans were allowed to enter it, though they were warned by inscriptions in various languages not to venture beyond a certain stone barrier.

18. Beyond this barrier rose the second terrace, elevated some twenty cubits beyond the first. On this was erected a second court, which was reserved for the Jews, and was known as the Porch of the Israelites. From this second enclosure a last stairway of fifteen steps led to the uppermost terrace, to which Levites only might ascend.

19. Here, in a third court, which was known as the Porch of the Priests, stood the great brazen Altar of Holocausts. As this was the only altar which the law of Moses sanctioned for all the tribes of Israel, its size required to be such, as to enable it to consume numerous victims at the same time. And so rapidly did this altar perform this work that it was known as Ariel, or the Lion of the Lord.

20. In this court also stood the Sea of Brass, which rested on the backs of twelve brazen oxen, and held two thousand gallons of water for the ablutions of the priest before the sacrifice. To the right and left of this court were two brass pillars thirty feet in height with lilies and palms embossed upon them.

21. Beyond this court lay the temple itself, with its whole surface covered with plates of gold, so that from the first rays of dawn till the last gleam of daylight, it blazed like the sun.

22. Doors of cedar overlaid with gold afforded entrance, and before these hung veils of blue, purple and scarlet linen, wrought with curious flowers. The inner walls were lined with cedar, on which cherubim and palm trees, and blooming flowers were carved with so much skill that they seemed to stand out from the surface.

23. The walls and floor of the Holy of Holies were covered with plates of gold, fastened by gold nails. All the furniture, including ten tables and ten candlesticks, were of the same precious material.

---

18. What stood on the second terrace? 19. What was on the third terrace? 20. What also stood in this court? 21. What lay beyond? 22. Describe the doors and interior. 23. Continue.

CHAPTER II.

THE REIGN OF SOLOMON—CONTINUED.

Palmyra (pal-mī'ra), also known as Tad'mor, was situated in the Syrian desert, 120 miles northeast of Damascus. It is now in ruins.

1. THE temple took seven years to build, and at the Feast of Tabernacles which followed close upon its completion, Solomon commanded the Ancients of Israel and the princes of the tribes, to assemble in order to bear the Ark of the Covenant to its final resting-place in the Holy of Holies.

2. Magnificent indeed must have been that triumphal procession from the Tabernacle on Mount Sion, to the glorious edifice which crowned the heights of Mount Moriah! First came the multitude of Israel, and then King Solomon, arrayed in his richest robes, and the Levites, rendering the ground moist with oblations, and filling the air with incense, as they chanted hymns in praise of the Lord, to the music of lutes and harps and cymbals.

3. Then, their approach announced by the blast of one hundred and twenty silver trumpets, came the body of Levites in the midst of whom was born the Ark of the Covenant. As they drew near the gates of the temple, the people fell back, and the priests alone entered in and placed the sacred deposit within the Holy of Holies.

4. After setting all in order, the priests came forth again, and then the king falling on his knees before the Altar of Holocausts, prayed as follows. "Lord God of Israel, there is no God like Thee in heaven or on earth. If heaven and the heaven of heavens cannot contain Thee, how much less this house which I have built.

5. O Lord, my God, hear the hymn and the prayer which Thy servant prayeth before Thee this day, that Thy eyes may

---

1. What did Solomon command when the temple was finished? 2. Describe the procession. 3. Who came next? 4. What did the king do after the priests had come forth? 5. Continue King Solomon's prayer.

THE DEDICATION OF THE TEMPLE.

be open upon this house night and day, that Thou mayst hearken to the prayer which Thy servant prayeth to Thee in this place. Mayest Thou hearken to Thy people when they pray in this place. Mayest Thou hear them and show them mercy."

6. When Solomon's prayer was ended, fire fell from heaven and consumed the holocausts. And when the Israelites saw this miracle by which Jehovah signified his pleasure in the temple erected in His honor, they fell prostrate on the ground praising his awful name, and retired from the holy place filled with awe.

7. Soon after the dedication of the temple, the Lord appeared a second time to Solomon and said to him, "I have heard thy prayer, and I have sanctified the house which thou hast built and My Eyes and My Heart shall be always there."

8. After the completion of the temple, Solomon built himself a magnificent palace. His throne was of ivory, and at either end of the six steps which led to it, stood a carved lion, the emblem of the tribe of Juda. At either side of the throne itself was placed another lion. All the king's table furniture and decorations of this palace were of gold.

9. In the time of Solomon the Hebrew nation touched its highest point of wealth and splendor. The great districts which David had conquered were organized, and secure in the possession of the land, the Hebrews turned their attention to the arts of peace.

10. The woodmen upon Lebanon felled timber for the architects, who built new cities as the people multiplied. The sword was turned into the plough-share, and every Israelite dwelt in happiness and prosperity "under the shadow of his own vine and fig tree."

11. Solomon also erected a summer palace on Mount Lebanon, and a separate palace in Jerusalem for his queen, the

---

6. What miracle took place? 7. When did God appear again to Solomon? 8. What else did he erect? 9. What of the Hebrew nation under Solomon? 10. Give some proof of this. 11. What did Solomon also build?

THE REIGN OF SOLOMON—CONCLUDED.

daughter of the Egyptian Pharaoh. He also constructed aqueducts to supply Sion with water, and several store-cities or depots for commerce.

12. In order to further his commercial enterprises, he erected the city of Tad'mor, afterwards the celebrated Palmyra, in the desert, and built a superb navy, which he stationed in the ports on the eastern arm of the Red Sea.

13. He strengthened his alliance with Tyre, which gave him a share in the great commerce of Phœnicia, and obtained from the Egyptians the city of Gaza, thus gaining command of the ancient highway between Egypt and Assyria. Thus, powerful by sea and land, Solomon was in truth the greatest of all eastern monarchs.

14. The gorgeousness of his court and the fame of his transcendent wisdom drew visitors from all parts of the world to Jerusalem. One of the most famous of these was the queen of Sa'ba.

15. After she had seen Jerusalem and the court, and listened to the discourse of Solomon she confessed to him: "The report is true which I heard in my own country, but I would not believe. Blessed are thy servants who stand before thee, and hear thy wisdom."

16. But wisdom and knowledge that enlighten the mind, are different gifts from divine grace which purifies the heart. Little by little Solomon fell away from God. Led on by his love of splendor, he disregarded the law of Moses which required that the future king should not multiply horses to himself, nor have strange wives, nor amass immense sums of gold and silver, and did all of these things.

17. He had forty thousand horses in his stable, his treasure was enormous, and he had seven hundred wives, many of whom were chosen from nations with whom marriage was strictly prohibited by the law of Moses.

---

12. What did he do for commerce? 13. What other prudent steps did he take? 14. Whom did his fame attract. 15. What did she confess? 16. Did Solomon retain his first fervor? 17. What had he in opposition to these commands?

18. He finally became what would now be called "a man of liberal views," attached to no particular religion, and went with his wives to burn incense before Baal, Mo'loch, As-tar'te or whatever other idol they wished to adore, and even built temples for some of these deities.

19. While the blinded king led this depraved life, revolt and seditions broke out among the people whom he had cruelly overtaxed and oppressed in order to provide palaces and luxuries for his vast array of heathen wives.

20. Then for the third time the Lord appeared to Solomon. But on this occasion no words of benediction came from the lips of Jehovah; but instead a terrible warning that in consequence of his sin, his kingdom was about to be divided.

21. "For David thy father's sake," said the Most High, "I will not do this in thy days, neither will I take away the whole kingdom, but I will give one tribe to thy son for the sake of David, my servant, and for the sake of Jerusalem which I have chosen."

22. Not long afterwards, this king whose wisdom it was once a blessing for others to hear, but who had lost the way of wisdom for himself, died in the fortieth year of his reign, without honor, though it is to be hoped, repentant.

23. In the book of Ecclesiastes, which he wrote, and on whose expressions the hopes of his repentance are founded, he acknowledges the truth which has been confirmed by so many other illustrious men through the ages, the utter insufficiency of the things of this world to satisfy the immortal soul of man.

24. At the pinnacle of his greatness, after declaring that he had withheld his heart from the enjoyment of no pleasure, this king who was the envy of the world, sadly confesses that he had found "in all things nothing but vanity and vexation of spirit."

---

18. What did he finally become? 19. What took place among the people? 20. Did the Lord appear again to Solomon? 21. What did the Lord do for David's sake? 22. What happened not long afterwards? 23. What does Solomon acknowledge in the Book of Ecclesiastes? 24. What does he declare?

CHAPTER III.

DIVISION OF THE KINGDOM OF ISRAEL.

1. After the death of Solomon, his son Ro-bo'-am ascended the throne. The people at once assembled and sent a deputation, headed by Jer-o-bō'am, a young man who had been in the service of Solomon, to the new king, to beseech him to lighten the grievous yoke which his father had laid upon them, and promised in return to serve him faithfully.

2. Roboam received them graciously, and bade them return in three days for his answer. During this time, he took counsel with the ancients of the nation as to what course he should pursue. They counselled him to yield to the people, and so retain their allegiance.

3. Not satisfied with this advice, Roboam consulted the young men who had been brought up with him and composed his retinue. They advised him to say to the people, "My father laid upon you a heavy yoke, and I will add more weight to it; my father beat you with scourges, but I will beat you with scorpions."

4. The counsel of these haughty young nobles was more in harmony with Roboam's own views, so he followed it. In consequence, ten of the tribes revolted against his authority, and chose for their king, Jeroboam, who had headed the deputation to the king.

5. The kingdom of Jeroboam was known as the kingdom of Israel, and its capital was the city of Sam'a ri'a. Only the two tribes of Juda and Benjamin remained faithful to Roboam, and his realm, which retained the city of Jerusalem as its capital, was known as the kingdom of Juda.

6. As Juda, therefore, retained the temple—the only place where the law of Moses permitted the Hebrews to offer sacri-

---

1. Who became king on his death? 2. How did Roboam receive them? 3. Whom else did he consult? 4. Whose advice did he take? 5. How were the two kingdoms known? 6. What wicked act did Jeroboam commit?

fice—Jeroboam, who was a shrewd, worldly-wise man, began to fear lest the people might go up to Jerusalem for this purpose, and thus be induced to return to their allegiance to Roboam. So he resolved to give the kingdom of Israel an established church of its own.

7. He had two golden calves made, and set up one at Dan, and one at Bethel. Then he said to the people, "Go ye up no more to Jerusalem; behold thy gods, O Israel, who brought thee out of the land of Egypt." And they obeyed him, and adored these idols.

8. Roboam never ceased, throughout his life, to make war on Israel, in the hope of conquering the revolted tribes. This warfare was maintained by their successors, who frequently called upon the surrounding idolatrous nations, to assist them and thus caused much sin and misery among their people.

9. In order to rouse the old Hebrew spirit among the people of both Israel and Juda, God raised up holy men, called prophets, who stimulated the indifferent, denounced the apostate, and threatened with God's vengeance those in high places who were guilty of injustice.

10. On the death of Jeroboam, his son, Nadab, succeeded him. Bā'-a sa' conspired against him, and after slaying him and the whole house of Jeroboam, reigned till his death. Baasa's son succeeded him, but Zam-bri, an officer of his household, formed a conspiracy, and seized the throne.

11. Am'-ri, a second conspirator, murdered Zambri, and reigned in his stead. At Amri's death, A'-chab, his son, ascended the throne. This king surpassed all his predecessors in wickedness.

12. He married Jez'-a-bel, the daughter of the king of the Sidonians, an idolatrous nation. This wicked queen introduced the worship of the god Bā al into Israel, and erected a temple to his worship, with four hundred and fifty priests consecrated to his service.

---

7. What did he do? 8. Were the two kingdoms at peace? 9. Whom did God now raise up? 10. Who succeeded Jeroboam on the throne of Israel? 11. Who murdered Zam-bri? 12. Whom did Achab marry?

THE KINGDOM OF ISRAEL—CONTINUED. 123

13. Achab, prompted by his wicked queen, then put the priests of the true God to death, and tried in every way to destroy the last traces of the true faith among the people of Israel.

14. One day the venerable prophet, E-li'-as, clad in a rough sheepskin, and bearing a staff in his hand, appeared before Achab, and told him that in punishment of his sins, a drought should fall upon the land for three years.

15. Achab was angry at the prophet for his stern rebuke, and resolved to put him to death. But the Lord directed Elias to conceal himself near the brook Car'-ith, in the vicinity of the Jordan. Here he was fed by ravens till the brook ran dry, when the Lord told him to go to Sa-rep'ta, a city of the Sidonians.

16. When he drew near the gate of this city, he met a woman gathering sticks, and asked her for a drink. As she was going to bring it, he called after her, "Bring me also a morsel of bread."

17. The woman answered, "As the Lord, thy God liveth, I have no bread, but only a handful of meal in a pot, and a little oil in a cruse; behold, I am gathering two sticks that I may go in and dress it for me and my son, that we may eat and die.

18. Then the prophet said to her, "Fear not, but go and do as thou hast said, but first make for me of the same meal a little hearth-cake, and bring it to me, and after that, make for thyself and thy son."

19. For thus saith the Lord God of Israel, "The pot of meal shall not waste, nor the cruse of oil be diminished, until the day wherein the Lord God will give rain upon the earth."

20. The woman did as the prophet told her, and from that day forth she had meal in her pot, and oil in her cruse, and there was no want in her house during the famine. But some time after, her son died, and she said to Elias, "What have I

---

13. What other wicked act did Achab commit? 14. Who appeared before Achab? 15. Was Achab angry? 16. Whom did he meet at Sarepta? 17. What did the woman answer? 18. What did Elias say to

done to thee, thou man of God? Hast thou come to me that my iniquities should be remembered?"

21. Moved with compassion, Elias took the child, and laid it on his own bed, in the upper chamber. And he cried to the Lord, and said, "O Lord, my God, hast thou afflicted also the widow, with whom I am after a sort maintained, so as to kill her son?"

22. Then he stretched and measured himself upon the child three times, and prayed, "O Lord, my God, let the soul of this child, I beseech thee, return into his body." And the Lord heard the voice of Elias, and the soul of the child returned to him, and he revived.

23. Then the prophet carried the child to the mother, and said, "Behold, thy son liveth." Full of joy and gratitude, the woman exclaimed, "Now by this I know that thou art a man of God, and the word of the Lord in thy mouth is true."

In Elias, the full-grown man, stretching and measuring himself upon the small body of the dead child, we have a figure of the Incarnation, when the Son of God adapted himself to our human nature, without ceasing to be God.

CHAPTER IV.

THE KINGDOM OF ISRAEL—CONCLUDED.

1. AFTER the earth had remained three years and six months without rain, the Lord told Elias to go and show himself to Achab. He obeyed, and Achab said to him, "Art thou he that troublest Israel?"

2. The prophet answered, "I have not troubled Israel, but thou, and thy father's house, who have forsaken the commandments of God, and followed Baal." Then he told the king to

---

21. What did the prophet do? 22. What further did he do? 23. What did the prophet then do?
1. What did the Lord command Elias to do at last? 2. What did the prophet answer?

THE KINGDOM OF ISRAEL—CONTINUED.

gather together all the people and the prophets of Baal on Mount Carmel.

3. Achab dared not disobey Elias on account of the terrible famine which was raging in the land, and even went himself to the mountain. And when all were assembled, Elias said to the people, "How long do you halt between two sides? If the Lord be God, follow Him; but if Baal, then follow him."

4. The people felt the justice of his reproaches, and were silent. Elias continued, "I only remain a prophet of the Lord, but the prophets of Baal are four hundred and fifty men.

5. "Let two bullocks be given us; and let them choose one bullock for themselves, and cut it in pieces, but put no fire under, and I will dress the other bullock, and lay it on wood, and put no fire under it.

6. "Then call ye on the names of your gods, and I will call on the name of my Lord, and the God that will answer by fire, let Him be the God." And all the people answered, "A very good proposal."

7. Then the priests of Baal, clad in their richest robes, and crowned with laurel, slew their bullock, and placed it on an altar. Then they danced around the altar from morning till noon, crying, "Baal, hear us." But no fire came to consume their sacrifice.

8. Then Elias mocked them, saying, "Cry out with a louder voice, for he is a god, and perhaps he is talking, or is in an inn, or perhaps asleep, and must be waked." So the priests of Baal cried louder than ever, and hacked themselves, as was their wont, with knives and lancets, till they were covered with blood, but all in vain.

9. When evening came, Elias told the people to come to him. Then taking twelve stones, according to the number of the tribes of Israel, he built an altar to the Lord, and laid wood upon it.

---

3. Did he do so? 4. Did the people answer? 5. What did he propose? 6. What further directions did he give? 7. What did the priests of Baal do? 8. What did Elias say? 9. What did he do at evening?

10. Then he cut the bullock in pieces, and laid it on the wood, and poured water on it till a stream ran down on every side and filled a trench which he had dug about the altar.

11. Then he offered the holocaust, praying, "O Lord God of Abraham, and Isaac, and Israel, show this day that Thou art the God of Israel, and that according to Thy commandment I have done all these things. Hear me, O Lord, hear me! that the people may learn that Thou art the Lord God, and that Thou hast turned their hearts again."

12. And instantly fire came down from heaven, and consumed not only the holocaust, but even the wood and the stones, and the water in the trench. And when the people saw this awful manifestation of Jehovah's power, they fell on their faces, crying out, "The Lord, He is God! The Lord, He is God!"

13. Then Elias went up alone to the top of the mountain, and returned thanks to God, and besought Him to refresh the earth with water. And as the holy man prayed, a little cloud, no bigger than a man's hand, appeared in the blazing sky that arched over the dying earth, and spread until all the heavens were dark, and the rain fell in torrents.

14. Elias slew the prophets of Baal, and when Jezabel heard it, she resolved to put him to death. So the prophet fled into the desert, and lay down to rest under a juniper tree. And sad at heart at the thought of Israel's idolatry he said, "It is enough for me, Lord; take away my soul, for I am no better than my fathers."

15. Then he fell asleep. He was aroused by an angel of the Lord, who said to him, "Arise and eat, for thou hast yet a great way to go." And he arose and walked in the strength of that food, which the Lord had provided, forty days and forty nights till he came to the mount of God, Horeb.

16. There God appeared to him, and told him of the judg-

---

10. What did he place on the altar? 11. What did he pray as he offered the holocaust? 12. What wonderful thing took place? 13. Whither did Elias go? 14. Why did Jezebel determine upon Elias' death? 15. Who roused him from sleep? 16. What did God reveal to him?

THE FLIGHT OF ELIAS.

ments that were to be executed on the house of Achab, and bade him go to Damascus, to anoint Ha′zael king of Syria, and make Eliseus (E-liz′-e-us) prophet in his place.

17. Meanwhile, Achab had added another to his long list of crimes. Near his palace at Jez′-ra-hel was the vineyard of a man named Na′both. The king had long coveted this vineyard, and finally asked Naboth to sell it to him, or exchange it for a better vineyard.

18. But Naboth who was steadfast in the true faith, and abhorred the king for his idolatry, answered, "The Lord be merciful to me, and not let me give thee the inheritance of my fathers." For the law of Moses forbade the son to sell the property which he had inherited from his forefathers.

19. So great did Achab's longing for the vineyard become, that he could neither eat nor sleep. But Jezabel rallied him and told him to be of good cheer, for she would secure what he desired. So she directed the chief men of the city to find some false witnesses to testify to Naboth having blasphemed against God and the king.

20. These creatures of the wicked queen obeyed her command, and Naboth was tried, condemned, and stoned to death. Jezabel then bade her husband go and take possession of the vineyard, as Naboth was dead.

21. The Lord directed Elias to go and meet Achab on his way thither, and announce to him that His vengeance was about to fall upon him. The prophet did so, and when Achab saw him, he said, "Hast thou found me, my enemy?"

22. Elias answered by reproaching him for his crime, and told him that the dogs would lick his blood on the very spot where Naboth was slain, and that Jezabel would be devoured by dogs in the same field.

---

17. What had Achab done, meanwhile? 18. Did Naboth refuse? 19. Did he still long for it? 20. Were Jezabel's commands obeyed? 21 What did God direct Elias to do? 22. What did Elias answer?

CHAPTER V.

THE KINGDOM OF ISRAEL—CONTINUED.

1. When Elias had gone to seek Eliseus according to God's command, he had found him ploughing with oxen. And he cast his mantle on Eliseus, who at once left his plough, and went with Elias, and ministered unto him.

2. But the time had now come when the Lord wished to remove Elias from the earth. The spirit of God led him to the Jordan, and Eliseus accompanied him. And Elias said to him: "Ask what thou wilt have me do for thee, before I be taken away from thee." And Eliseus asked for a double portion of his spirit.

3. Elias answered that he asked for a hard thing, but that if Eliseus saw him when he was taken from earth, he might know it was granted. And as they went on, a fiery chariot, and fiery horses, parted them, and Elias was carried in it up to heaven.

4. And as Eliseus saw him ascending, he cried out "My father! My father!" And he took up the mantle of Elias that fell from him, and going back to the Jordan, struck its waters with the garment. And the stream was divided, and he passed over to Jericho, where the disciples of Elias saluted him as their master.

5. Soon after this, as Eliseus went up to Bethel, to denounce the worship of the golden calf, which was set up there, some boys came out of the city, and said to him, mockingly, "Go up, thou bald-head! Go up, thou bald-head!"

6. Eliseus, knowing that in insulting him, they insulted the Almighty, turned, and cursed them in His Name. And immediately two bears came out of the neighboring forest, and tore forty-two of the boys to pieces.

---

1. How had Elias summoned Eliseus? 2. What had now come? 3. What did Elias answer? 4. What did Eliseus cry out as he saw him vanishing? 5. Who insulted the prophet on his way to Bethel? 6. How

7. Eliseus soon became celebrated throughout Israel for the miracles which he worked. Among the most striking, may be named his multiplication of a few loaves to feed one hundred men, his changing of the waters of the fountain near Jericho from bitter to sweet, and his restoration to life of the son of the Su'na-mite woman, who had given him a lodging in her house.

8. Whilst he was working these wonders in Israel, it chanced that a band of robbers from Syria invaded the land of Israel, and carried off among their captives, a little maid, who was taken to Damascus, and sold as a slave to the wife of Na'a-man, the general of the army of the king of Syria.

9. Now Naaman was a rich and valiant man, who had done much to make Syria powerful, and was consequently in high esteem with the king. But he was a leper.

10. One day the little Israelite maid said to her mistress, "I wish my master had been with the prophet that is in Samaria; he would certainly have healed him of the leprosy which he hath."

11. The wife of Naaman at once told him what the maid had said, and he immediately set out, in great state, with chariots and horses, and rich gifts, to seek the promised healer.

12. But when he reached the door of the prophet's dwelling, and sent in a messenger to tell his name, and why he had come, Eliseus merely sent him back a message to bathe seven times in the Jordan, and he should be healed.

13. When Naaman heard this, he was angry, and exclaimed, "I thought he would have come out to me, and standing, would have invoked the name of the Lord, his God, and have touched with his hand the place of the leprosy, and have healed me. Are not Ab'a-na and Phar'par, rivers of Damascus, better than all the waters of Israel, that I may wash in them and be made clean?"

---

7. What of the miracles wrought by Eliseus? 8. What took place about this time? 9. What was Naaman's character and disease? 10. What did the little maid say to her mistress? 11. What did Naaman do in consequence? 12. How did Eliseus receive him? 13. What did Naaman say?

THE KINGDOM OF ISRAEL—CONTINUED.

14. But as he was thus angrily turning homeward, his servants said to him, "Father, if the prophet had bidden thee do some great thing, surely thou wouldst have done it; how much rather what he now hath said to thee, 'Wash, and thou shalt be made clean.'"

15. Naaman recognized the justice of their words, and going down to the Jordan, bathed seven times, as the prophet had commanded. "And his flesh was restored, like the flesh of a little child, and he was made clean."

16. Naaman at once hastened back to the prophet, and declared that there was no God, save the God of Israel. He then pressed rich gifts on Eliseus, but the holy man refused to accept anything.

17. Naaman then departed homeward. But he had not gone far when he was overtaken by Gĭ-e′-zĭ, a servant of Eliseus, who said that his master desired a talent of silver, and two changes of raiment, to bestow on two young men who had just come to him from Mount Ephraim.

18. Naaman gladly gave him what he asked, and Giezi took them home and hid them. But when he came into the presence of Eliseus, the prophet, to whom God had made known his treachery, reproached him for his deception, and told him that in punishment for it, the leprosy of Naaman should abide with him till his death.

19. The list of Eliseus' miracles did not end even with his death. Once, when some men were digging a grave, near that of Eliseus, robbers from Moab rushed upon them.

20. In their terror, they thrust the corpse into Eliseus' sepulchre and fled. But no sooner had the dead man touched the prophet's bones, than he was restored to life, and came forth from the tomb.

---

14. What did his servants say to him? 15. Did he follow their advice? 16. What did he do? 17. What deception did Giezi practice? 18. Did Naaman give him what he asked for? 19. What miracle did Eliseus' remains work? 20. What did they do in their terror?

CHAPTER VI.

THE KINGDOM OF ISRAEL—(CONTINUED).

Nin-e-veh (nin'i-vay). This splendid city, the capital of the great Assyrian Empire, was situated on the Tigris River. Its streets were broad, its architecture was magnificent, and "it shone like the sun." Its population numbered about 600,000.

1. A SHORT time before Elias had been taken up alive into heaven, Achab had been killed in battle with the Syrians. His son, Joram, had succeeded him, but the time had now come when God's vengeance was to descend upon his house.

2. Eliseus, therefore, inspired by God, sent one of his disciples to anoint Jĕ'hu, king of Israel. Jehu at once proceeded with an armed force to Joram's palace, and after approaching the king with the wickedness of Jezabel, his mother, drew his bow and shot him dead.

3. Jehu then went through the city of Jezrahel. And Jezabel heard that he was approaching, and having donned her richest attire, and painted her face, and adorned her head, took up her station at a window of her palace.

4. And when Jehu saw her, he ordered her servants to throw her out of the window. They did so, and she fell on the spot where Naboth had been slain, and where the blood of Achab, her husband, had been licked from his chariot wheels by the dogs, when it had been driven home after the fatal battle.

5. In this spot, too, the second part of Elias' terrible prediction was now accomplished. After Jehu had eaten, he said to his servants, "Go and see after that cursed woman, and bury her, for she is a king's daughter."

6. But when they reached the place, they found nothing save her skull, and feet, and the extremities of her hands. The dogs had eaten her flesh. And when they returned and told

---

1. What had become of King Achab? 2. What did Eliseus do? 3. What was Jezabel's fate? 4. What did Jehu command his servants to do? 5. What was now to be accomplished in this spot? 3. What did they find?

Jehu, he said, "It is the word of the Lord, which he spake by his servant, Elias."

7. Jehu accomplished his mission of destruction upon the house of Achab faithfully. He also destroyed the temple of Baal, and put his priests to death. But he could not bring his mind to touch the state church of Israel, and restore his kingdom to the unity of the temple of Jerusalem.

8. So the golden calves remained in Dan and Bethel, and for this unfaithfulness, God punished the house of Jehu, though in reward for his good deeds, he permitted his children to sit on the throne of Israel, to the fourth generation.

9. While the house of Jehu was reigning in Israel, the Lord, who had wished to show mercy to the Gentiles, directed Jo'nas, a prophet who had arisen in Israel after the death of Eliseus, to go to Nineveh (nin'i-vay), and preach penance to its inhabitants.

10. Nineveh was the capital of the empire of Assyria, which had been a province of the great empire of Chaldea, but about the year 1250 B. C. had supplanted it, and for six hundred years was the ruling power of the ancient world.

11. Jonas, who knew how easily the Lord's anger is appeased, feared lest if he foretold to the Ninevites, as he had been told to do, that the Lord would destroy their city in forty days, they would do penance, and obtain forgiveness, and thus come to regard him as a false prophet, embarked for Thar'sis, instead of Nineveh.

12. The ship sailed from the port of Joppa, but on the way, the Lord sent a great storm, so that the ship was in danger of being lost. The sailors threw all the freight on board into the sea, in order to lighten her, and called on their gods for help.

13. Meanwhile Jonas lay asleep in the inner part of the ship. And the ship-master went to him and said, "Why art thou

---

7. In what was Jehu faithful, and in what unfaithful? 8. What remained in Bethel? 9. What did the Lord command Jonas to do? 10. Of what was Assyria the capital? 11. What reason kept Jonas from obeying? 12. What happened on the voyage? 13. Where was Jonas meanwhile?

asleep? Rise up, sleeper, call on thy God, if so be that God will think of us, that we may not perish."

14. The storm increased in violence, and at last the sailors determined to cast lots to know why this evil had come upon them. The lot fell on Jonas, who confessed his sin, and said, "Cast me into the sea, and the sea shall be calm to you."

15. The crew of the ship were at first very unwilling to do this, and strove very hard to reach the shore to land him. But the tempest increased in fury, and at last they cast him into the sea. And at once the wind and waves grew calm.

16. The Lord had sent a great fish which swallowed Jonas as soon as he was cast into the sea. And he remained for three days and three nights in the whale's belly, while he unceasingly called on God to save him.

17. His prayer was heard, and on the third day, the whale threw him out of its mouth on dry land. The Lord now commanded him once more to go to Nineveh. He at once obeyed and walked through its streets for one entire day, crying out, "Yet forty days, and Nineveh shall be destroyed."

18. The inhabitants of the stately and splendid city were greatly terrified at this prophecy, for they well knew that their guilt justified such a doom. A general fast for man and beast was proclaimed; during which all, even the king himself, put on sackcloth and ashes, and strove to appease the wrath of the Almighty.

19. Meanwhile Jonas had retired to a short distance from the menaced city to watch the course of events. As he had feared, the repentance of the Ninevites disarmed the divine justice, and the beautiful city was spared. And he grew angry and troubled, lest he should pass for a false prophet in consequence.

20. Then the Lord, to show him how unreasonable was his anger, caused a large vine to spring up during the night, and

---

14. Did the storm increase? 15. Did they do so? 16. What happened to Jonas in the sea? 17. Was his prayer heard? 18. Did the inhabitants believe Jonas? 19. Whither did Jonas go? 20. What did the Lord do to Jonas to convince him of his unreasonableness?

shelter him from the scorching rays of the next day's sun. Then on the following morning he caused a worm to eat its root, so that it withered away.

21. When the sun rose, God sent a burning wind also, which caused the prophet, no longer protected by the grateful shade of the ivy, to suffer so much with the heat, that he desired to die.

22. Then the Lord said to him, "Thou art grieved for the ivy for which thou hast not labored, and shall not I spare Nineveh, in which there are more than one hundred and twenty thousand persons that know not how to distinguish between their right hand and their left?"

Jonas, lying three days in the whale's belly, was a figure of Christ lying three days in the tomb, as his coming forth alive prefigured the Resurrection of the Savior.

CHAPTER VII.

END OF THE KINGDOM OF ISRAEL.—THE SAMARITANS.

1. As time went on, the kingdom of Israel became more and more corrupt. Its princes went on building their palaces of ivory, and rolled in wealth and luxury, while the people sank lower and lower in ignorance and vice.

2. In the midst of this general wickedness, the Lord raised up the prophet A′mos, who sternly denounced both the king and the priesthood, and foretold the punishment which God was soon to send on them. But the king, Jeroboam, drove him out of Israel, and he had to take refuge in Juda.

3. The prophet O′see took the exiled prophet's place, and continued his warnings to Israel. But he was no more heeded than Amos had been, and so God resolved to punish them in his wrath, and utterly destroy them.

---

21. What did God send to increase his suffering? 22. What did the Lord then say to him?

1. Did Israel grow worse or better as time went on? 2. What prophet did the Lord raise up? 3. Who took the place of Amos?

4. The Almighty chose as the instrument of his vengeance on Israel, the great empire of Assyria, which had repented at the warning of Jonas, and was now reaching its utmost point of power and glory.

5. In the reign of king O'see, in Israel, the Assyrian king Salmanas'ar led his armies into Israel, and besieged the strong city of Samaria. For three years the city struggled, and then it fell beneath the Assyrian battering-rams.

6. According to inscriptions on recently discovered slabs in the ruins of Nineveh, the number of families, whom the Assyrian king carried into captivity from Samaria, was 27,280. Of these, some went to augment the splendor of Nineveh with the labor of their slavery; while others were sent to people barren regions far to the east.

7. These are known as the ten lost tribes of Israel, because from this time they disappear utterly from the light of history, and their land became a wilderness.

8. After a time however, the Assyrian king resolved to people it with his subjects, and sent thither a number of families from all parts of Assyria and placed them in the cities of Samaria. As time went on, the people which sprung from these Assyrian colonists were known as Samaritans.

9. The religion of these new colonies was a monstrous union of all sorts of idolatry. And the Lord was angry at their defilement of the holy soil of Israel with this new worship, and He sent lions which ravaged the whole country, and forced them to cease from troubling the Almighty with its practice.

10. They then turned to the scattered remnants of the nation of Israel who had escaped being driven into captivity, for knowledge of the true God; and one of the captive priests was also sent back from Assyria, to instruct them in the faith of Israel.

---

4. What power did the Almighty choose as his instrument of vengeance? 5. What king reigned in Israel at the time of the invasion? 6. How many families did the Assyrian king carry into captivity? 7. How are these known? 8. How did it become peopled with pagans? 9. What was the religion of these new colonies in Israel and how was it punished? 10. To whom did the Samaritans turn?

11. But instead of the pure law of the Lord, this priest taught the new settlers the schismatic rites which had prevailed in Israel before the captivity. His first care was to reestablish the High Places on Bethel where Jeroboam had once raised up the Golden Calf.

12. The consequence was, that though the Assyrian colonies adored Jehovah, they served their own gods at the same time, according to the custom of the nations from whose midst they had been transported into Samaria.

13. This mixing up the worship of the God of Israel with that of their own idols by the Samaritans, made them an object of such abhorrence to the Jews of Jerusalem that it was forbidden for a Jew to so much as speak to a Samaritan.

14. As time went on, the Samaritan worship was gradually freed from its superstitions, and brought more in accordance with the Jewish ceremonial; a Temple almost as magnificent as that of Jerusalem was erected on Mount Gar'-i zim, and confused hopes of the Messias began to be cherished among them.

CHAPTER VIII.

THE STORY OF TOBIAS.

1. AMONG the captives carried off to Assyria, was Tobias, an upright and pious Israelite who had never adored the Golden Calf, but had gone regularly to offer his tithes and first fruits in the temple at Jerusalem. He was married to a virtuous wife of his own tribe named Anna, and they had one son, Tobias.

2. Tobias won the favor of Salmanasar, and was permitted by him to go from city to city, as he wished. On one of these journeys, he found in Rages, (ra'jes) a city of Media, one of

---

11. What did this priest teach them? 12. What was the consequence? 13. What effect had their idolatry on the Jews of Jerusalem? 14. Was the Samaritan worship ever brought more in accordance with the Jewish ceremonial?

1. What good man was carried off among the captives to Assyria? 2. Did he prosper?

his countrymen, named Gab'e-lus, in great want, and loaned him ten talents of silver.

3. When Salmanasar died, his son Senacherib (sen-ak'er-ib) succeeded him. He was not favorable to the Israelites, and the soldiery took advantage of this fact to gratify their own hatred of the captive people, and stabbed numbers of them in open day, and left their corpses in the streets.

4. On such occasions Tobias, whose life was spent in works of charity, would go out and bring the bodies of his murdered countrymen to his house, and bury them by night. This was against the king's commands, and when he heard of it, he sentenced Tobias to death.

5. Tobias managed to escape, and remained in concealment till the death of Senacherib, when he returned to Nineveh, and resumed his works of charity. But one day, when he was greatly fatigued, he lay down beneath the wall of his house to sleep, and the drippings from a swallow's nest fell on his eyes and destroyed his sight.

6. This affliction did not cause the pious Tobias to murmur, though, as time went on, he fell into deep poverty. His wife, Anna, became the support of the family and went out every day to work.

7. Tobias' son had now grown up, and so the father resolved to send him to Rages to recover the sum of money which he had lent to Gabelus. So he gave him good advice, and then sent him out into the city to find a guide for his journey.

8. The young Tobias went out and soon returned with a beautiful youth, who told him his name was Az-a-ri'-as, but who was in reality the arch-angel Raphael, whom God had sent to accompany him.

9. Tobias blessed the two youths and they set out on their journey. They rested the first night by the river Tigris, but, as Tobias went to wash his feet in its waters, a monstrous fish

---

3. What happened to the Israelites when Salmanasar died? 4. Would Tobias bury these? 5. Did Tobias escape? 6. Did this cause him to murmur? 7. Whither did Tobias resolve to send his son? 8. What

came up to devour him. In terror, he called to his companion, "Sir, he cometh upon me!"

10. The angel said to him, "Take him by the gill and draw him to thee." Tobias did so, and when the fish lay panting on the land, the angel told him to take out its heart, liver and gall, for they were useful medicines.

11. Then Tobias made a fire and broiled some of the fish for their evening meal, and after they had finished, salted a portion of what remained to serve as provision for the journey.

12. At length they reached a city where a kinsman of Gabelus dwelt, named Ragū'el. They went to lodge in Raguel's house, and the angel directed Tobias to ask his host for Sara, his daughter, as his wife.

13. Tobias objected that she had already been given to seven husbands in turn, whom the devil had killed on the night of the wedding, and that if such a fate should overtake him, the only son of his aged parents, it would bring down their old age with sorrow to the grave.

14. The angel answered that the devil had such power only over those, who, in marriage, shut out God from their hearts, and thought only of the gratification of their evil passions, and that he would avoid it by passing three days with his wife in prayer, after their marriage.

15. Tobias accordingly asked Raguel to give him Sara in marriage. He hesitated, but the angel told him not to fear, because the young man feared the Lord. So Raguel joined the hands of Tobias and Sara, saying, "The God of Abraham, the God of Isaac, and the God of Jacob, be with you and fulfil His blessing in you."

16. While the marriage was being celebrated the angel went to the city of Rages, to Gabelus, who paid him the debt and

---

10. What did the angel tell him to do? 11. What did Tobias do with the fish? 12. What place did they at length reach? 13. What objection did Tobias make to this? 14. What did the angel answer? 15. Did he ask for Sara in marriage? 16. Whither did the angel go during the

returned with him to the house of Raguel, which they reached before the conclusion of the festivities.

17. And when Gabelus saw Tobias he wept with joy, and embraced him, saying, "The God of Israel bless thee, because thou art the son of a very good and just man that feareth God and doeth alms deeds. And may a blessing come upon thy wife."

18. Tobias was now anxious to return home. "I know that my parents count the days," he said to Raguel, "and their spirit is afflicted within them." So his father-in-law, after vainly entreating him to stay a little longer, gave him the half of what he possessed, and dismissed him and Sara with his blessing.

19. Meanwhile, Tobias' parents had grown exceedingly sad at the long absence of their son. And his mother cried, "Woe, woe is me, my son, why did we send thee to a strange land, the light of our eyes, the staff of our old age, the comfort of our life, the hope of our posterity!"

20. Tobias said to her, "Hold thy peace, our son is safe." But she would not be comforted, but went out into all the ways, that she might see him coming afar off. And at last one day she saw him approaching and ran with the joyful news to her husband.

21. By the angel's desire, Tobias had left his wife and attendants some distance behind. As he drew near his home, he met his father, who had groped his way forth to meet him, and they all wept for joy.

22. And after they had adored God and given Him thanks, Tobias rubbed his father's eyes with the gall of the great fish which he had preserved. And at once his sight was restored, and he cried out, "I bless thee, O Lord God of Israel, because Thou hast chastised me, and Thou hast saved me, and behold I see Tobias, my son!"

23. Seven days later, Sara arrived, and completed the joy of

---

17. What did Gabelus do when he saw Tobias? 18. What was Tobias very anxious to do? 19. How fared it with his parents meanwhile? 20. Did Tobias succeed in comforting her? 21. What had Tobias done by the angel's desire? 22. What did Tobias do after they had adored God? 23. What completed their joy?

TOBIAS RETURNING THANKS.

the happy household. Nothing now remained but to reward Azarias for his devotion and the benefits which he had conferred upon Tobias.

24. So they told him that they could never repay him, but besought him to accept half of the money which Gabelus had paid, as some slight token of their gratitude.

25. The angel answered, "Bless ye the God of heaven, and give glory to Him in the sight of all that live; because He hath shown His mercy to you. Prayer is good with fasting and alms, more than to lay up treasures of gold.

26. When thou didst pray with tears, and didst bury the dead, I offered thy prayer to the Lord. And because thou wast acceptable to God it was necessary that temptation should prove thee. The Lord hath sent me to heal thee, and to deliver Sara, thy son's wife, from the devil.

27. "For I am the angel Raphael, one of the seven who stand before the throne of God." As soon as the household heard this, they fell prostrate at his feet, in fear. But he told them not to fear, but to bless and thank God, and then vanished from their sight.

28. The elder Tobias lived forty-two years after these wonderful events, and passed away at the age of one hundred and ten years. Tobias, his son, also lived to a very great age, and saw his children's children to the fourth generation.

CHAPTER IX.

THE KINGDOM OF JUDA.

1. UNLIKE the kingdom of Israel, none of whose kings were faithful to the Lord, Juda had some rulers who strove to walk

---

24. What did they say to him? 25. What did the angel answer? 26. Repeat the angel's words when he told Tobias he had offered his prayer to the Lord. 27. Tell how he revealed his identity, and how did it affect the household? 28. How long did the elder Tobias, and the younger live?

1. Had Israel any good kings?

THE KINGDOM OF JUDA. 143

in the footsteps of King David, and maintain the worship of God in its purity.

2. Before his death, Roboam fell into idolatry and vice, and was punished by having his kingdom invaded by the king of Egypt, who carried off the public treasure. His son A bi' as, who succeeded him, was at first faithful to the Lord, but afterwards imitated the infidelity of his father.

3. Abias was succeeded by his son A'sa, who was contemporary with the first seven kings of Israel from Jeroboam to Achab. At first he did what was pleasing in the sight of God, and defeated the Ethiopians who had invaded his kingdom, but afterwards fell away from the service of the Almighty.

4. Asa was succeeded by his son Josh' a phăt, who was one of the most religious monarchs that ruled over the kingdom of Juda. His power was respected at home and abroad, and during his reign his kingdom reached a degree of splendor approaching to that which it had attained under David and Solomon.

5. He was succeeded by his son Jo'ram, whose first act was to slay all his brothers and marry Ath a-lī'-ah, the daughter of Achab and Jezebel, of Israel. Athaliah brought the idolatrous practices of Israel into Juda. God punished Joram by causing him to perish slowly of a loathsome disease.

6. He was succeeded by his son O-cho-zi'-ah, who was slain after a reign of one year by Jehu the king of Israel, who had invaded Juda, because he was of the blood of Achab.

7. His mother Athaliah at once usurped the throne, and ordered all the house of her son Ochoziah to be put to death. But a new-born son of Ochoziah (Jo' as) was saved by his aunt Jos' a-bĕth, and brought up in secret in the Temple till his seventh year.

8. Then Jehoiada (je-hoy'-ă-dă) the high-priest, having

---

2. What befell Roboam? 3. By whom was Abias succeeded? 4. Who succeeded Asa? 5. Who succeeded Joshaphat? 6. By whom was Joram succeeded? 7. What did Athaliah do then? 8. What did Jehoiada then do for the prince?

collected the Levites in the Temple, showed the young prince to the people, who acknowledged him as king.

9 Athaliah, hearing the acclamations, hurried to the Temple, but was seized and led without the sacred precincts to beyond the western gate. Here, at the entrance to her own palace, she was put to death.

10. Joas reigned for forty years. As long as Jehoiada lived, he was guided by his counsels, and remained firm in the faith. But after that holy man's death, Joas fell into idolatry.

11. More than one prophet called the king to repentance, but in vain. At length the spirit of God came upon Zacharias, the son of Jehoiada, and he sternly rebuked both prince and people for having forsaken the worship of the true God.

12. Enraged at the holy priest's boldness, Joas commanded him to be stoned to death. God's punishment for this crime was speedy; the Syrians invaded the land, and plundered Jerusalem. Joas fell ill, and was murdered by his servants in his bed.

13. Joas was succeeded by his son Amasias. During the first years of his reign, this king observed the laws of Moses, but afterwards brought idols into Jerusalem, and burnt incense before them.

14. God sent a prophet to rebuke him, but Amasias threatened to kill him. The holy man departed, and God soon punished the wicked king. After being defeated in a war with Jehu, king of Israel, he was murdered by his own servants.

15. Amasias was succeeded by his son Ozias. For many years this prince governed the kingdom in a religious manner. But at length his prosperity became so great that he was puffed up by it, and resolved to minister as high-priest in the Temple.

16. The king went to the Temple with his attendants, intending to enter the house of the Lord. But the priests and Levites, with

---

9. Relate Athaliah's fate. 10. How did Joas act as king? 11. Who rebuked the king? 12. Relate Joas's crime and punishment. 13. Who succeeded Joas? 14. What became of Amasias? 15. What did Ozias attempt? 16. Did he succeed?

the high-priest at their head, prevented him from burning incense upon the altar.

17. Filled with anger, Ozias threatened to strike the priests. But as he raised his hand to do so, he was stricken with leprosy. The priests thrust him out of the sacred precincts, and he dwelt in retirement for the rest of his life, his son Jŏ′ a tham acting as regent.

18. At the death of Ozias, Joatham ascended the throne, and reigned in peace for sixteen years. Then he died, and was succeeded by his son A′ chaz. Idolatry had been rife during the previous reign, but grew worse under Achaz, who openly professed it.

19. This wicked king, the bad son of a good father, publicly offered his son in sacrifice to Moloch, and covered the land with idols. In punishment for this, God caused the army of Israel to defeat that of Juda, and slay one hundred and twenty thousand men in one day.

20. Achaz, fearing for his kingdom, sought the alliance of the king of Assyria. He sent messengers to him saying, "I am thy servant and thy son, come and save me out of the hands of Syria and Israel." The king of Assyria sent an army to his help and for the moment he was relieved.

CHAPTER X.

THE KINGDOM OF JUDA—(CONTINUED).

1. LIKE the kingdom of Israel, the kingdom of Juda had had during all this time her prophets, whose warning voices had denounced the sins of the people and summoned them to repentance.

2. As the years went on, and these returns to penitence grew

---

17. What did he threaten and how was he punished? 18. Did Joatham ascend the throne? 19. Give some proofs of this and tell how he was punished. 20. Whose alliance did the wicked Achaz seek?

1. Had the kingdom of Juda prophets? 2. What change came over the prophets' warnings as time went on?

fewer and briefer, the prophets began sorrowfully to announce to the rebellious people the destruction of their kingdom. The only consolation left to these holy men was the thought of the Messias, whose coming each one prophesied more and more clearly.

3. Up to the reign of Joatham, the most noted of the prophets of Juda, were Jo'el, who foretold the destruction of Jerusalem, and Mī chē'as, who foretold that Bethlehem should be the birthplace of the Redeemer.

4. In the reign of Achaz appeared the prophet Isaias, (ī sā'yas) the first of the four Major or Greater Prophets, as they are called, from the fullness and clearness of their prophecies in regard to Our Saviour.

5. Isaias strove to prevent Achaz from forming the alliance with Assyria, declaring that it would be the instrument used by God for the destruction of Juda. And when Achaz refused either to listen or to ask a sign from God, Isaias uttered his memorable prophecy of the coming of Christ.

6. "Behold," he said, "a virgin shall conceive, and bear a son, and his name shall be called Emmanuel, that is, God-with-us. And there shall come forth a rod out of the root of Jesse, and a flower shall rise up out of his root.

7. "And the spirit of the Lord shall rest upon Him, the spirit of wisdom and of understanding, the spirit of counsel and of fortitude, the spirit of knowledge and of godliness. And He shall be filled with the spirit of the fear of the Lord."

8. Both king and people turned a deaf ear to the prophet's assurances that God would protect them by His own arm, without the assistance of the great pagan empire. But they were soon to find how little trust was to be placed in their new ally.

9. Glad of the opportunity of extending his empire west-

---

3. Mention the most noted of Juda's prophets up to the time of Joatham. 4. What great prophet appeared in the reign of Achaz? 5. What did Isaias strive to prevent? 6. Repeat this prophecy. 7. What did Isaias declare would be the characteristics of the Messias? 8. Did Juda heed the prophet's assurances of God's protection? 9. What did the king of Assyria do after he conquered Israel and Syria?

THE KINGDOM OF JUDA—CONTINUED. 147

ward, the king of Assyria led his armies to attack Israel and Syria, but after he had conquered them, he came and plundered Jerusalem, and Achaz was forced to buy him off by giving him the sacred vessels of the temple and all the royal treasure.

10. After this, Achaz, in a fit of blind despair, shut up the temple, and began to sacrifice to the gods of Syria and Damascus. In this state of apostasy, he died, and was succeeded by his son Ezechias (ez-e-ki′as).

11. Ezechias was a very different man from his father. Full of piety and zeal, and firmly believing that the hope of Juda was in the God of their fathers, he overthrew the idols of Achaz, and ordered the Levites to purify the temple from the defilements it had suffered during the preceding reign.

12. When this had been done, and the solemn sacrifice offered in his presence, the king prepared to celebrate the Feast of the Pasch with due solemnity, and sent invitations to Israel to join Juda in its observance.

13. Such terrible progress, however, had unbelief made in Israel, that the message was received with laughter, and only a very few responded. But the proud and godless kingdom of Israel was even then nearing its doom; and in a few short years it had vanished from among the nations.

14. The pious Ezechias, after seeing the children of Israel driven into captivity, was confirmed in his resolve to trust to God alone.

15. In his reign much of the old power of Juda had been restored, many neighboring countries had been brought beneath his sceptre, and he now determined to throw off the yoke of Assyria, and refused to be any longer a tributary of that power.

16. The reigning king of Assyria at this time was Senach-

---

10. What did Achaz then do? 11. Was Ezechias like his father? 12. What further proof of piety did Ezechias give? 13. Did Israel heed his invitation? 14. What effect had the doom of Israel on Ezechias? 15. What did the renewed power of Israel lead Ezechias to do? 16. Who was now king of Assyria, and what did he do?

erib (se-nak' er-ib). A proud and mighty monarch, holding all the nations of Asia as tributaries, he did not long brook such an insult, but set out with his armies to punish the audacious king who had dared to offer it.

17. He crosses the Jordan at its source, and so mighty is his host that the waters of the river are diminished to a feeble thread, after the men and animals had drunk of it. City after city is taken and he rapidly nears Jerusalem.

18. Ezechias, seized with terror, for a moment wavers in his faith in God, and endeavors to buy the invader off by the payment of an immense treasure, though to accumulate it, he has to tear even the gold plates from the doors of the temple.

19. But Senacherib, who has determined to establish his idols on the sacred soil of Mount Sion, haughtily demands that Jerusalem be given up to him. When Ezechias heard this he sent to beseech Isaias to intercede for Juda with the Lord, then, clothing himself in sackcloth and ashes, went up into the temple to pray.

20. Isaias sent back word to Ezechias not to fear, for that God had heard his prayer and would destroy the Assyrians, and that on his return to his own country, Senacherib should perish by the sword.

21. That evening as the sun set, it rested on the purple and gold of the vast array of the Assyrians, as they lay encamped about Jerusalem. If the magnificent sight struck terror into some hearts, the greater number of the Jews remembered the mighty miracles worked by God in behalf of their fathers, and felt confident that He would not now desert them.

22. So when at twilight the drums and dulcimers of the Assyrians sounded, they were answered from the Jewish battlements by a trumpet blast of defiance. And then the night fell

---

17. Where does he cross the Jordan, and what happens? 18. Does Ezechias waver? 19. Does this treasure satisfy Senacherib? 20. What word did Isaias send back to the king? 21. What was seen at sunset and what emotion did it rouse in Jerusalem? 22. What answered the Assyrian drums at twilight?

—the night which was to have no morning for so many of the warriors of Assyria.

23. For during it the Angel of the Lord descended into the camp of the Assyrians and slew one hundred and eighty-five thousand of them. And when Senacherib saw this terrible sight, he at once departed for his own country, where shortly after, as he was worshipping in the temple of his god at Nineveh, he was put to death by his own son.

CHAPTER XL.

THE KINGDOM OF JUDA—CONTINUED.—JUDITH.

1. Ezechias died in peace after a prosperous reign, and was succeeded by his son Manasses. During this king's long reign of fifty-five years, he undid all the reforms of his good father and restored the worship of idols.

2. During the reign of Manasses Isaias continued to prophesy regarding the coming of the Messias, and to describe the marks of his person and of His Kingdom.

3. But in so doing he was brought into collision with the most deeply-rooted predjudices of the Jewish race, or, as he himself says, "with the iron sinew of their neck, and their forehead of brass."

4. For the Jews expected the Messias, when he came, to be exclusively for themselves, whereas Isaias said that God had given Him "for a leader and a master to the Gentiles," and declared that their temple, into which none save their own race might then enter, was to be made common to all nations.

5. Still more bitter to the haughty Jews, secure in the conviction that they were God's chosen people, and looking for

---

23. What took place during the night?
1. Who succeeded Ezechias, and what wickedness was he guilty of?
2. Did Isaias continue to prophesy during Manasses' reign? 3. Were his prophecies in harmony with the Jewish idea of the Messias? 4. For whom did the Jews expect the Messias to come? 5. What was still more bitter to the haughty Jews?

the coming of a king who should be greater than either David or Solomon, was the portrait that Isaias held up to their contemplation.

6. Despised, and the most abject of men; a man of sorrows and acquainted with infirmity, "who should be wounded for our iniquities, and bruised for our sins; who should be led as a sheep to the slaughter, and be dumb as a lamb before His shearer;" such Isaias declared, should be the deliverer they longed for.

7. In their anger, they heeded no further revelations of the prophet, and turned to worship false gods. Then Isaias told them that God would punish their idolatry by causing them to be led into captivity where they should remain for seventy years, and that only a small remnant should return, like the gleaning of grapes when the vintage is over.

8. Manasses was so enraged by this warning of Isaias that he declared him guilty of treason, and had him sawn in two.

9. The wicked king's punishment was speedy. The Assyrians again attacked Jerusalem and bore him off to Nineveh, where he remained in captivity for many years.

10. Whilst their king was thus languishing in an Assyrian dungeon, a brother of As-sur-ban'-i-pal, the king of Assyria, instigated Juda along with all the other kingdoms of the west that were subject to that monarch, to revolt against him.

11. Assurbanipal at once sent his general, Hol-o-fer'-nēs, at the head of an immense army, to chastise the rebellious provinces. Crossing the Euphrates, he swept westward, destroying the cities and ravaging the fertile plains with fire and sword, till at length he drew near to the kingdom of Juda.

12. At the news of his approach, E-li' a kim, the high-priest of Jerusalem, in whom was vested the supreme power, during

---

6. How did Isaias picture the Messiah? 7. What did their anger lead them to do? 8. What was the fate of the holy prophet Isaias? 9. Relate Manasses' punishment. 10. Who stirred up all the western provinces of Assyria to revolt during Manasses' captivity? 11. Whom did Assurbanipal send to chastise them? 12. What did Eliakim do at his approach?

the captivity of Manasses, went round the cities of Juda, exhorting the Jews to humble themselves in sackcloth and ashes, and pray to the Lord their God for deliverance, while the men of war prepared to defend their country.

13. At length Holofernes reached Bethu'-li-a, a town on one of the mountain-roads leading to Jerusalem. He laid siege to it, and the town held out bravely till he destroyed the aqueducts which supplied it with water.

14. This caused the inhabitants of the town to suffer from thirst to such a degree that at the end of twenty days they implored the elders to surrender. The latter promised to do so at the end of four days, should no aid come from the Lord in that time.

15. THE STORY OF JUDITH.—Now there dwelt in Bethulia at this time a devout widow named Judith. Though beautiful and wealthy, she lived retired from the world, and spent her life in prayer and good works. But now, touched with compassion by the woes of her people, she came to the elders of the city and spoke as follows:

16. "What is this word by which you have consented to give up the city in four days? You have set a time for the mercy of the Lord according to your pleasure. This is not a word that may draw down mercy, but rather indignation. Let us therefore be penitent for this same thing."

17. Other noble words Judith also spoke, until at length the ancients became infused with the spirit of her sublime faith, and implored her to pray for the people. Judith therefore returned home and retired into her oratory, and while entreating God to spare her country, suddenly thought of a plan for its deliverance.

18. Hastening once more to the elders, she briefly informed them that she and her maid would go to the Assyrian camp. They made no objection, so Judith returned home, and after

---

13. What town did Holofernes at length reach? 14. What did this cause? 15. Who dwelt in Bethulia at this time? 16. Repeat her address to the elders. 17. What else did Judith say, and what was the result? 18. Relate her proceedings.

praying to God in sackcloth and ashes, rose and clothed herself in her richest attire, and anointed herself with her sweetest perfume.

19. Then leaving the town by night with her maid, she took her way to the Assyrian camp. They were soon stopped by the sentinel of the Assyrians, to whose questions Judith replied that she was a Jewess who had fled from the besieged city, knowing it must fall, and that she had important intelligence for Holofernes.

20. The sentinel had her conducted at once into the presence of the general. So charmed was the Assyrian with her majestic beauty, that he had a tent provided for her, and gave orders that she was to come and go as she pleased.

21. On the fourth day Holofernes gave a grand banquet to the officers of his army, and invited Judith to be present. Judith consented, on condition that she should not be required to partake of the Assyrian meats, which her religion forbade.

22. In the course of the banquet Holofernes drank deep, and when his guests at length retired, he fell back on his couch in the heavy sleep of intoxication. Judith had remained, and finding herself at last alone with the threatened destroyer of her country, resolved to kill him.

23. "Strengthen me, O Lord God of Israel," she prayed, "and in this hour look upon the work of thy hands, that I may bring to pass that which I have purposed, having a belief that it might be done by Thee." Then she took down Holofernes' own sword from where it hung, on a pillar near by, and cut off his head.

24. Early in the morning she stood before the gates of Bethulia, and cried, "Open the gates, for God is with us." She was conducted before the elders of the city, who, on seeing the head of Holofernes, gave glory to God for their deliverance.

---

19. Did she go to the camp? 20. Was she conducted to Holofernes? 21. What did Holofernes give on the fourth day? 22. What did Holofernes do during the banquet, and what did Judith resolve? 23. Repeat Judith's prayer, and relate how she killed Holofernes. 24. What did Judith say in the morning to the watch at Bethulia?

JUDITH WITH THE HEAD OF HOLOFERNES.

25. Judith then counseled the people to make an assault at once on the Assyrian camp. They did so, and as Judith had foreseen, the Assyrians were seized with panic on finding Holofernes dead, and fled, leaving their camp with all its rich spoils in the hands of the Jews.

26. After this the high priest of Jerusalem came to visit Judith, and all the elders who came with him, said to her with one voice, "Thou art the glory of Jerusalem, thou art the joy of Israel, thou art the honor of our people." Judith responded by singing a canticle in praise of the Lord.

27. The rejoicings for this splendid victory were prolonged for three months. Judith was held in the highest honor by all Israel throughout her long and devout life, and deeply mourned at her death.

Judith, in some degree, prefigures the Blessed Virgin. Judith saves her people, as Mary is the chosen instrument of the Incarnation by which mankind is saved. Judith was praised as the pride and ornament of Israel; Mary is called blessed by all mankind as the glory of the human race, the mother of the Man-God.

CHAPTER XII.

THE PROPHET JEREMIAS—FALL OF THE KINGDOM OF JUDA.

1. AFTER the death of Manasses, his wicked son A'mon reigned for a few years, and then his son Josias succeeded him. God had now raised up another great prophet named Jer-e-mi'-as, and Josias listened to his counsel, and forbade idolatry.

2. Early in life, however, Josias was slain in battle, and Jeremias wrote Lamentations for his death which were sung in Israel. Jō'a-kin, his son, abandoned all Josias' reforms, and

---

25. What did Judith counsel the people to do at once, and what was the result? 26. Who came to visit Judith after this? 27. How long did Israel rejoice for this victory?

1. Who succeeded Manasses? 2. What was the fate of Josias, and who succeeded him?

FALL OF THE KINGDOM OF JUDA.

built a grand palace of cedar, where he lived in great luxury, and adored false gods.

3. Jeremias therefore rebuked the king in public for his wickedness, and the people for following his example. Incensed by his plain speaking, the people endeavored to stone him to death, but some of the elders assisted him to escape.

4. As he faithfully continued his mission as prophet, however, and threatened both king and people with the wrath of the Lord, King Joakin had him imprisoned.

5. But Jeremias sent from his prison for another prophet, named Bā′ruch, and gave him a scroll on which he had written all his prophecies, and told him to read it aloud in the temple on the occasion of a public fast.

6. Baruch did so, and when the elders heard that the great bulk of the nation were to be carried into captivity and the temple and city destroyed by fire, they were filled with fear and astonishment, and ordered Judi, a scribe, to take the scroll to the king and read it in his presence.

7. Judi accordingly took the scroll and went to the king's winter palace, where he found him seated before a hearth full of burning coals. Judi began to read, but when he had read a few pages, the king took the scroll from him, cut it into pieces with his penknife and cast it into the fire.

8. The great empire which bore first the name of Chaldea and then of Assyria, was now known as Babylon, because that province had revolted, and conquered the rest of the empire.

9. The magnificent city of Nineveh, as many of the prophets of Israel had foretold, had been utterly destroyed, and the seat of government established at the city of Babylon, on the Euphrates river. (B. C. 625.)

10. The second king of Babylon, Neb-uch-ad-nez′-zar, was the

---

3. What did Jeremias do? 4. Did he continue his mission? 5. How did Jeremias now manage to communicate with the people? 6. When Baruch did so, what did the elders command Judi to do? 7. Did Judi go, and was the king moved? 8. What great empire ruled the civilized world at this time? 9. What city had been destroyed? 10. Who was the instrument chosen by God to chastise Juda?

instrument chosen by the Almighty for the destruction of Jerusalem. The very year after Joakin had burnt the scroll of Jeremias, Nebuchadnezzar attacked Jerusalem, and while repelling an assault, Joakin was slain and his body cast without the gates.

11. Nebuchadnezzar then led away the chief inhabitants of Jerusalem to people his city of Babylon. This is called the Great Captivity, and the seventy years of the Jewish exile date from it. (B. C. 605.)

12. The king of Babylon left the least desirable portion of the Jewish population in Jerusalem, and placed Sed-e-ci-as, a brother of Joakin, to rule over them as his deputy. After some years, Sedecias revolted and endeavored to effect the independence of Juda.

13. This remnant of Juda's population had not been converted to God by the fate of their brethren. On the contrary, their lives had been such that the measure of their iniquity was full, and the patience of the Almighty exhausted.

14. Nebuchadnezzar's armies swiftly encompassed Jerusalem, and soon made a breach in its walls. Sedecias was taken, and after his eyes had been put out, he was sent as a prisoner to Babylon, where he died.

15. Jerusalem was then burnt to the ground, the temple destroyed, and those of the inhabitants who were not put to the sword, led captive to Babylon. Thus, at length, was fulfilled the judgment which had been so long withheld.

16. Jeremias, the faithful prophet, remained for a time amid the ruins of the holy city, and made many lamentations over its fall. These form a separate book of the Holy Scriptures. He then went to Egypt to exhort the Jews who were settled in that country, and remained there till his death.

17. Jeremias is the second of the Major prophets. He au-

---

11. Whom did Nebuchadnezzar lead into captivity? 12. Did he leave any in Jerusalem? 13. Had this remnant of Juda's population repented? 14. What was the consequence? 15. What happened to Jerusalem and its inhabitants? 16. Where did Jeremias remain for a time? 17. What is Jeremias and what did he prophesy of the Messias?

nounced the birth of the Messias from the family of David, His mission as a Prophet of the Gentiles, and the new covenant He would make with His chosen people.

The *New* Covenant of which Jeremias speaks is the Christian religion in which greater grace is bestowed on men, for which reason it is called the law of grace, while the Old Covenant was the law of fear.

CHAPTER XIII.

THE JEWS IN CAPTIVITY IN BABYLON.—EZEKIEL—DANIEL.— THE STORY OF SUSANNA.

1. THE captive Jews were treated kindly by the king of Babylon, and Jeremias wrote to them as follows: "Build ye houses and dwell in them; plant orchards and eat the fruit of them, and be ye multiplied. Seek the peace of the city."

2. Under the great king Nebuchadnezzar, Babylon became one of the most wondrous of all the beautiful Oriental cities. It covered an area of seventy square miles on each side of the Euphrates, and was surrounded with walls of burnt brick two hundred cubits high, and fifty thick.

3. Huge gates of bronze, sixty in number, gave entrance and egress on the land, and guarded the streets which led to the river. Extensive tracts within the great city were devoted to grazing purposes, so as to guard against famine during long sieges, while its superb palaces and sumptuous temples, rose from the midst of beautiful gardens.

4. Babylon's grandest temple was the tower of the god Bel, which was considered one of the seven wonders of the world. It consisted of eight separate towers, constructed one over the other. The topmost was the chamber of the god and contained furniture of solid gold.

5. Nebuchadnezzar's palace was a huge structure of plain and

---

1. Were the captive Jews treated kindly? 2. What did Babylon become? 3. Describe it. 4. What was its grandest temple? 5. Describe the king's palace.

enamelled bricks, with bronze gates, and surrounded by hanging gardens. Those gardens which were the glory of the East, were laid out in open terraces, raised on arches of masonry and supplied with water from the Euphrates, by means of buckets and pulleys.

6. But all the glory and beauty of Babylon could not make the Jewish captives cease to sigh for Jerusalem. We read in the Psalms that "upon the rivers of Babylon we sat down and wept when we remembered Sion. On the willows in the midst, we hung up our harps, for there they that led us into captivity, required of us the words of songs.

7. "How shall we sing the song of the Lord in a strange land? If I forget thee, O Jerusalem, let my right hand be forgotten. Let my tongue cleave to my jaws if I do not remember thee, if I make not Jerusalem the beginning of my joys."

8. During the chastisement of his chosen people, God did not forget them, but sent another great prophet, Ezechiel (E-ze' ki-el) to instruct and sustain them. He consoled them greatly by relating a wonderful vision which God had vouchsafed to him.

9. The spirit of the Lord conducted him to a vast plain filled with bones. At the command of God, Ezechiel bade the bones to come together. This was done and they were clothed with flesh, but there was no spirit in them.

10. At the command of the Lord the prophet then spoke again and commanded a spirit to enter into each of the bodies and cause them to live. And then they stood forth an exceeding great army, and the Lord made known to him that the vision prefigured the restoration of the Jews from their seemingly hopeless captivity to the land of Juda.

11. Out of the ranks of the Jewish captives, Nebuchadnezzar chose several young men of high rank for his personal service.

---

6. Did the Jews forget Jerusalem in this beautiful city? 7. Continue the words of the Psalms. 8. Whom did God send to sustain the Jews during this trial? 9. Relate Ezechiel's vision. 10. What took place at the prophet's word? 11. Whom did the king set apart from the ranks of the Jewish captives?

Among these youths were Daniel, An-a-nī' as, Mis' a-el and Az-a-rī' as.

12. They were conducted to the king's palace, clothed in rich apparel and furnished with food from the king's own table. But as the Jewish law forbade the most of these dishes they begged the steward to serve them with vegetables and water only.

13. The steward said he had no objection to doing so, only he feared that they would lose all their beauty on such a diet, and then the king would punish him severely for consenting to it.

14. But Daniel entreated him to try it for ten days, and be guided by the result. He did so, and at the end of that time the faces of the Jewish youths were fresher and fairer than those of the other youths of the court.

15. So from that time the steward served them with the food they desired, and God permitted them to grow so beautiful and so wise that when Nebuchadnezzar saw them he was charmed with them and retained them about his person.

16. THE STORY OF SUSANNA.—Among the rich and influential Jews who had been brought to Babylon was Joakin. His house was a great resort of his countrymen who were received with great hospitality by himself and his beautiful and virtuous wife, Susanna.

17. Among these visitors were two of the ancients who had been appointed judges for that year. Under the appearance of virtue and benevolence, these two old men masked wicked and depraved hearts, and one day when Susanna was walking in the orchard at noon, sought to induce her to commit sin.

18. Filled with horror, Susanna spurned the proposal of the wretched hypocrites. But they declared that if she persisted

---

12. Whither were they conducted? 13. What did the steward answer? 14. What did Daniel entreat him? 15. Did he thenceforth give them the food they desired? 16. Who was among the rich Jews of Babylon and who was his wife? 17. Who were among these visitors? 18. What did the virtuous Susanna do?

in her refusal they would publicly accuse her of having committed such a crime.

19. Then in her anguish Susanna cried, "I am straitened on every side, for if I do this thing it is death to me, and if I do not I shall not escape your hands. But it is better for me to fall in your hands without doing it, than to sin in the sight of the Lord."

20. She then made a great outcry, which drew a throng of people about the orchard gates. Then the elders opened it and accused her before the multitude of a most wicked act. And the next day Susanna was brought before the tribunal of justice, tried, and sentenced to be stoned to death.

21. As she was led away, weeping, to her terrible fate, the Lord, in whom she was full of confidence, inspired Daniel, who was present, to cry out, "I am clear of the blood of this woman."

22. The people inquired his meaning, whereupon he told them to return to judgment, because the elders had borne false witness against Susanna. This was done, and Daniel ordered her accusers to be brought in separately before the tribunal.

23. Then Daniel said to the first, "O thou that art grown old in evil days, now are thy sins come out. Tell me, under what tree didst thou see Susanna?" He said, "Under a mastic tree." Daniel answered, "Thou hast lied against thy own head."

24. The first elder was then led away and the second one brought in. Daniel said to him, "Tell me, under what tree didst thou see Susanna?" He answered, "Under a holm (home) tree," Daniel answered, "Thou hast lied against thy own head."

25. The people saw from these contradictory statements how false was the testimony of these wicked old men. Rising up

---

19. What did she exclaim? 20. What did she then do, and what followed? 21. What did the Lord inspire Daniel to do as she was led away? 22. What did the people ask, and what did he answer? 23. Relate Daniel's interview with the first elder. 24. Who was then brought in? 25. What did the people see from this?

against them they gave them the death intended for Susanna, who was restored to her joyful husband and children. And from that time Daniel was held in high estimation in Babylon.

CHAPTER XIV.

DANIEL INTERPRETS NEBUCHADNEZZAR'S DREAM.—THE GOD BEL.—THE THREE YOUNG MEN IN THE FIERY FURNACE.

1. About this time Nebuchadnezzar had a dream which terrified him. The dream itself he could not remember, and when he found that none of the wise men of Babylon could bring it back to his mind he ordered them all to be put to death.

2. The Jewish wise men had not been consulted, but Daniel, fearing lest they should be included in the general destruction, went to the king and begged for time to solve the question. It was accorded, and Daniel returned home and bade his companions to beseech God to reveal it to him.

3. The next day Daniel stood before the king and told him that God in heaven had revealed to him his dream and its interpretation. He then told the king that he had seen a large statue with a head of gold, breast and arms of silver, belly and thighs of brass, legs of iron, and feet, part iron and part clay.

4. Then the king, Daniel continued, had seen a great stone rolling from a mountain, and this stone struck the statue and shattered it, and then the stone became a great mountain and filled the whole earth.

5. This statue, Daniel explained, signified the great empires of the world that should succeed one another. The head of gold betokened Nebuchadnezzar, a glorious and powerful king; the breast and arms of silver, the empire of the Medes and Persians which should succeed him.

---

1. What had the king about this time? 2. Had the Jewish men been consulted? 3. Did Daniel reveal it to the king? 4. What had the great stone done in the vision? 5. What did this statue signify?

6. The belly and thighs of brass prefigured the empire of Alexander the Great, which should conquer the Persians, and the legs and feet of iron, the great Roman empire which was to conquer all the others.

7. The stone that fell from the mountain signified a kingdom which God himself should found on earth, and which from a small beginning, would gradually spread all over the earth, and last forever.

8. Then the king fell on his face before Daniel, and exclaimed, "Verily, your God is the God of Gods, and Lord of Kings, a revealer of hidden things, seeing thou couldst discover this secret." And he made Daniel chief magistrate over all the wise men of Babylon.

9. One day, not long after this, the King asked Daniel why he did not adore his God, Bel. Daniel answered that he adored no gods made by hands, but only the living God who had created heaven and earth, and had power over all flesh.

10. Surprised, the king asked if he supposed that Bel, for whom large quantities of food were every day provided, were not a living God? But Daniel answered that Bel was but clay and brass and had not eaten at any time, as he would prove to the king.

11. Much disturbed, the king made Daniel accompany him to the temple of Bel, and told the priests of the god that if Daniel could prove his assertion they should die, but that if, on the contrary, they could prove that Bel did consume the provisions placed in the temple, Daniel should be put to death instead.

12. The priests at once requested the king to set the meats and place the wines for the god, and then to shut the temple and seal it with his own ring; then to return in the morning and punish them with death if the food were not consumed.

---

6. What empires did the brass and iron portions prefigure? 7. What did the great stone signify? 8. What did the king exclaim? 9. What did the king ask Daniel about Bel? 10. Relate the King's answer. 11. What did the king say to the priests? 12. What did the priests answer?

13. The priests then retired, and the king set out the god's repast. Then Daniel bade his servant bring ashes and strew the floor with it. They then left the temple and the king sealed its doors with the royal seal.

14. The following morning the king returned to the temple with Daniel. The seals were broken in their presence and they entered to find that all the provisions had disappeared. And the king cried out in triumph, "Great art thou, O Bel, and there is no deceit with thee."

15. But Daniel only laughed and pointed out to the king the print of the footsteps of men, women and children in the ashes on the floor.

16. They then investigated the place and discovered the secret doors by which the priests were accustomed to enter the temple every night with their wives and families, and eat the food provided for the god. The king, enraged by the long deceit which had been practised on him, had all the priests put to death.

17. The Babylonian counselors of the king, fearing that the Jews were gaining too much ground with him, and that it would end in the destruction of their idols, persuaded Nebuchadnezzar to have a great statue of gold set up in the plain of Babylon, with the command that whenever the sound of music was heard, all should fall down and adore it.

18. Scarcely had it been set up than Ananias, Misael, and Azarias, Daniel's companions, refused to bow down and adore it. Filled with fury, the king commanded his servants to cast them, without even waiting to remove their clothing, into a fiery furnace.

19. This was done, but the angel of the Lord descended with the Jews into the furnace, and caused its atmosphere to become as cool and refreshing as that of a pleasant valley; while

---

13. What did the king and Daniel do in the temple? 14. What did they find in the morning? 15. What did Daniel point out to the king? 16. What did they find? 17. How did the Babylonian counselors of the king seek to ruin the Jews? 18. Who were the first to refuse to adore it? 19. What miracle took place?

the flames darted out and consumed the men who had executed the king's cruel order.

20. Filled with gratitude for their wonderful preservation, the young men intoned a glorious canticle of praise and thanksgiving, which the Church of God still makes use of in divine service.

21. The sound of their glorious anthem reached the king, who hastened to the spot with his courtiers. And when he saw the young men walking about in the midst of the fire, he cried out "Ye servants of the Most High God, come forth."

22. They obeyed, and when they stood before the king safe and sound without even the smell of fire on their garments, he cried out, " Blessed be the God of Ananias, Misael, and Azarias, who has sent His angel and delivered His servants that believed in Him."

23. He then decreed that if any one in his kingdom dared to blaspheme the God whom these young men adored, he should be put to death, for that there was no other God who had power to save. He then raised the three to high positions in the kingdom.

The stone falling from the mountain which Nebuchadnezzar saw in his dream signified the Catholic Church which Christ established on earth. In the beginning it was small, but kept on increasing, and will continue to increase till the end of the world.

CHAPTER XV.

CAPTURE OF BABYLON BY CYRUS.

1. AFTER a time, Nebuchadnezzar had another dream which troubled his spirit, and Daniel interpreted it to him, and told him that it was a warning that in consequence of his sins the

---

20. How did they express their gratitude to God? 21. What reached the king, and what did he do? 22. What did the king say when they stood before him unharmed? 23. What did he decree?
1. What did the king's second dream portend?

CAPTURE OF BABYLON BY CYRUS.

Most High was about to afflict him with madness for seven years.

2. He therefore advised the haughty monarch to appease God's wrath with alms, and works of mercy, but the king paid no heed to his advice, and went his way.

3. Twelve months later, as he was walking in his palace at Babylon, and pluming himself on the beauty and magnificence which he had given the city, he was suddenly stricken with madness, and fleeing from his court, dwelt with the beasts of the field for seven years.

4. During this time he ate grass like an ox, and his body was wet with the dew of heaven; his hair grew like the feathers of eagles, and his nails like the claws of birds. At the end of seven years, he regained his senses, and glorified God, who thereupon made him even more powerful than he had been.

5. After a reign of forty-two years, this great king died, (B.C. 561) and with him passed away the true greatness of the empire of Babylon. Several of his line succeeded him, but none of them inherited his genius, and it began to decline.

6. This nation which both as the Assyrian and the Babylonian empire, had so long served as an instrument in the hands of the Most High to chastise his people, was now about to be punished for its own pride and cruelty.

7. The power destined to humble the empire of Babylon was the empire of the Medes and Persians—the second of the four great empires of Nebuchadnezzar's dream,—which under the great king Cyrus, had now reached its climax of power.

8. After conquering a large part of Asia, Cyrus turned his arms against Babylon. For several years the Babylonians bravely resisted his advances, but he surely, though slowly gained, and at length laid seige to the city of Babylon itself.

---

2. What did Daniel advise? 3. What terrible fate overtook him twelve months later? 4. What did he do during this time? 5. When did Nebuchadnezzar die? 6. What was now about to befall the nation? 7. What power was destined to humble Babylon? 8. When did Cyrus attack Babylon?

9. Bal-tas'-sar, the grandson of Nebuchadnezzar, was then reigning. Knowing that against the military engines of those days, the fortifications of Babylon were impregnable, and that the city possessed ample resources against famine within its limits, he felt little apprehension of the result.

10. In fact, month after month glided away, until nearly two years had passed, without having seen any progress on the side of Cyrus. To make a breach in the walls, or starve out the inhabitants, seemed utterly hopeless, yet to retire from the seige was to confess that Persia had reached the limit of her conquests.

11. In this dilemma, the magnificent military genius of Cyrus conceived the idea of turning from its bed the great river Euphrates. In the vicinity of Babylon there was a lake which had been excavated by Nebuchadnezzar to receive the waters of the river through a canal.

12. But since that time, an embankment had been built between the river and the canal, and both it and the lake were now dry. On a long dark night in winter therefore, Cyrus ordered a division of his men to break down the embankment, while other large detachments continued to advance through the dry bed of the river to the heart of the city.

13. Meanwhile, within the city, one of the great Babylonian festivals was in progress. Unmindful of the foe at their gates, all the inhabitants had given themselves up to enjoyment. Baltassar himself, surrounded by the nobles of his empire, sat at a splendid banquet in the pillared hall of his palace.

14. Myriad lights shone on the gold and silver dishes and drinking vessels, while the beat of timbrels rose and fell in the perfumed air, and nothing indicated that the end of Baltassar's life, and of his long dynasty, was at an end.

15. In the midst of the feast, Baltassar bethought himself of

---

9. Who was reigning and what did he feel? 10. Did Cyrus make any progress? 11. What did the genius of Cyrus conceive in this dilemma? 12. Were the canal and lake dry? 13. Meanwhile, what was in progress within the city? 14. Describe the scene? 15. What did Baltassar order to be brought forth?

the gold and silver vessels which Nebuchadnezzar had brought away from the temple of Jerusalem, and commanded the attendants to place them on the table. And when this was done, the king and all present drank from them, and gave praise to their false gods.

16. But suddenly, on the walls of the banqueting chamber, there appeared strange words written in characters that blazed like fire. In vain the terrified king summoned the wise men of the empire, and promised them rewards to decipher their meaning; the mysterious warning continued to blaze upon the wall, unread.

17. At length the queen thought of the holy Jew, Daniel. He was sent for, and filled with the spirit of God, fearlessly told the haughty king that the downfall of his empire was at hand.

18. Even while this scene was taking place, platoons of Persian troops were investing the city, and soon a fearful cry rose that the foe was upon them. But resistance was in vain. From house to house, and street to street, the Persians swarmed, and slew the revellers.

19. The royal palace was surrounded, and Baltassar was slain on the steps of his throne. Babylon was made a province of the Persian empire, and Cyrus put his father-in-law, Darius the Mede, to govern as regent while he pursued his conquests. B. C. 539.)

CHAPTER XVI.

DANIEL CAST INTO THE LIONS' DEN.—HIS PROPHECIES OF THE MESSIAH.—RETURN OF THE JEWS TO JERUSALEM.

1. DARIUS showed great favor to Daniel, who had been a confidential minister of state during the preceding dynasty, and

---

16. What appeared on the walls of the banqueting chamber? 17. Who read it? 18. What was taking place even then in the city? 19. What was the fate of Baltassar and of Babylon?

1. Did Darius favor Daniel?

advanced him to the highest office in the kingdom. This roused the jealousy of the other princes, and they resolved upon his destruction.

2. With this end in view, they persuaded Darius to sign a decree, that any one who, for the space of three months, should ask any petition of any God or man, save Darius himself, should be cast into the den of lions.

3. Then carefully watching Daniel, they found the holy man praying three times a day, as he was wont to do, with his face turned towards the temple at Jerusalem; and so they hastened and accused him before Darius of having broken the law.

4. The king was deeply grieved, and labored till sunset to save Daniel, but the princes reminded him of the law of the Medes and Persians, that no decree of the king might be altered, and so he was obliged to order Daniel to be cast into the den of lions.

5. This was done, and then the king sealed the stone which was laid upon the mouth of the den with his ring, and went away. For seven days, the prophet was kept in the den, during which time, the lions received no food. But they did not harm Daniel.

6. At this time there was a prophet named Habacuc (hab'-a-knk) in Juda. And the Angel of the Lord appeared to him, and said: "Carry thy dinner to Daniel, who is in the lions' den at Babylon." But Habacuc replied, "Lord, I never saw Babylon, nor do I know the den!"

7. Then, the Angel transported Habacuc to Babylon, and placed him over the lions' den. And the prophet called to Daniel, "Thou servant of God, take the dinner that God hath sent thee." Daniel thanked the Lord, and arose and ate, while the angel bore Habacuc back to his own place.

8. On the seventh day, the king came to bewail Daniel.

---

2. How did they accomplish this? 3. Did they find Daniel praying to God as usual? 4. Did the king try to save him? 5. Was it done, and what followed? 6. What did the angel tell Habacuc to do, and what did he answer? 7. Was he taken to Babylon? 8. What took place on the seventh day?

DANIEL IN THE LION'S DEN.

And when he removed the seal, and looked in, and saw Daniel sitting among the lions, he cried with a loud voice, "Great art thou, O Lord, the God of Daniel!" Then he bade him come forth, and restored him to his old place.

9. Then in his anger at those, who had led him to expose the holy man to such a fate, he had them cast into the den, where the lions instantly tore them to pieces.

10. Up to this time, Isaias, Jeremias and other prophets had described the person and characteristics of the expected Messias, but had revealed nothing positive respecting the time of his coming. To do this was the special mission given to Daniel.

11. Daniel determined this by describing the four great empires which were to precede Him, and which were revealed to the prophet in a vision under the form of four great beasts; the Babylonian as a lioness, the Persian as a bear, the Greek as a leopard, and the Roman as a strange, strong beast, with iron teeth and ten horns.

12. Daniel also determined the coming of the Savior by deducing it from a date in Jewish history. He foretold that the Jews should return to Jerusalem, and declared that from the day on which the order should be given to rebuild Jerusalem, till the death of the Messias, there should be only seventy weeks of years; that is 490 years.

13. In the second year of his regency, Darius the Mede died; on the following year (B. C. 536) Cyrus returned and assumed the government of the empire. He then issued a decree authorizing all the Jews who so desired to return to Jerusalem and rebuild the temple. Thus was accomplished the prophecy of Isaias.

14. By this time however, the majority of the people had come to possess houses and lands in Babylon, and preferred the ease and prosperity of a life there, under the mild rule of the

---

9. What punishment did he inflict on Daniel's enemies? 10. What was Daniel's special mission among the prophets? 11. What was the first way in which Daniel determined this? 12. How else did he determine it? 13. What took place after Darius died? 14. Did all respond?

Persian kings, to the toils and anxieties attending the rebuilding of the temple.

15. According to the prediction of the prophet, therefore, "that only a small remnant should return and again take root," comparatively a small number assembled under Zor-a-ba'-bel, who had been appointed to lead them back. But these made up in zeal what they lacked in numbers.

16. They arrived at Jerusalem and set to work at once to rebuild the temple. But they soon found that. while the first building had been a work of joy and peace, this was to be one of strife and danger.

17. The Samaritans first sent to say that they were of their kindred and that they desired to join with them in building. But when Zorababel refused their aid, they joined in league with several of the surrounding peoples and hired agents in the Persian court to endeavor to have the decree of Cyrus reversed.

18. During the reigns of Cyrus, and of his son Cambyses (kam-bī'-ses), they were unable to accomplish this, but when Smerd'is usurped the throne on the death of Cambyses, they succeeded in having him issue a decree forbidding the building of the temple to proceed. (B. C. 522.)

19. But the prophets Ag-gĕ'-us and Zach-a-rī'-as whom God had then raised up among His people, bade the people persevere. They did so, and when the Samaritans attacked them, the matter was once more brought before the court of Persia.

20. The great Darius was now on the throne, and he confirmed the decree of Cyrus, and ordered that if any man offered opposition to the work, he should be hanged. Zorababel therefore pushed the work forward, and at length in the sixth year of the reign of Darius, it was completed.

21. When only the altar had been erected, and sacrifice was offered, the old people had wept to think of the glory of the

---

15. What of the number who assembled under Zorababel? 16. What did they find the second building of the temple to be? 17. What did the Samaritans do? 18. Did they effect their purpose? 19. Who urged the Jews to persevere? 20. What king was now on the throne of Persia? 21. What had been foretold by Aggeus?

first temple. But Aggeus had consoled them by the assurance that the Desired of all nations, should honor it with his presence.

22. So now at its solemn dedication, the remembrance of this prediction formed the crown of their joy, and consoled them for all the anxieties, dangers and struggles they had undergone during the work of rebuilding.

CHAPTER XVII.

QUEEN ESTHER.

1. DARIUS continued to favor the Jews and after his death, his successor, Xerxes (zerks-ēz´) continued the same policy. This king is the As-su-ē´-rus of Holy Scripture, who raised a beautiful Jewish maiden named Esther to the throne.

2. Esther, who was an orphan, had been brought up by her uncle Mardochai (mar´ do-kāi), a devout Jew, and when she was chosen by the king, from among a throng of beautiful maidens, to fill the place of his haughty wife Vashti, whom he had repudiated, she kept secret the fact that she was a Jewess by her kinsman's desire.

3. Mardochai, in his desire to know if all went well with the queen, obtained the office of porter at the king's palace. In this capacity, he learned of a plot to kill the king, and revealed it to Esther who at once told the king.

4. On examination, her story proved to be true, and the conspirators were put to death. The story of the plot, and the fact that Mardochai had discovered it, were duly recorded in the chronicles of the kingdom, and then the matter was forgotten.

5. In place of one of the officials who had conspired against him, Assuerus appointed A'man the Mede, as prime minister,

---

22. What did this prediction excite at the dedication?
1. Who was Xerxes, the successor of Darius? 2. Who was Esther?
3. What did Mardochai do? 4. What was done to the conspirators?
5. Who was appointed prime minister?

and ordered all his servants to bend the knee and worship him. Mardochai alone withheld this homage which his religion forbade him to pay to any one save God.

6. This omission on Mardochai's part, and the fact that he was a Jew were soon told to Aman, who from that time knew no rest in his desire to compass his ruin. At length by persuading the king that the Jews were planning a revolt, he prevailed on him to issue a decree that all the Jews in his empire should be put to death and their property confiscated.

7. Mardochai at once sent a copy of the edict to Esther. She knew what was expected of her, but sent back word to him that it would be death for her to enter the king's presence, unless he held out the golden sceptre in token of clemency.

8. To this remonstrance of Esther, Mardochai sent back the message, "Who knowest whether thou art not therefore come to the kingdom that thou mightst be ready for such a time as this?" Esther therefore hesitated no longer and bade Mardochai tell all the Jews in the city to join her in a fast of three days.

9. When this was finished, Esther rose and attired herself in her richest robes, and adorned herself with her rarest jewels. Then attended by her handmaids, she entered the king's presence. But when she saw his stern countenance, she almost sank to the earth with fear.

10. But the king extended his golden sceptre, and said to her, "What wilt thou, Queen Esther? What is thy request? If thou shouldst ask one half of my kingdom it shall be given thee." But Esther only asked him to come with Aman to the banquet which she had prepared.

11. The king graciously assented, and at the appointed time, came with Aman to the banquet. But when, during it, the king desired to know her request, she begged him and Aman to

---

6. What did Aman seek when he heard of Mardochai's omission? 7. What did Esther say when she heard the decree? 8. What did Mardochai answer? 9. What did Esther do when this was finished? 10. Was the king angry? 11. Did the king go?

come to her banquet on the following day, when she would make it known.

12. Aman was delighted at this second invitation, but as he left the palace his joy was marred by perceiving that Mardochai, who was in his usual post at the gate, showed him not the slightest sign of honor as he passed.

13. He hastened home, but while he was recounting to his wife and friends all the marks of favor that had been shown him, he declared in a transport of rage, that all these things seemed as nothing so long as he saw Mardochai the Jew, sitting in the king's gate.

14. Then his wife and friends advised him to have a gibbet prepared fifty cubits high, and in the morning to go to the king and get leave to hang Mordocai on it, "so that he might go full of joy with the king to the queen's banquet."

15. That same night, the king was afflicted with sleeplessness, and ordered that the records of his kingdom be brought and read to him. And when he heard the plot which Mardochai had discovered, he asked what reward he had received, and heard, none at all.

16. Early in the morning Aman came to the king to make his request. But before he could speak the king said to him, "What ought to be done to the man whom the king is desirous to honor?"

17. Never dreaming that the king meant any one but himself, Aman answered that such a man should be clothed in the king's apparel, with the royal crown on his head, and be led through the city on the king's horse by one of the first nobles, while a herald proclaimed, "Thus shall be honored whom the king hath a mind to honor!"

18. Then the king bade him go and do exactly as he had said to Mardochai the Jew! Aman did as he was commanded, but after it was finished, and Mardochai had returned to the palace

---

12. What of Aman? 13. What did he acknowledge to his wife and friends? 14. What did they advise him to do? 15. What did the king order that same night? 16. What did he say to Aman next morning? 17. What did Aman answer? 18. What did the king command?

gate, Aman hastened home where he mourned with his head covered, until a summons to the banquet arrived from the palace.

19. While the banquet was in progress, the king again pressed Esther for her request. She answered, "If I have found favor in thy sight, O king, give me my life, for which I ask, and my people, for which I request. For we are given up, I and my people, to be destroyed, to be slain, and to perish."

20. In surprise, the king asked, "Who is this, and of what power, that he should dare to do these things?" Esther answered, "It is Aman that is our most wicked enemy." Then the king rose up in great wrath, and being told by one of the attendants of the gibbet Aman had prepared for Mardochai, ordered Aman himself to be hanged on it.

21. That same day Assuerus raised Mardochai to Aman's place, and revoked the edict against the Jews. The Jews rejoiced greatly at their unexpected deliverance, and many of the heathens were converted by this wonderful proof of God's care of His chosen people. The feast of Pur'im commemorates this event.

Esther is a figure of Mary, Queen of Heaven. As Esther alone was exempted from the law of death, so Mary was alone preserved amongst human creatures from original sin. As Esther saved her people from death so Mary saves all who love and serve her, from everlasting death.

---

19. Relate Esther's answer to the king at the banquet? 20. What did the king ask? 21. How did the king reward Mardochai?

CHAPTER XVIII.

ESDRAS, "THE SECOND MOSES" — NEHEMIAS—THE GREEK EMPIRE SUCCEEDS THE PERSIAN.

Gran-i-cus River. A small river in the northwestern part of Asia Minor.

Is'-sus. A town on the coast of Northern Syria, on the Mediterranean Sea.

Al'-ex an–dri-a. A seaport city of Egypt, on the Mediterranean Sea 112 miles N. W. of Cairo. It was founded by Alexander the Great, and was a great centre of learning.

1. XERXES was succeeded on the throne of Persia by his son, Ar'-tax-erx'-ēs, surnamed "the Long-handed." From this king, Es'-dras, "a ready scribe in the law of Moses," obtained permission to lead back a second band of Jews to Jerusalem, (B. C. 458.)

2. They were received with open arms by the Jews of Jerusalem, but Esdras soon found that though the temple had been built, a serious work of reform had still to be accomplished, in order to restore the observance of the Law of Moses.

3. While Esdras was endeavoring to bring about this reform it pleased God to send the Jews another friend in Ne he mī' as. He was cup-bearer to the Persian king, when he heard that the walls of Jerusalem were still broken down, as they had been left by Nebuchadnezzar.

4. Nehemias therefore obtained permission from the king to build up the walls of the holy city, with an order to the keeper of the king's forests to supply him with timber for the purpose.

5. In order to resist any attempt of the surrounding hostile nations to prevent them from doing the work, half the people remained under arms while the other half labored, girt with their swords, and after a few months of continuous labor, the wall was finished and the gates hung up.

---

1. By whom was Xerxes succeeded? 2. What did Esdras find after their welcome at Jerusalem? 3. What other friend did God send the Jews? 4. What did Nehemias obtain? 5. How were the builders of the wall protected?

6. Esdras now thought that the time had come for a solemn thanksgiving to God for their restoration. A general assembly of all Israel was proclaimed, and during it Esdras read and explained the sacred writings which he had collected into one volume, while the people alternately wept and rejoiced.

7. The Feast of Tabernacles, which lasted an entire week, and the Day of Atonement, were observed with appropriate rites. All the time the reading of the scriptures went on, and at their close the people made a new covenant with God, which was recorded in writing, and signed by the princes, priests and Levites.

8. They bound themselves by this not to intermarry with the heathens, to abstain from traffic on the Sabbath, to keep the Sab-bat'ic, or seventh year, with its release of all debtors from their obligations; to pay a yearly tax for the sanctuary, and to offer to the Lord their first-fruits, and their first born, and to pay the tithes due to the priests and Levites.

9. In order to keep the people true to this covenant, Esdras founded the synagogue worship, as it exists among the Jews to this day. In the synagogue the law of Moses, and the books of the prophets were publicly read and expounded to the people on the Sabbath and other festivals of the Law.

10. Esdras also erected schools for the young, in which the basis of instruction was Jewish history, founded on the Sacred Scriptures. His work would seem to have borne great fruit, for during the existence of the Persian Empire, the temple of Jerusalem was held in high honor even among distant nations.

11. The Jews remained under the dominion of Persia for two hundred years after the time of their return to Jerusalem under Cyrus (B.C. 536). Then the sceptre of empire passed to the western branch of the Aryan race, and the Greeks,—the

---

6. For what purpose did Esdras now assemble Israel? 7. What did the Jews enter into after the Day of Atonement? 8. What did they bind themselves to? 9. What means did Esdras take to keep the people true to the covenant? 10. What else did Esdras erect? 11. How long did the Jews remain under the dominion of Persia?

third great kingdom, prefigured in Daniel's vision as a spotted leopard—supplanted the Persians.

12. In the year 334 B. C., Alexander the Great, king of Greece, invaded Asia with his armies and defeated Da-ri-us, king of Persia, at the river Granicus. The following year Alexander defeated him still more completely at Issus.

13. Instead of marching directly on the great cities of Persia, Alexander then turned down the coast of Syria in order to conquer the entire coast line of the Persian Empire. Punishing severely the cities which had held faithful to Persia, Alexander at length drew near Jerusalem, which had also maintained its allegiance to that power.

14. Jad-du'-a, who was then high priest, was in an agony, not knowing how to meet the invader. But God bade him in a dream, take courage, adorn the city, and open its gates, and meet the strangers in the robes of his office, while the people followed in white garments of peace.

15. At length, from the heights of Sion, the watchmen gave notice of the approach of the Greeks. According to the Divine command, the gates of Jerusalem were at once thrown open, and through them passed a long procession.

16. First came the priests in their linen robes, and then the High Priest clothed in purple and scarlet, with the great breast plate of judgment on his breast, and on his head the mitre bearing a plate of gold on which was engraved the name of God. The people followed, attired in their white garments.

17. When Alexander saw the immense multitude in the distance, he rode forward to meet them, attended by his generals. When he reached the High Priest, he saluted him, and adored the Name which was graven on the mitre. Then hand in hand with him, he rode into the city and offered sacrifice in the Temple.

---

12. When did Alexander the Great invade Asia? 13. In what direction did Alexander turn after defeating Darius? 14. How did God direct Jaddua to receive the Greeks? 15. Did the Jews go to meet them? 16. Describe the procession. 17. What did Alexander do?

18. On learning from Jaddua that his victories over the Persians were predicted in the Sacred Scriptures, he confirmed and even augmented the privileges conferred upon the Jews by the Persians, and ever afterwards held their temple in the highest veneration as God's sanctuary.

19. The Greeks were at this time the most refined and intellectual people of the whole world, and looked upon all other nations as barbarians. By Alexander's conquests, the language, arts, and literature of the Greeks were introduced into Asia, and thus prepared it intellectually for the spread of the Gospel, as the Roman conquest did materially.

20. Another means of preparation for the Gospel was also afforded the pagans by the translation of the Holy Books of the Jews into Greek. At the request of the King of Egypt, the Jewish High Priest sent to Alexandria, then the capital of Egypt, seventy-two men deeply versed in Greek and Hebrew, who did the work.

21. It was about this time in the history of the Jews that God inspired a holy man, named Jesus, the son of Sirach (si' rak), to write a book of religious and moral instructions. It is the Book of Ecclesiasticus in the Catholic Bible, and contains many wise and beautiful maxims.

MAXIMS OF JESUS THE SON OF SIRACH.—The fear of the Lord is the beginning and a crown of wisdom.

The word of God is the fountain of wisdom, and her ways are everlasting commandments.

The fear of the Lord shall delight the heart, and shall give joy, and gladness and length of days.

It shall go well with him that feareth the Lord, and in the days of his end he shall be blessed.

My son, my son, from thy youth up receive instruction, and even to thy gray hairs thou shalt find wisdom.

Take all that shall be brought upon thee, and keep patience, for gold and silver are tried in the fire, but acceptable men in the furnace of humiliation.

---

18. What led him to treat the Jews with favor? 19. What were the Greeks at this time? 20. What other means of preparation was afforded the Jews for the reception of the Gospel? 21. What holy man wrote a book at this time?

Hear the judgment of your father, and grieve him not in his life.

The father's blessing establisheth the houses of the children, but the mother's curse rooteth up the foundation.

Despise not a man in his old age, for we also shall become old.

Despise not the discourse of them that are ancient and wise, but acquaint thyself with their proverbs.

Praise not a man for his beauty, neither despise a man for his looks.

The bee is small among flying things, but her fruit hath the choicest sweetness.

Be at peace with many, but let one in a thousand be thy counsellor.

Nothing can be compared to a faithful friend, and no weight of gold and silver is able to countervail the goodness of his fidelity.

If thou wouldst get a friend, try him before thou takest him. And do not credit him easily. For there is a friend for his own occasion, and he will not abide in the day of thy trouble.

A lie is a foul blot in a man. In no wise speak against the truth, but be ashamed of the lie in thy ignorance.

Let not the naming of God be used in thy mouth, and meddle not with the names of saints.

A man that sweareth much shall be filled with iniquity, and a scourge shall not depart from his house.

Before thou hear, answer not a word, and interrupt not others in the midst of their discourse.

Hast thou heard a word against thy neighbor, let it die within thee, trusting that it will not burst thee.

Hedge in thy ears with thorns; hear not a wicked tongue, and make doors and bars to thy mouth. Melt down thy gold and silver and make a balance for thy words.

Flee from sin as from the face of a serpent.

All iniquity is like a two-edged sword; there is no remedy for the wound thereof.

Observe the time and fly from evil.

He that loveth danger shall perish therein, and he that toucheth pitch shall be defiled with it.

In every work of thine, regard thy soul in faith, for this is the keeping of the commandments.

In all thy works remember thy last end, and thou shalt never sin.

CHAPTER XIX.

EVIL INFLUENCE OF GREEK LITERATURE AND CUSTOMS ON THE JEWS. THEIR PERSECUTION BY ANTIOCHUS, KING OF SYRIA.

An'-ti och. This great and beautiful city had been built by Se leu' cus, one of the generals of Alexander, to whom fell Syria. It stood on the river O-rontes, and its lovely situation, fine seaport, splendid water supply, and fairy-like suburbs, made it one of the world's favorite resorts for the people of all nations who could enjoy the fruits of Greek culture. It is now a commercial city.

1. ALEXANDER died young, and his generals divided his empire into four parts—Greece, Asia Minor, Syria, and Egypt. Thus Judea, as Juda was now called, lay between the new Greek kingdom in Egypt, and the Syrian-Greek kingdom, of which it was made a tributary.

2. The Jews were thus brought into close contact with the Greeks, and imbibed their culture. Unhappily, this led to an evil spirit of contempt for the learning and knowledge to be found in the Sacred Scriptures.

3. At length a wicked wretch named Ja'son, went to Antioch, the capital of Syria, and by means of an immense bribe, succeeded in having himself appointed by the king, high priest, in place of his brother O ni' as, the true high priest.

4. Jason then resolved to convert his countrymen utterly, to the customs and ideas of the Greeks, and to this end erected a Gymnasium, or large Government College in Jerusalem, in which pagan schoolbooks were exclusively used. Thus we see how education, which should be the handmaid of religion, can be perverted from her true office.

5. The customs of the Greeks sanctioned immorality and excesses of the most degrading kinds, which were strictly forbidden in the Jewish code, as most abominable in the sight of

---

1. Into how many parts was Alexander's empire divided after his death? 2. What was the result? 3. What did Jason do? 4. What did Jason then resolve? 5. What did the Greek customs sanction?

God. These things were now encouraged among the young Jews, so as to make them hate the Law of Moses.

6. Such was the fearful condition with which God's chosen people were menaced by following the dictates of a culture which had not the true faith for its basis! But God had not forgotten them, and as in the days of old, chastisement and affliction were to recall them to their faith.

7. The early kings of Syria did not coerce the Jews in matters of religion, trusting to the slower but surer means of Greek civilization and culture to destroy their faith.

8. But in the year 168 B. C., Antiochus IV. (an-tī'-o kus), enraged at the failure of his campaign against Egypt, was moved to discharge his anger on the Jewish nation, so large a part of which still stubbornly clung to their ancient faith, and root out the Law of Moses.

9. He therefore seized Jerusalem on the Sabbath, a day on which the Jews were forbidden by the Law of Moses even to defend their own lives, and gave the city up to fire and sword, till multitudes had been slaughtered.

10. He then proceeded to defile the temple by erecting a statue of Jupiter before the altar, and offering to it sacrifices of swine's flesh. An edict was then published, enjoining uniformity of worship throughout the king's dominions, and requiring Jews to sacrifice to the Greek gods.

11. One of the severest persecutions recorded in history, followed. Unhappily, many of the Jews, whom Greek influences had only too well prepared for such apostasy, yielded to the test of eating swine's flesh after it had been offered in sacrifice, thus doubly breaking the Law of Moses, which forbade it to be eaten at any time.

12. On the other hand, persecution revived much of the old Jewish spirit, and numbers, by their heroic endurance of cruel

---

6. What menaced the nation in consequence? 7. Had the early kings of Syria treated the Jews indulgently in matters of faith? 8. What king reversed this? 9. When did he seize Jerusalem? 10. What did he then proceed to do? 11. What followed? 12. What did the persecution revive?

MARTYRDOM OF THE MACCABEES.

torments, and death, made one of the most glorious pages in the annals of either Jewish or Christian martyrology.

13. One of the first to refuse was the venerable Eleazar, the chief of the Scribes, and ninety-nine years of age. Some friends advised him to feign compliance, but he answered that the Almighty would surely punish him for such hypocrisy, and was scourged to death.

14. Shortly after, a certain widow and her seven sons, known as the Maccabees (mak'-a-bees) were brought before Antiochus. Each son in turn, told the king that he would rather die than transgress the law of God, and each was put to death with the most horrible torments, till it came to the last.

15. So young and fair was this seventh Maccabee that even the cruel king found it in his heart to pity him, and promised him riches and happiness if he would yield. Seeing that his words had no effect, the king, as a last resource, turned to the mother, and bade her counsel her son for his own good.

16. This noble Hebrew mother promised to do so. Then, turning to her son, she solemnly adjured him to remain true to the God of heaven and earth, and thus earn a martyr's death, and reunion with herself and his brothers in eternity.

17. She had scarcely finished speaking when the youth cried, "For whom do ye stay? I will not obey the commandment of the king, but the commandment of the law given to Moses."

18. Then he turned to Antiochus, and said to him, "Thou who hast been the author of all mischief against the Hebrews, shall not escape the wrath of the Almighty God, who beholdeth all these things."

19. Enraged by the heroic youth's boldness, the tyrant had him subjected to the most terrific torments till he died. The mother was then put to death, leaving a noble example of the highest maternal love to the mothers of all ages.

---

13. Who was one of the first to refuse? 14. Who was brought before Antiochus shortly after? 15. What effect had the appearance of the seventh Maccabee on the king? 16. Did she agree to do so? 17. What did the youth exclaim? 18. What did he say to Antiochus? 19. How did he die?

CHAPTER XX.

THE ASMONEANS—MATHATHIAS—JUDAS MACCABEUS.

1. EXCEPTING a few striking cases of apostasy, the tribe of Levi remained steadfast in the faith under the persecution of Antiochus, and from them were now to spring a line of valiant warriors who were to deliver Juda, and obtain for her a brief period of national independence, and splendor.

2. At the beginning of the persecution, an aged priest named Mathathias withdrew from Jerusalem, with his five sons and other kindred, and retired to his own city of Mŏ din; where, in due time, came the king's officers to enforce the royal edicts in regard to religious worship.

3. The statue of Jupiter was set up in the synagogue, and all were commanded to partake of swine's flesh after it had been offered in sacrifice. But Mathathias boldly rose up in the synagogue, and exhorted the people to refuse to transgress the commandment of the Lord.

4. Scarcely had he finished, when a Jew approached the altar with the king's officer to sacrifice to the idol. Unable to endure the sight, Mathathias rushed upon them, and slew them both; then, inviting all who were for the Law of God to follow him, fled with his sons to the mountains.

5. A small army soon gathered around them, and from these fastnesses they made descents on the cities of Juda, throwing down the Greek altars, destroying the idols, and executing the vengeance of God on the apostates.

6. At the end of a year, Matathias died, bequeathing his son Judas Macabeus, or "The Hammerer," to his people for their leader. The wisdom of his choice was soon manifest, for it was at once seen that the new captain was as great as the mighty champions of old, Joshua, and Gedeon and David.

---

1. Did the tribe of Levi remain faithful? 2. What Levite withdrew from Jerusalem to Modin? 3. What was set up in the synagogue, and what did Mathathias do? 4. What followed? 5. What did the small army do? 6. Whom did Mathathias leave as leader to his people?

7. So rapid and signal were his successes that Antiochus, stung with rage, resolved to blot out the Jews from among the nations. He was himself obliged to go to Persia, but he ordered his viceroy Lysias, to take an army with elephants, and conquer Juda, enslave its population, and destroy Jerusalem.

8. Lysias at once took the field, and with an immense army, accompanied by merchants with money to buy the Jewish slaves, and chains to bind them, advanced on the small force of Jewish patriots. But Judas bade the latter not to be dismayed, but to array themselves in sackcloth and pray to Jehovah.

9. As the armies drew near each other, Judas placed his men in order of battle, and made a brief address to them, telling them not to fear the Grecian host, but to put their trust in the God who had brought their forefathers dry-shod through the Red Sea, to save them from the power of Pharaoh.

10. The Greek general waited an opportunity to surprise the Jews by night. Judas found this out by means of his spies, and accordingly left his camp fires burning brightly in order to lure forward the detachments commissioned to attack him, while he led his army forth in the shadow, surprised the main army of the foe, and defeated it utterly.

11. Turning back, he met the returning detachments, and routed them completely also. He then led his army homeward with their rich booty, singing as they went, hymns of praise and gratitude to God, as was done in the days of old.

12. Equally decisive victories followed, so that during the following year, Judas recovered Jerusalem. The sight of the temple, with its desolate sanctuary, its profaned altar, burned gates, and grass-grown courts, caused the Jews to put ashes on their heads, and lament.

---

7. What did Antiochus order? 8. Were his orders obeyed? 9. How did Judas encourage his men when the armies met? 10. What was the plan of the Greek general, and how did Judas foil him? 11. Did he defeat the detachments who had been sent to attack him also? 12. Did his success continue?

13. They then set to work to purify it. After this was done, the altar was dedicated again, and the lamps in the Temple porches were lighted anew to the sound of harps and lutes and cymbals, and the joyful chants of the Levites.

14. A solemn sacrifice was then offered. A magnificent festival of eight days then celebrated Judas' victories, and it was decreed that this festival should be kept for a perpetual remembrance. It is still observed by faithful Hebrews as the Feast of Lights.

15. The splendid victories of Judas roused Antiochus to fury, and he returned in haste from Persia to Jerusalem. But the time had come when this tyrant was to furnish a memorable example of God's justice. On the way he was seized by a terrible disease.

16. So frantic was his desire to be revenged on the Jews, however, that he continued to urge his steeds forward till they attained such speed that he was flung from his war-chariot and so much injured that he had to be borne on a litter.

17. His disease rapidly grew worse, and he was soon so foul to sight and smell, that his very slaves refused to carry him. In vain he cried to the God of the Jews, declaring there was no God save Him; the Almighty heeded not this repentance which proceeded from fear only, and the wretched king died in torment.

18. The successors of Antiochus continued to send armies against Judas. During one of these conflicts, the Greek and Syrian host beheld in the air above the Jews, five horsemen, clad in shining armor, fighting for them. The spectacle struck them with so much terror that they fled, leaving thirty thousand warriors dead on the field.

19. On another occasion, when a great number of the Jews were slain in battle, it was found, when their bodies were pre-

---

13. Describe the proceedings in the temple after it was purified. 14. What celebrated Judas' victories? 15. What of Antiochus? 16. Did this deter him? 17. Did he grow worse? 18. What took place during one of the conflicts between the armies of Antiochus' successor and the Jews? 19. What caused the death of many Jews in another battle?

pared for burial, that they wore amulets or heathen charms, which the Law forbade a Jew even to touch. And the reason why they had lost their lives was thus made manifest to all.

20. In pity for his unhappy brethren, Judas sent 12,000 drachms (drams) of silver to Jerusalem, to have sacrifices offered for them, "for" says the Scripture, "it is a holy and wholesome thought to pray for the dead that they may be loosed from their sins."

21. Judas continued to fight bravely against the Greeks, but at last came to believe in the necessity of human protection against them, in addition to that of God, and decided to seek an alliance with a new power, far to the west—Rome—of whom the Oriental world was just beginning to hear.

22. The Roman Empire was the fourth great kingdom of Daniel's vision, figured as a beast with iron teeth and ten horns. Judas' embassadors made their way thither, and for the first time, the Jew and the Roman beheld each other. The Roman Senate received them kindly, and met the proposal of the alliance with favor.

23. A friendly letter, in which the terms of the alliance were fully set forth, was graven on tables of brass, and sent back to the Jewish nation. Thus began the connection with Rome, which was to end in the crucifixion of the Messias, by the sentence of an officer of this people, and in the total destruction of their holy city and their nation.

24. No sooner was the alliance concluded, than the army of Judas seemed to lose its supernatural courage. When the Greek general Bachides (bak'ki des) came against them soon after with a great army, a vast number deserted from the Jewish ranks, and left the valiant leader with but eight hundred men at his command.

25. Judas felt that the hour had come to sacrifice his life for

---

20. What did Judas do for the repose of their souls? 21. Whose aid did Judas invoke? 22. Who were the Romans and how did they receive the Jews? 23. What did the Romans send to the Jews? 24. What effect had the Roman alliance on Judas' army? 25. How did Judas act in the strait?

the honor of God and the holy law of his nation, so he led his little force to meet the foe. The battle was hard fought, but at last Judas was overcome by numbers, and slain, and the remnant of the Jewish force fled. (B. C. 161.)

26. The body of the dead hero was borne to his own city, Modin, amid the solemn lamentations of all Juda, who cried, "How is the valiant man fallen who delivered Israel!" It was there interred in the sepulchre of his father.

CHAPTER XXI.

ASMONEAN PRIEST-PRINCES.

1. WHILE the Syrian general was hunting down the Jewish patriots, Jonathan, the youngest brother of Judas, held out in the wilderness, until he grew strong enough to assume the defensive. At length, eight years after the death of Judas, he was installed in the high priesthood, at the Feast of Tabernacles. (B. C. 153.)

2. Thus began the line of Asmonean priest-princes, who governed Israel. They were of the family of Judas Macabeus, and their proper name was As mo nē ans, from Asmon, the great-great-grandfather of Judas and his brethren.

3. Ten years later, the Syrian king succeeded in having Jonathan put to death. His brother Simon, the last of the sons of Mathathias, succeeded him as high-priest. Taking advantage of the internal disorders of Syria, he succeeded in securing the recognition of Jewish independence. (B. C. 142.)

4. Under Simon's just and firm government, the golden age of Israel is renewed. Peace rests upon the land, the splendor of Jerusalem is restored, messengers from the neighboring nations seek the Jewish favor and alliance, with

---

26. Where was Judas buried?
1. Who held out in the wilderness while the Syrians held Juda? 2. What began with Jonathan? 3. What was Jonathan's fate, and who succeeded him? 4. What is renewed under Simon's rule?

vessels of silver, purple garments, buttons of gold, and other rich gifts.

5. Unhappily for Judea, Simon was treacherously murdered by his son-in-law, Ptolemy, a creature of the Syrians. This man called in the enemies of his country, Jerusalem was surrounded, and forced to surrender, and thus became once more a tributary of Syria. (B. C. 133.)

6. Fresh troubles in Syria enabled John, the son and successor of Simon, to re-establish Jewish independence. Juda was enlarged by the conquest of land beyond the Jordan, and Idumea and Samaria, and began to be known by its Grecian or Roman appellation of Judea.

7. From this time, the kingdom of Judea comprised Galilee in the north, Samaria in the centre, Judea proper in the south, and Per ê' a beyond the Jordan.

8. The high priesthood of John witnessed the rupture of the religious unity of the nation by the rise of the opposing sects of the Pharisees and the Sad'-du-cees.

9. The name of Pharisee, which signifies Separatist, was given by the more liberal Jews to those ardent souls who had resisted all the tendencies of Greek culture, and had fought nobly for the freedom of their country under Mathathias and his sons, but who had now become fanatics.

10. The Pharisees' love for fatherland had narrowed into a fierce hatred of strangers—to fly from the impure contact of the Gentiles became for them a law which they desired to impose on all Israel. They had made 1,279 rules which the Jew must observe, if he would avoid contamination.

11. Neither the Asmonean priest-princes, nor the priests who surrounded them, followed the Pharisee in his views. Obliged to maintain political relations with other countries, and yielding to the seductions of power and wealth, they con-

---

5. What happened after Simon's death? 6. Who restored Juda's independence? 7. What did the kingdom of Judea thenceforth comprise? 8. What two great sects rose in the time of John? 9. What was the origin of the Pharisees? 10. What had their love for fatherland become? 11. Who were the Sadducees?

fined their observance to the letter of the law, and thus got the name of the Sad'du-cees, or The Just.

12. John was succeeded by his son Judas, who changed his name to the Greek form of A-ris' to bu'lus. Hitherto the Asmonean priest-princes had been content with that dignity, and being acknowledged by foreign potentates as Princes of the Jews. But this prince would be satisfied with nothing less than the regal name, and assumed the title of king as Aristobulus I.

13. By this time the high, pure spirit of Judas and his first successors, had departed from the Asmonean race. In their lives they set the example of vices which speedily communicated themselves to the people. The outward observances of the Law of Moses were indeed observed to an extreme point, but the spirit had utterly departed.

14. Four hundred years before, the prophet, Mal'a chi'as, had told the Jewish priests that their offerings had ceased to please the Lord, and that their Temple should be closed, and the fire on their altar extinguished forever.

15. "From the rising of the sun," said the prophet, "even to the going down of the same, My Name is great among the Gentiles, and in every place there is sacrifice, and there is offered to My Name a clean oblation."

16. This refers to the Holy Sacrifice of the Mass, of which, as the earth's rotation brings the morning hours successively from point to point on its surface, the sun is a constant witness.

17. Aristobulus I. was succeeded by his son, Alexander Jannae-us (Jan' nĕ us). After a life of cruelty and ambition, he died, and his two sons, Hyr cā' nus and Aristobulus, disputed the succession. Hyrcanus, the elder, had the people on his side, but Aristobulus, by his talents, gained over the priests and chief men of the nation.

---

12. By whom was John succeeded? 13. Were the later Asmoneans like Judas? 14. What had Malachias told the Jewish Priests four hundred years before? 15. Repeat the further prophecy of Malachias. 16. To what does this refer? 17. Who succeeded Aristobulus?

18. The Roman general, Pompey, was then in Asia, and to him both brothers appealed for aid, denouncing each other in bitterest terms. But as the Roman deferred his decision, Aristobulus seized Jerusalem and declared his independence.

19. Pompey at once marched to Jerusalem and besieged the city. Aristobulus lost courage and went out to offer terms of submission, and a large sum of money. Pompey accepted his terms, and sent his lieutenant to receive the money.

20. Those inside Jerusalem, however, refused to stand by the agreement, declaring it had been made without their consent. Pompey therefore laid siege to the city, and after three months, succeeded in taking it.

21. The adherents of Aristobulus took refuge in the temple. Pompey laid siege to it, and took it. Then, accompanied by the officers of his staff, he went through the sacred building, even going so far as to lift the veil which screened the Holy of Holies, and profane the sacred spot by his presence.

22. Pompey carried Aristobulus a prisoner to Rome, and nominated Hyrcanus High Priest, and Prince of the country, on condition of his submitting to Rome, paying tribute, and promising never to assume the crown or add to his territories.

23. The reign of Hyrcanus was far from being peaceful however. The son of Aristobulus, Alexander, made desperate efforts in the cause of his father, till the latter himself escaped from Rome, and headed his party in person.

24. Rome herself, distracted by the rival claims of Pompey and Julius Cæsar (sē′ zar), could not restore order, because Pompey gave the protection of his legions to Hyrcanus, while Cæsar favored Aristobulus. But at length the latter prince and his son were put to death by the adherents of Pompey.

---

18. To whom did both brothers appeal? 19. What did Pompey do? 20. What did those inside Jerusalem declare? 21. How did Pompey profane the temple? 22. How did he treat Aristobulus and Hyrcanus? 23. Did Hyrcanus reign in peace? 24. Was Rome not able to restore order?

CHAPTER XXII.

THE REIGN OF HEROD—LAST DAYS BEFORE CHRIST.

Id′u mếa, or E′dom, the settlement of Esau, lay on and about the mountain ranges to the south-east of the Dead Sea. Here the race of Esau became great and numerous, and at last in the person of Herod, held the sceptre over the proud Jewish nation, who held them in contempt. Idumea is now utterly deserted, save for some Arab tribes who feed their flocks in its valleys.

San′he drin. The Great Council of the Jews, which served as Parliament, High Court of Justice, and the supreme resort of instruction. It was composed of seventy members, headed by the High Priest, and represented the three classes of the nation, the Priests, the Scribes or Doctors of Law; and the nation at large, by the Ancients chosen from among the elders of each tribe and family.

1. ONE of the most ardent partisans of Hyrcanus, was an Id′u mē′an named An tī′pas, who had changed his name to the Greek form of An tip′a-ter. He soon rose to high distinction, and introduced his son Her′od to political life at an early age.

2. After the death of Aristobulus, Antipater took advantage of Cæsar's friendship, which he had carefully cultivated, to have the feeble prince, Hyrcanus, made High Priest, and himself appointed Proc-ū-rā′tor, or governor of the whole province of Judea.

3. Soon after, Antipater had his son Herod made governor of Judea proper. Herod, who was quick to see that the Roman interest was the only way to power, assiduously courted it, while at the same time he sought to win the favor of the Jews by wedding Mā ri′-am-nĕ, the grand-daughter of Hyrcanus.

4. The Sanhedrin soon perceived that this foreign adventurer, as ambitious as he was unscrupulous, aimed at the sovereignty of Judea. In the hope of thwarting him in his

---

1. Who was an ardent partisan of Hyrcanus? 2. What did Antipater secure for Hyrcanus and for himself? 3. What post did he secure for Herod? 4. Who opposed Herod?

THE REIGN OF HEROD—LAST DAYS BEFORE CHRIST. 193

designs, they therefore formed a party in favor of An tig' o-nus, the sole remaining son of Aristobulus, and raised an army.

5. Herod promptly took the field with an opposing force, and succeeded in defeating Antigonus. He then went to Rome, where, through the influence of Mark Antony, he was declared king of Judea by the Senate, and did homage to the Romans for his crown. Thus were the words of the prophecy fulfilled, "the sceptre passed away from Juda." (B. C. 40.)

6. For more than ten years after Herod's return to Judea as its king, Antigonus bravely carried on the struggle, but at length with the aid of the Romans, Herod succeeded in defeating him utterly. Antigonus was then put to death, and with him the male line of the Asmoneans came to an end.

7. Herod now held undisputed sway, and peace returned to the land. But as he had laid the foundations of his throne in blood, so he never shrank from any crime which would preserve it to him. Thus he murdered his own sons, Mariamne his wife, and lastly, the Holy Innocents, fearing in each a possible rival.

8. Herod was a man of great abilities, and brilliant success crowned both his foreign and domestic policy. His passion for architecture led him to adorn Jerusalem with magnificent buildings and to stud Judea with superb cities, filled with gorgeous palaces. One of these he called Cesarêa, and colonized entirely with Greeks.

9. He then turned his attention to the temple, which the passage of five hundred years, and repeated sieges, had ruined in many parts. At first the zealous Jews feared, when they saw the workmen tearing it down, that he only intended to demolish it, but they were relieved by seeing it rising anew from its ruins, and crowning Moriah with "masses of white marble and pinnacles of gold."

10. But while he thus pleased the Jews, he maintained his

---

5. What was the result of Herod's victory ? 6. Did the Jews struggle against Herod ? 7. To what crimes did Herod's ambition lead him ? 8. What of his character as a king ? 9. Did he restore the temple? 10. How did he support his character of Rome's vassal ?

character of vassal king of Rome by fostering all the Roman customs and amusements. A theatre was built within the walls of Jerusalem, and an amphitheatre without, and chariot racing, boxing, the drama, even gladiators and wild beasts, were introduced, in the hope of heathenizing the Jews.

11. At length he placed a gilt eagle, the Roman ensign, at the entrance to the temple. The Jews, irritated beyond endurance at this insult to the Almighty, rose in tumult, and tore it down. This act cost three thousand of the people their lives.

12. Such was the pitiable condition of the faithless Jewish nation as the time of the Messias approached. They had killed God's prophets, and forgotten his repeated chastisements, and now were ground beneath the heel of a master of the despised race of Esau, himself a vassal of a foreign power. Truly the sceptre had indeed departed from Juda!

13. Meanwhile, as the years went by, the expectation of the promised Redeemer, the long looked for Messias, quickened many hearts, but with what different emotions! The Jews panted for a great leader who should renew the splendor and power of Israel, while Herod on his blood-stained throne, watched to murder Him when he should appear!

14. Only a few faithful hearts, among the Jews, and a few more among the Gentiles, longed for His coming as One who should establish the spiritual kingdom of God on earth, and prayed that the clouds might rain down the Just One, and the earth bud forth the same.

15. The great, proud pagan world was steeped in wickedness and corruption. The great empire of Rome had changed masters till at length Octavius, the nephew of Julius Cæsar, became its sovereign under the title of Augustus (B. C. 29).

16. Augustus restored order and tranquillity to the world, so long rent by Rome's warring factions. The temple of the god

---

11. How did Herod insult the Almighty? 12. What is to be said of the condition of the Jews at this time? 13. Was the Redeemer looked for by many? 14. Who viewed His character rightly? 15. What of Rome and Augustus? 16. What good did Augustus accomplish?

Janus at Rome, which was open only in time of war, was by him closed for the first time in over two hundred years.

17. The promises made by God to Abraham had been fulfilled; the prophecies of Daniel had been accomplished, and the time was now at hand for the advent of Him who had been expected for nearly five thousand years, the Messias, the Redeemer of the World, OUR LORD JESUS CHRIST, TO WHOM BE HONOR AND GLORY FOR EVER AND EVER!

---

17. Had all things now been accomplished that prefaced the advent of the Savior?

PART SECOND.
HISTORY OF THE NEW TESTAMENT.
I.—BIRTH AND CHILDHOOD OF JESUS CHRIST.

CHAPTER I.

ANNUNCIATION OF THE BIRTH OF JOHN THE BAPTIST.

1. DURING the reign of Herod, there dwelt in Yout-tah, a town in the heart of the mountains of Judea, a holy Levite named Zach'-a-ry, and his wife, Elizabeth. "They were just in the sight of God, and walked without reproach in the ways and commandments of the Lord," although they had to endure the sore trial of childlessness.

2. The time for the birth of the Redeemer was almost at hand, when the turn of Zachary came round to fulfil his functions, as a Priest of the Most High, in the temple, and he went up to Jerusalem.

3. Zachary's office was that of Incense-Burner—the highest of the sacerdotal duties. Everything was made ready beforehand and at a signal from a prince of the priesthood, the officiating minister entered the Holy Place and cast the precious perfumes on the flames; then bowing to the veiled Holy of Holies, he withdrew backwards, that he might not turn his face from the altar.

4. Meanwhile the people prayed beneath the porches, waiting

---

1. What holy pair dwelt in Youttah during the reign of Herod? 2. When did Zachary go up as usual to Jerusalem? 3. What was his office? 4. What did the people do meanwhile?

for the bell which gave warning of his withdrawal, and of the Benediction which he bestowed on the people, and at whose sound the Levites intoned the sacred hymns and the music of the Temple.

5. Although this ceremonial was observed twice every day, it was always with secret anxiety that the Jews beheld the officiating priest disappear within the sanctuary. He was their representative, and should Jehovah reject his offering, then indeed should be accomplished the ruin of Israel.

6. For this reason, the officiating minister never made any unnecessary delay, but as rapidly as reverence would permit, discharged his functions and re-appeared, so as not to prolong the anxiety of the people. But on this especial day, their fears were increased to utter terror, for after a long absence, Zachary appeared pale, trembling, and dumb.

7. The cause of this terrible agitation, which he did not reveal for a long time afterwards, was that within the sanctuary he had seen, amid white clouds of incense, a mighty angel, who said to him: "Fear not at all, Zachary! Thy prayer is heard; thy wife Elizabeth shall bear a son, and thou shalt give him the name of John.

8. "This child shall be thy joy and thy gladness; and the multitude shall rejoice at his birth. For he shall be great before the Lord; he shall not drink of wine nor of aught that doth inebriate, and he shall be filled with the Holy Spirit even from his mother's womb.

9. "He shall convert many of the children of Israel to the Lord their God, and he himself shall walk before Him in the spirit and might of Elias, that he may turn the unbelieving unto the wisdom of the righteous, and prepare for the Lord a perfect people."

10. This revelation was too lofty for the human wisdom of

---

5. How did the Jews regard this familiar ceremonial? 6. Did this cause the minister to hasten? 7. What was the cause of his agitation? 8. What goodness and greatness did Gabriel predict for John? 9. What did he predict of his ministry? 10. Did Zachary believe without questioning?

Zachary to comprehend, yet he was too haughty to receive it with the strong, simple faith which the Lord required, and presumed so far as to ask, "How shall I know the truth of these words? For I am old now, and my wife is advanced in years."

11. The angel answered, "I am Gabriel, one of the ministering spirits standing even in the presence of God, who has been sent to speak to thee, and announce to thee these good tidings.

12. "Look thou therefore, thou shalt be dumb, and shall not be able to speak until the day wherein these things shall take place, because thou hast not believed my words which shall be accomplished in their time." Having spoken thus, he disappeared. Zachary accomplished his duties in the temple, and then returned home.

The prophet Malachias had foretold that two forerunners should herald the Messiah's appearance; one, John the Baptist, was to announce His first Advent; before His second, Elias will descend to prepare men for his coming.

CHAPTER II.

THE ANNUNCIATION OF THE BIRTH OF CHRIST.

1. Six months later, Gabriel received of God a new mission. This time it was to Nazareth, an obscure village of Galilee—to a virgin named Mary, a young kinswoman of Elizabeth. She was the daughter of a virtuous pair named Joachim and Anna, and had one sister, who, according to a Jewish custom, was named, like herself, Mary.

2. A light which had never before shone on the maidens of Israel had revealed to the first of these Marys, the holiness of virginity, and she had resolved therefore, the first of womankind, to dedicate her virginity to God.

---

11. Repeat the angel's answer. 12. What punishment did he foretell for Zachary?
1. On what new mission was Gabriel sent soon after? 2. What had been revealed to Mary?

3. As they were without male offspring, however, her parents, in order to secure the legal transmission of their property, had been obliged to betroth her to Joseph, who was, like herself, descended from the royal house of David, and her sister to another young man of the same lineage.

4. The poverty and obscurity into which these scions of the royal blood of Israel had sunk, was the best possible protection for them, and no doubt was so designed by God. Although the prophecies which promised the throne to a son of David, were well known to Herod, he never thought of seeking him here.

5. Gabriel found Mary praying in the solitude of her own chamber, and saluted her with the words, "Hail, full of grace, the Lord is with thee; blessed art thou among women."

6. But the meek and humble virgin was troubled at these strange words, and wondered what could be the meaning. The angel continued, "Fear not at all, Mary, for thou hast found favor with God. And behold, thou shalt conceive in thy womb, and shall bear a son, and thou shalt give him the name of Jesus.

7. He shall be great, and shall be called the Son of the Most High, and the Lord God shall give him the throne of David, his father, and he shall reign in the house of Jacob forever, and of his kingdom there shall be no end."

8. Mary had meditated much on the Prophecies, and she understood, therefore, from the angel's words that God had chosen her to be the mother of the long-expected Messias. But as she prized her virginity even beyond this unspeakable honor, she asked him how this could be, seeing that she was a virgin.

9. Gabriel answered: "The Holy Ghost shall come upon thee, and the power of the Most High shall overshadow thee; therefore the Holy One that shall be born of thee, shall be called the Son of God. And behold, thy cousin Elizabeth hath

---

3. To whom had she and her sister been betrothed? 4. For what did their obscurity serve? 5. How did Gabriel find Mary? 6. Repeat the further speech of the angel. 7. Continue. 8. Did Mary understand and submit? 9. How did Gabriel reassure her?

THE ANNUNCIATION.

conceived a son in her old age, because no word shall be impossible with God."

10. Reassured on this point, Mary abandoned herself utterly to the will of the Almighty; and bowing down before the seraphic messenger, replied, "I am the handmaid of the Lord; be it done unto me according to thy word." And "at once the WORD WAS MADE FLESH, and took up its habitation with us."

11. A short time after this wonderful event, Mary journeyed to Youttah, to congratulate her cousin Elizabeth on her approaching happiness. No sooner had she entered her kinswoman's dwelling, than Elizabeth, realizing the presence of the Incarnate God, cried out, "Blessed art thou among women, and blessed is the fruit of thy womb.

12. And whence is this to me that the mother of my Lord should come to visit me? Blessed art thou that hast believed, because these things shall be accomplished that were spoken to thee by the Lord."

13. In a transport of joy, Mary answered in the sublime words of the Magnificat, beginning, "My soul doth magnify the Lord, and my spirit hath rejoiced in God my Saviour. Because he hath regarded the humility of his handmaid; for behold, henceforth all generations shall call me blessed. For He that is mighty hath done great things to me, and Holy is His Name."

14. Mary remained with her cousin for three months, and then returned to Nazareth. Shortly after, an angel appeared to Joseph, and told him not to fear to espouse Mary, for the child which she had conceived was of the Holy Spirit. "And thou shalt call His name JESUS," concluded the angel, "for He shall save His people from their sins."

---

10. Did Mary then consent? 11. Whom did Mary visit shortly after? 12. How did Elizabeth express her sense of Mary's condescension in visiting her? 13. What was Mary's answer? 14. What message did the angel bear to Joseph after Mary's return to Nazareth?

CHAPTER III.

BIRTH OF JOHN THE BAPTIST.

1. In due time, Elizabeth gave birth to a son. Eight days after, all her neighbors and kinsfolk assembled for the ceremony of the child's circumcision. This office was usually performed by the father, but as the dumb Zachary could not utter the accompanying benedictions, his place had to be filled by one of his relatives.

2. At the close of the ceremony, when according to ancient Jewish custom, the child received a name, they would have called the infant Zachary after his father. The latter neither heard nor understood, but Elizabeth declared the child should be called John.

3. They objected, declaring that none of her kindred had borne that name. But Elizabeth was firm, and turning to her afflicted husband, asked him by signs what name he wished to give the child. Zachary took up his tablet, and wrote, "John is his name."

4. Then, before they had recovered from their astonishment, the old man's tongue was loosened, and he spoke aloud in thanksgiving to the Lord. The amazement of those present now deepened into awe, and they said, "What an one, think you, shall this child be? For the hand of the Lord was upon him."

5. With his hearing and speech, Zachary received the Divine favor, and filled with the Holy Spirit, began to prophesy in a canticle which still bears his name and is sung in our churches. In it the holy old man foretells the Redemption of the human race.

CANTICLE OF ZACHARY.—Blessed be the Lord God of Israel; because He hath visited and wrought the Redemption of His people,

---

1. What usual ceremony took place at the birth of John the Baptist? 2. What name did Elizabeth insist on giving the child? 3. Who decided this point? 4. What miracle then took place? 5. Did Zachary also receive the Divine favor?

And hath raised up a horn of salvation to us, in the house of David his servant.

And he spoke by the mouth of His holy Prophets, who are from the beginning.

Salvation from our enemies, and from the hand of all that hate us,

To perform mercy to our fathers, and to remember his holy Testament.

The oath which he swore to Abraham our Father, that He would grant to us,

That being delivered from the hand of our enemies we may serve Him without fear,

In holiness and justice before Him, all our days.

And thou, child, shalt be called the prophet of the highest; for thou shalt go before the face of the Lord to prepare His ways;

To give knowledge of salvation to His people, unto the remission of their sins.

Through the hands of the mercy of our God, in which the Orient, from on high hath visited us,

To enlighten them that sit in darkness, and in the shadow of death; to direct our feet into the way of peace."

CHAPTER IV.

BIRTH OF OUR LORD JESUS CHRIST.

Beth'-lĕ-hem. A village situated five and a half miles southwest of Jerusalem, and a distance of four days' foot-travel from Nazareth. It lies upon a succession of natural terraces, crowned with vines, and olive and ng trees. On the summit now stands the Church of the Nativity, surrounded by the Latin, Greek and Armenian convents.

Khan (kan). The inns of Oriental countries are known by this name. They are still to be seen in the East, much as they were in the time of Our Lord, and consist of a huge square enclosed by porticoes. Here, on slightly raised platforms, sheltered by galleries, the travellers spread their rugs for beds, while their beasts of burden occupied the courtyard.

1. WHEN the time was drawing near for the birth of the Messias, the Roman Emperor Augustus issued a decree that all the people of his vast empire should be registered.

---

1. What decree did the Emperor Augustus issue?

2. Now the Jews were in the habit of taking an account of their population, not according to residence or birth-place, but by assembling according to the Family or Tribe, whence each one had sprung. Thus Joseph and Mary were obliged to go to Bethlehem, where David had been born, for they were of the "Tribe and Family" of that "Great King."

3. So then, to inscribe himself in the Public Registers, the carpenter of Nazareth and his spouse, set out on their four days' rough winter journey to Bethlehem, which, like most of the poorer class, they made on foot.

4. On arriving at Bethlehem, the travellers found the khan or inn, already crowded, and were refused admittance. Doubtless their fatigue was too great to permit them to seek further for lodgings; for according to the testimony of tradition, they found refuge close by the inn.

5. The chalk-hills of Judea are honey-combed with countless caves. One of these excavations was used as a shelter for such beasts as the public stables were unable to hold. In this rude spot, Joseph and his holy spouse now found shelter, and here at midnight, OUR LORD JESUS CHRIST WAS BORN INTO THE WORLD. And the virgin mother wrapped him in swaddling clothes and laid him in the manger.

6. On that memorable night, some shepherds were keeping guard over their flocks, in the valley to the east of Bethlehem. Suddenly, "an Angel of the Lord appeared before them, the glory of God enveloped them with light," and they were filled with a great terror.

7. But the angel said, "Be not afraid; I am come to announce good tidings of great joy unto you and unto all your people. To-day, in the city of David, is born to you a Saviour, the Christ, the Lord! And behold the sign by which you shall know him: you shall find an Infant, wrapped in swaddling-clothes, and laid in a manger."

---

2. How were the Jews accustomed to number their population? 3. Did Joseph and Mary go to Bethlehem? 4. What did they find at Bethlehem? 5. Describe the cave in which Our Lord was born. 6. Who appeared to the shepherds? 7. How did the angel reassure them?

BIRTH OF OUR LORD JESUS CHRIST.

8. And so, at last, while ambitious, carnal Israel is lost in dreams of a great earthly conqueror like David, the Messias comes, and reveals Himself, in the straw of His manger, not to the proud Doctors of the Law, but to these simple, docile hearts, in which still lingered the faith of Abraham, of Isaac, and of Jacob!

9. These shepherds were still pondering upon the angel's wonderful tidings, when they saw a great multitude of the hosts of heaven, and heard their angelic voices singing in the clear midnight, those joyous words which the church delights to repeat every day in the Holy Sacrifice of the Mass, "Glory to God in the highest, and on earth peace to men of good will!"

10. When the glorious anthem had ceased, and the angelic choir had vanished, the shepherds exclaimed, "Let us go to Bethlehem, and see this which the Lord has made known to us." They soon found the cave; amid the straw in the dumb beasts' manger, lay an infant wrapped in swaddling clothes; over Him knelt the young mother, and a thoughtful, silent man.

11. In a transport of joyful faith, they too bowed down in adoration, before the Divine Child; then going forth, they recounted to those whom they met all they had heard concerning Him. "And all were in admiration at this tale which the shepherds related." They then returned to their flocks.

12. Eight days after His birth, the Divine Child was circumcised by His foster father, St. Joseph, and received the name of JESUS, which signifies, One who has loved us even to dying for us.

13. Forty days after his birth, Joseph and Mary went up to the temple at Jerusalem, in order that according to the law of Moses, Mary might undergo the ceremony of purification, and her first-born be consecrated to the Lord. On this occa-

---

8. Why had these shepherds merited the revelation of the Messias' presence on earth? 9. What did the shepherds hear? 10. Did the angels go to the cave? 11. What did they do after adoring the Divine Babe? 12. What ceremony took place eight days after the birth of Jesus? 13. What ceremony took place forty days after?

sion, two turtle-doves —the Sacrifice of the Poor—were offered for both.

14. Now there was at this time in Jerusalem a just man, and one who feared God, named Simeon, who lived in expectation of the consolation of Israel. The Holy Spirit was with him, and had revealed to him that he should not die till he had seen the Messiah.

15. At the time when Mary and Joseph were approaching the temple, the Holy Spirit led Simeon thither also, and revealed to him in the helpless babe who lay within his mother's arms, the long-expected Messiah. In an ecstasy of joy, Simeon took Him in his arms, and intoned the following canticle:

16. "Now thou dost dismiss thy servant, O Lord, in peace, because my eyes have seen Thy salvation which Thou hast prepared before the face of all peoples; a light to the revelation of the Gentiles, and the glory of thy people, Israel."

17. Then looking upon Mary, with prophetic eyes, the holy man saw all that the virgin mother was to suffer. Holding up the Divine Child, he said to her, "He whom you now look upon, is for the ruin and the resurrection of many in Israel. He shall be a man rejected and denied."

18. "As for thee," he went on to Mary, "a sword of sorrow shall pierce thy heart, and thus the thoughts which many hide in their hearts shall be revealed." This meant that the Lord would distinguish in this way those who sought the Messiah in the hope of riches, glory, and temporal happiness, and those who would welcome Him, under whatever form He might appear.

19. At this moment there happened to approach, a prophetess named Anna. This holy woman was eighty-four years of age, and had dwelt in the Temple for many years, serving God by night and day, in fasting and prayer.

---

14. Who dwelt at this time in Jerusalem? 15. What led Simeon to the temple? 16. Repeat Simeon's Canticle. 17. What did Simeon say to Mary? 18. What did Simeon predict for Mary? 19. Who happened to approach at this moment?

20. Anna at once recognized the Child whom Simeon had blessed, and having thanked God for unveiling to her eyes the Mystery, praised him as the Lord, her God, and spoke of Him to all those who awaited the redemption of Israel.

21. To Anna belongs, therefore, the signal honor of having been the first to announce to Jerusalem the Divinity of Christ, which other most illustrious witnesses were soon to publish to the world. The Holy Family now quitted Jerusalem, and returned to Bethlehem.

CHAPTER V.

THE ADORATION OF OUR DIVINE LORD BY THE MAGI.

1. OF all the pagan lands of the East, Persia was most free from idolatry. From the earliest days, the Persians had raised shrines and temples, undefiled by the presence of idols, to One Supreme Being, to whom they sent up their solemn chants and prayers.

2. This noble belief they bore to Babylon when led by Cyrus, they conquered that empire. There, the Persian priests, or Magi had passed under the potent influence of the Captive Hebrew priests, and heard the predictions of the prophet Daniel concerning the time of the coming of the Messiah.

3. From Daniel too, the Magi learned that the Saint of Saints was that very One Whom, more than 1600 years before, on the mountain overlooking the camp of the Israelites, the unwilling lips of Balaam had prophesied should arise from Jacob, like a Star.

4. The knowledge of these prophecies gradually spread from country to country, throughout the East, and in the time

---

20. Did Anna recognize the Divine Child, also? 21. What honor belongs to Anna?

1. What may be said of Persia? 2. Where did the Persians come in contact with the Jews? 3. What prediction did the Persians learn from Daniel? 4. What did it give rise to, throughout the East?

of the birth of Our Lord, there was a settled conviction that a king was to arise from Judea, who should conquer the world.

5. Nowhere had the remembrance of the prediction been more carefully cherished than in Persia, and as the time of its fulfilment drew near, the Magi, who always followed the courses of the stars attentively, watched with renewed eagerness, from their lofty towers, the movements of the heavenly host.

6. At length their patience was rewarded—one night, there swam into their sight, on the clear blue sky of the Orient, a new Star, that outshone in its serene splendor, all the other orbs of heaven. At once, faith entered their hearts, and three of their number resolved to journey in search of Him of whose approach the heavens were telling.

7. Guided by the Star, they set out on their long journey. He who had created it had suspended the laws which governed its motion; its orbit was His will. And so it moved—a blazing splendor—westward on its solemn way, till it stood over the city of Jerusalem—then disappeared.

8. The Holy Family were just quitting Jerusalem, after the Purification, when the rich caravan of the Magi entered it. The inhabitants of the Holy City were well accustomed to see travellers from far distant countries within their gates, so that no surprise was felt at the presence of the Persians, till they were heard to inquire for the newly-born King of the Jews, that they might adore Him.

9. This question passing from lip to lip, at last reached the ears of Herod, in his marble palace. It was now thirty-four years since this tyrant had ascended the throne, and his bloodstained course was almost run. But his ruling passion—ambition—was still as strong as ever, as new crimes were soon to testify.

---

5. Had the remembrance been cherished in Persia? 6. Did they perceive the Star, at last? 7. Whither did the star proceed? 8. When did the Magi enter Jerusalem, and what did their request excite? 9. Whom did the news of their coming at last reach?

10. Hastily convening a council composed of High-priests and Scribes, he desired to know where the Messiah was to be born. They at once answered, "In Bethlehem of Juda, for so it is written by the prophet."

11. Herod therefore summoned the Magi to him in secret, and inquired minutely about the Star. When he saw there was nothing more to learn, he feigned deep faith, and bade them depart at once for Bethlehem, and as soon as they had found the Child, to make the fact known to him, that he too might go and adore Him.

12. He dismissed them thus secretly at night, in order that no one might hear of their interview, and by warning the Magi, rob him of his victim. The Magi departed, but scarcely had they passed beyond the gates of Jerusalem, when the star shone out anew upon their gaze.

13. With solemn joy they followed their restored heavenly guide as it moved to Bethlehem and stood still over the spot where the Divine Child was. Christian tradition tells us that this was not the stable in which He had been born, but a humble dwelling.

14. Reverently entering, they fell prostrate at the feet of the Child who rested within his mother's arms, and adored the Godhead enshrined within this helplessness. Then their attendants brought to them from their camels, treasures of gold, incense, and myrrh (mer), which they offered to Jesus.

15. After their pious duty was discharged, the Magi returned to the inn, no doubt, to rest after their long and difficult journey. But in a dream, God warned them not to return to Herod, but to travel back to Persia by another road than that which led through Jerusalem.

16. As soon as the Magi had departed homeward, the angel of the Lord appeared to Joseph while sleeping, and said to

---

10. What did Herod do? 11. How did Herod arrange to murder the Messiah? 12. What did the Magi see after they had left Herod? 13. Whither did it lead them? 14. What did the Magi do before our Lord? 15. What did God warn the Magi in a dream? 16. What did the Angel direct Joseph to do?

ADORATION OF THE MAGI.

him, "Arise, take the Child and His mother, and flee into Egypt. There you will dwell till such time as I shall declare to you, for Herod is searching for the Child, to destroy Him."

17. At once, while it was still night, Joseph rose up and took the Child and His mother and set forth. Mary rode on an ass bearing her Divine Son in her arms, while Joseph walked by her side. Three days' journey brought them from the mountains of Juda to the borders of Egypt, where they fixed their dwelling.

18. Meanwhile woe reigned in Judea. When the Magi failed to appear, as they had promised, the jealous fears of Herod were raised to their highest pitch, and found vent in an act of savage fury.

19. All that he had been able to learn of the Messiah led him to conclude that He must still be an infant; but, determined to make sure of His destruction, he ordered all the children under two years of age, in and around Bethlehem, to be put to death.

20. The cruel order was at once executed, and throughout the city of David and its environs, the dying cries of the little ones mingled with the despairing shrieks of their mothers. But Herod was even then dying of a loathsome disease, and soon followed these Holy Innocents to the grave.

21. At his death his kingdom was divided by the Roman emperor Augustus. Half of his territory, comprising Id′u mē′a, Judea, and Samaria, was given to his son Archelaus (ark e-lā′us). The remainder was divided between his two sons, Herod Antipas and Philip.

22. Thus Herod Antipas received a te′-trarch-y, or one quarter of his father's domains, comprising Galilee and Perea, the land beyond the Jordan ; while another tetrarchy, comprising the lands extending from the Lake of Ge nes′a reth, to the sources of the Jordan, was bestowed on Philip. (See map, page 210).

---

17. Did they go? 18. What raised the fear of Herod? 19. How did he seek to destroy the Messiah? 20. Was it done? 21. Was his kingdom divided? 22. How was this half divided?

CHAPTER VI.

RETURN OF THE HOLY FAMILY TO JUDEA.—JESUS IN THE TEMPLE.

1. As soon as Herod had passed away, the Angel of the Lord appeared to St. Joseph in Egypt, and said to him, "Arise, take the Child and the mother and return to the land of Israel, for they are dead who sought the life of the Child."

2. The Holy Family returned at once to Judea. It had been Joseph's intention to settle in Bethlehem, but on the road he learned that Archelaus was as bloodthirsty a tyrant as his father had been, so he changed his plans and retired into Nazareth in Galilee, that thus the prediction of the prophets in regard to the Messiah might be fulfilled. "He shall be called a Nazarene."

3. For some unknown reason, although Nazareth had its name of Netz'er or Flower, from the beauty of its site, a name which the prophets applied to the Messiah by declaring He should be the Netzer, a Flower of the Rod of Jesse, the name of Nazarene had become a term of contempt, and as such was used of Our Redeemer.

4. In this secluded village, the Divine Childhood passed away. Once and once only, is the veil which hangs over it, lifted in the Gospel, when Jesus at the age of twelve years, accompanies his parents to Jerusalem to celebrate the yearly festival of the Pasch.

5. This age witnessed some important changes in a young Jew's life. Then, for the first time, he took his place in the synagogue, and began to bind about his brows the phylacteries (fy-lac'ter-res), long bands of parchment covered with sacred

---

1. What did the Angel direct Joseph to do after Herod's death? 2. After returning to Judea, what led them to settle in Nazareth? 3. How were the Nazarenes viewed by the Jews? 4. What do we know of the Divine Childhood? 5. What did the twelfth year witness?

texts. Thus He became a Son of the Law, and so subject to its prescriptions.

6. One of the first of these was to visit Jerusalem at the Feast of the Pasch. Jesus, therefore, along with his parents, took their places in the caravan which started from Galilee, and after a journey of three or four days, arrived in the Holy City.

7. The seven days of the Passover went by, and on the day after its close the caravans were ready for departure. About midday, that of Galilee, composed of many thousands of persons, went out of the gates of Jerusalem. Mary and Joseph were of it, but to their consternation, when they halted at nightfall, they could not find Jesus.

8. In order to explain why they had not missed Jesus sooner, it must be remembered that Jerusalem was flooded at the time of the festival with millions of pilgrims. Caravans were consequently formed amid the greatest confusion, and it was only when the long files of camels and mules had got out into the open country, that it became possible to collect one's own party.

9. Mary and Joseph returned to Jerusalem and sought Jesus for three days and three nights in vain. The following day was the Sabbath, and they went to the Temple, and entered the lofty hall in which the Doctors of the Law were wont to meet, to solve any difficulties arising in its interpretation.

10. Here, seated amid these sages, holding them captive with the charm of His wondrous discourse, was He Whom they had sought for three days with such weariness and anguish! Around the group, pressed throngs of Jews from all over the world, who had come to be instructed by the Doctors, but now like them, hearkened in wonder and delight to the Divine Voice!

11. Marvellous as was the scene thus presented to Mary, it could not make her forget all that she had suffered, and she

---

6. What was one of the most important of the Law's prescriptions? 7. What took place the day after the close of the Festival? 8. Why had they not missed Him before? 9. Where did His parents seek Jesus? 10. Where did they behold Him? 11. What did Mary say to Jesus?

THE PRESENTATION.

said to Jesus, "My Son, why treat us thus? Thy father and I have sought Thee sorrowing."

12. The answer of the Saviour to this gentle reproach is the first of His utterances which have come down to us. "Why did you seek Me?" He asked. "Did you not know that indeed I must be about My Father's business?"

13. Jesus then left the temple with Joseph and Mary and returned to Nazareth, and "was subject to them." The veil has once more fallen, not to rise again till eighteen years have gone by.

---

12. What did Our Lord answer? 13. Did He return with them?

II.--PUBLIC LIFE OF OUR LORD JESUS CHRIST.

CHAPTER I.

MISSION OF JOHN THE BAPTIST, THE PRECURSOR OF CHRIST.

1. THIRTY years had gone by since the night in which the watching shepherds on the Judean hills, had heard the anthems of the angelic choir, and hastened to adore their Redeemer. They were now dead, along with most of those who had known of his birth.

2. Thus Zachary and Elizabeth, and holy Simeon and Anna, and even St. Joseph, had passed away. Gone, too, no doubt, were most of those who had seen or heard of the three Eastern sages who had come from a distant land with rich gifts, to seek the new-born Messiah.

3. The great Roman Emperor Augustus, whose edict had forced St. Joseph and Our Blessed Lady to go up to Bethlehem, and who had thus unconsciously served the true Master of the world by occasioning the fulfilment of the prophecies concerning the place of His birth, had also passed away, A. D. 14, and been succeeded by his step-son Tiberius.

4. From Judea proper, the very shadow of independence had departed. It had formed part of the kingdom of Archelaus, but after a mis-government of nine years, that prince had been deposed and exiled by Augustus, and the country made a mere Roman province under a Roman governor, or Procurator.

---

1. Relate some of the changes which had taken place since Our Lord's birth. 2. Who else had passed away? 3. Was the Emperor Augustus still reigning? 4. What had departed from Judea?

5. Two Roman knights, Cŏ pō′ ni us, and Va-ler-i-us Gratius, had successively held the post, until it was finally assumed, (A. D. 26), by Pontius Pilate, who was destined to achieve so terrible an immortality by his part in the most awful event in the annals of human history.

6. The hopes which had been stirred in many devout hearts by hearing of the wonderful events in Bethlehem, and in the temple, at the time of the birth of the Messiah, had faded as time went on, and He gave no sign of His presence among men.

7. The pagan world was sinking deeper and deeper into the foulest moral degradation, while the signs of dissolution in the chosen nation, grew more and more apparent. Thus we see that after the long ages during which God had prepared the Jewish people for His coming, they were still unready when He at last came.

8. God therefore sent John, the son of Zachary, to prepare the way for Him. From his early youth this holy man had dwelt in the wild hill country of Judea, called the Wilderness. Here, clad in camel's skin, with a leathern girdle, without any other shelter than the caves or thickets, or other food than locusts and wild honey, John prepared by prayer and penance for his great mission.

9. When he reached the age of thirty years, the Word of God came to him. Then quitting his solitude, he entered the Valley of Jericho, and began to preach and call on the people to do penance, for that the Kingdom of Heaven was at hand.

10. The consummate sanctity, and burning words of the great preacher appealed to the hearts of the people, who flocked from cities and towns and villages, first to listen to his warning voice, upbraiding them with their sins, and then to confess their sins with humble contrition, and receive baptism as a mark of public penance, and of faith in his mission.

---

5. Name the governors of Judea. 6. What of the hopes which the wonderful events attending the birth of the Messiah had aroused?' 7. What of the condition of the world and the Jewish nation? 8. Whom did God send to prepare the world for His coming? 9. When did the

11. John had taken up his station on the banks of the Jordan, at a ford where a large concourse of travellers were continually passing to and from Perea. His immersion in the stream of the body, was figurative of the cleansing of the heart. For this reason he is called the Baptist or Baptizer.

12. The two great sects of Pharisees and Sadducees at this time, divided the Jewish nation. The Sadducees represented the aristocratic, and cultured classes, whom intercourse with pagan nations had gradually made weaker and weaker in their faith.

13. At length they had rejected the immortality of the soul, the resurrection of the body, and the existence of the Angels, and believed that after Jehovah had once revealed to man the moral law, He had withdrawn into the repose of eternity, and left him to himself.

14. These Sadducees were a great scandal to the Pharisees. As we have seen, the latter had sprung from the more conservative orthodox Jews, who had grown Zealots, as time went on. "They multiplied hedge after hedge" about the law. But the ancient spirit had departed from them, their religious exterior masked for the most part, bigotry and hypocrisy.

15. In order to give the proper gravity to their carriage, they shortened their steps so that their feet almost met. In order to preserve a modest deportment, some kept their eyes so fixed on the ground as to often come in collision with walls, while others enveloped their heads in sacks, and walked the street like blind men.

16. Drawn by the fame of John's preaching, many of the Pharisees and Sadducees came out to hear him. But the Baptist, who had only words of encouragement for the sincere, of all ranks and occupations, had a terrible greeting for these proud hypocrites.

---

11. Where did John take up his station? 12. What of the two great Jewish sects? 13. What revealed truths did the Sadducees reject? 14. How did the Pharisees view them? 15. Mention some of the customs of the Pharisees. 16. Did any of the Pharisees and Sadducees go to hear John?

17. "Breed of vipers," he cried, "of whom have you learned to flee from the wrath that is to come? Show me some worthy fruits of repentance, and do not venture to say among yourselves, 'We have Abraham for our father.' For I say to you, God is able, of these stones, to raise up children unto Abraham.

18. Already the ax is at the root of the trees. Every tree which will not bear good fruit, shall be cut down and cast into the fire." Thus John declared that the ancient covenant was dissolved, and that Israel's glorious distinction—that of being the children of Abraham, the chosen people of God, had been forfeited.

19. But to those who sought him in sincerity, the austere Baptist was all mercy and kindness. When the people gathered about him, asking what they must do, he contented himself with pointing out to them the duties of almsgiving and fraternal love. "Let him who has two coats give to him who has none; and let him who has food use it in like manner."

20. To some publicans, who as collectors of the Roman tax, were hated and despised by the Jews, and who came to him and said, "Master, what shall we do?" he answered: "Demand nothing, above that which has been commanded you."

21. Certain soldiers, upon their march, who passed near the place where he was preaching, were also touched by grace, and sought counsel of him as to their conduct. He said to them: "Do not do any violence, nor any fraud; be content with your pay."

22. He thus prepared men for the coming of Christ, by preaching, not a visionary perfection, but a godly and upright fulfilment of man's daily duties, and the practice of the ordinary virtues of one's state of life.

23. Every day the excitement increased as the throng

---

17. Repeat his greeting. 18. How did John declare that Israel was no longer the chosen nation of God? 19. How did the Baptist receive the sincere? 20. What did he counsel the publicans? 21. The soldiers? 22. What is to be said of his preparation of men for Christ? 23. What idea began to prevail in regard to John?

grew greater about the Baptist. At first, it had been rumored that he was Elias come down from heaven, but at length the idea that he might indeed be the Messiah, began to be cherished among the people.

24. John heard this and answered: "As for me, I baptize you with water, but after me there cometh One who is mightier than I, the latchet of whose shoes I am not worthy to loose. He it is who shall baptize you with the Holy Ghost, and with fire.

25. "The fan is in His Hand, and He will cleanse His floor; He will gather together the good grain into his granary, and will burn the chaff in a fire which shall not be extinguished."

CHAPTER II.

BAPTISM OF OUR LORD BY ST. JOHN.—OUR LORD'S TEMPTATIONS.

1. John had begun to preach in the month of September, in the beginning of the seventh or Sabbatical Jewish year, during which there was a full remission of all debts, and the fields were left fallow, thus allowing the people to enjoy a protracted period of leisure.

2. Three months after John had begun his preaching, Our Lord quitted the humble home which had sheltered Him for thirty years, and journeyed southward through the Holy Land to the Jordan, on whose banks he one day presented Himself unannounced amid the surging crowds, to the Baptist.

3. The spiritual discernment of St. John, however, enabled him at once to recognize His Redeemer, and he exclaimed, "I ought to be baptized by thee, and comest thou to me?" But Jesus answered, "Suffer it now; for thus does it become us to fulfil all justice."

---

24. How did he receive it? 25. What terrible image did John make use of to depict the Saviour's judgment of men?
1. When had John begun to preach? 2. What did Our Lord now do?
3. Did John recognize Christ?

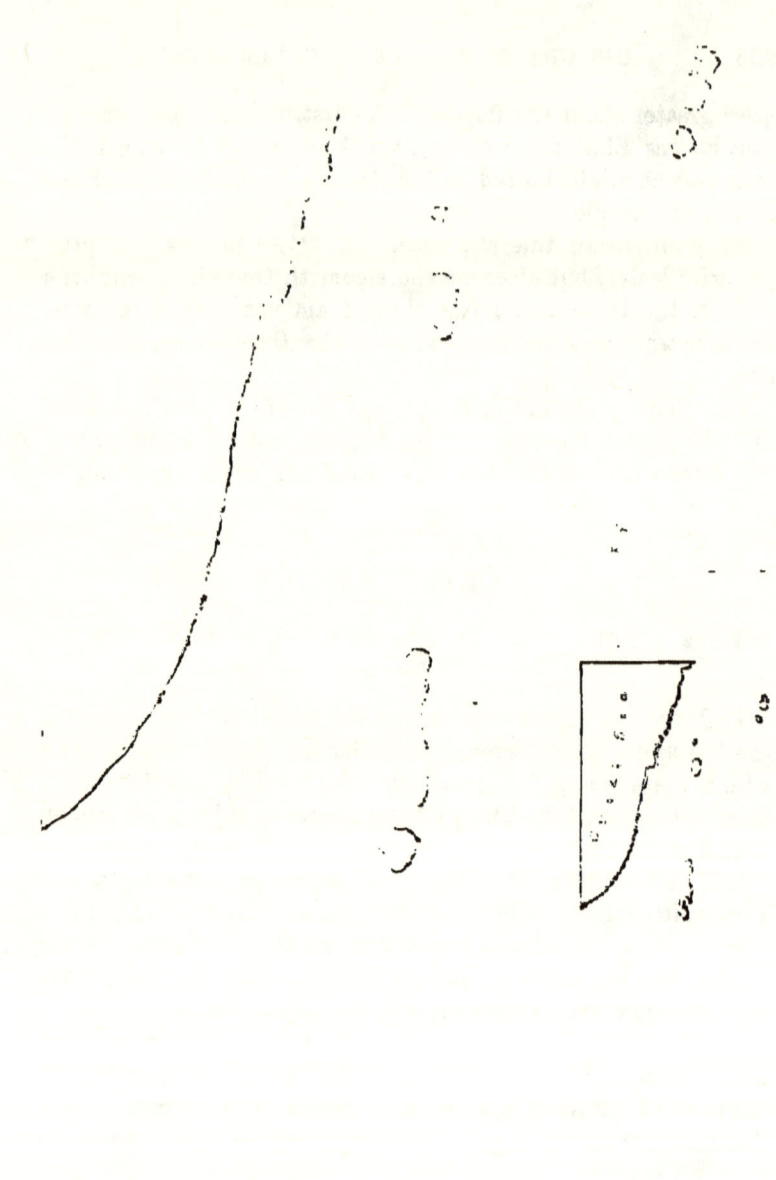

BAPTISM OF OUR LORD. 221

4. John resisted no longer, but immersed Jesus in the Jordan. Thus Our Lord sanctified the element of water, that it might become in his own sacrament of baptism the instrument of regeneration for mankind.

5. As Our Lord rose from the waters, the heavens opened, and the Holy Ghost descended upon Him in the form of a dove; while at the same time a Voice said, "This is my dearly beloved son; in whom I am always well pleased."

6. The Voice of God was not heard by the Jews, save as a sound of thunder. But St. John at once perceived the first manifestation of the mystery of the Trinity to man—the Father in the Voice from the heavens; the Son in Jesus, and the Holy Ghost in the Dove, the symbol of grace, whose reign was now begun on earth.

7. Directly after His Baptism, Our Lord was led by the Holy Ghost into the most savage part of the Wilderness of Judea. Here, amid wild beasts, dwelling in a cave, the Saviour passed forty days in fasting and prayer. "And when the forty days were spent," says St. Luke, "He was hungry."

8. Throughout the long ages during which the Jewish nation had looked for the coming of the Messiah, Satan had had the same expectation, though with far different feelings; for the coming of the Son of God in human form, to redeem the world, was the one event which he dreaded above all others.

9. As prophecy after prophecy was fulfilled, and the time for His Birth grew near, Satan grew doubly watchful, and, no doubt, was filled with alarm at the many wonderful circumstances attending that event. But there were other things which Satan was not allowed to know, and he was further baffled by the poverty, meekness, and hidden life of the Holy Family.

10. But when Our Lord left Nazareth and presented Himself at the Jordan, the Vision seen by St. John may have again

---

4. Did John obey? 5. What took place as Our Lord rose from the waters? 6. Was this vision seen by all? 7. Whither did the Holy Ghost conduct Our Lord after His Baptism? 8. Who else had watched for the coming of the Messiah? 9. Did Satan watch for His coming? 10. What alarmed Satan once more?

alarmed Satan, and made him resolve to assail Jesus in the desert, with the twofold object of discovering who He was, and at the same time of inducing Him to sin.

11. He therefore appeared before Our Lord in the extreme state of weakness to which he had permitted Himself to be reduced, and said to Him: "If Thou be the Son of God, command that these stones be made bread."

12. Satan thus made, not merely a sensual appeal to the appetite, but an appeal to the power of miracles, which as the Son of God He must have possessed, to save Himself from perishing of hunger in the wilderness, when Heaven seemed to have abandoned Him.

13. But Our Lord answered: "Man does not live by bread alone, but by every word which comes from the mouth of God." Thus He restored to God the honor which Satan's words had impaired, and baffled the latter's desire to know who He was, because His words applied to the humblest child of Adam, as well as to the Incarnate Son.

14. Satan then transported Our Lord to a pinnacle of the temple at Jerusalem. Then he said to Him, "If Thou be the Son of God, cast thyself down, for it is written that He hath given His angel charge of thee, and they shall bear thee up in their hands lest perhaps thou dash thy foot against a stone."

15. Satan imagined that to thus descend with celestial pomp and splendor, into the midst of the crowds which thronged the courts of the temple, would be too alluring a prospect for the Messiah to resist. But he was again baffled by Our Lord's calm answer: "It is written also, 'Thou shalt not tempt the Lord thy God.'"

16. Then Satan transported Our Lord to the top of a high mountain, whence he showed to Him all the empires of the world and their glory, and said to Him: "All these I will give thee, if, falling down before me, thou wilt adore me."

---

11. How did he tempt Our Lord? 12. What did Satan thus make an appeal to? 13. What did Our Lord answer? 14. Relate the second temptation of Our Lord. 15. What did Satan imagine? 16. Relate the third temptation of Our Lord.

17. Even this insult Our Lord bore calmly and meekly for our sakes, and answered, "Begone, Satan, for it is written, 'Thou shalt adore the Lord, thy God, and Him only shalt thou serve.'" Then the devil fled away; and angels came and ministered to Him.

Our Lord's temptations are our consolation, our strength, and our example. Our consolation, because they strengthen us under like trials; our strength, because He has won for us all the graces which are needed to enable us to triumph, and our example, because He teaches how calmly we should resist temptation, resting on our faith, and trusting in God.

CHAPTER III.

THE FIRST DISCIPLES OF OUR LORD.

1. DURING the absence of Our Lord in the desert, John continued to preach to the same great throngs, whose enthusiasm grew more and more intense. At length the Sanhedrin, or Great Council of the Jews, sent a formal deputation of Pharisees to him to ask who he was.

2. To their question as to whether he was the Messiah, John answered, "I am not." "What then?" they asked. "Art thou Elias?" "No," answered John. "Art thou the Prophet," they then asked, in allusion to the prophet whom Moses had foretold should come. But John answered again, "No."

3. "Who art thou then," asked the messengers, "in order that we may render an account to those who sent us here? What sayest thou of thyself?" John answered, "I am the Voice of one crying in the Wilderness, 'Make straight the ways of the Lord,' as hath said the prophet Isaiah."

---

17. How did Our Lord bear this insult?
1. Did John continue to preach? 2. What replies did John make to these questions? 3. What did the messengers then say, and what did John answer?

4. This response, far from impressing the Pharisees, seemed to them to deprive John of all right to preach, and purify by absolution. "Why dost thou baptize," they said; "if thou art neither Christ, nor Elias, nor the prophet?"

5. John replied, "As for me I baptize in water, but there hath stood One in the midst of you whom you knew not. He cometh after me; He Who hath been set above me, and I am not worthy to loosen the latchets of His shoes."

6. Thus did St. John bear formal and official witness to the presence of the Messiah among men. His steadfastness and humility, however, disconcerted the Pharisees, and they questioned him no further.

7. Shortly after the Saviour descended from the mount of temptation to the Jordan. When John beheld Him approaching, he cried out, "Behold the Lamb of God—behold Him Who beareth the sins of the world."

8. The Precursor continued, "Behold Him of whom I have said 'There cometh after me a Man Who hath been set above me, because He was before me. And I knew Him not; yet am I come, giving you the baptism of water, that so He may be made manifest in Israel.'"

9. On the following day John was walking with two of his disciples when Jesus passed on before them. John exclaimed again, "Behold the Lamb of God!" The two disciples, therefore, quitted John and followed Jesus. The Saviour soon turned, and seeing that they were following Him, said, "Whom are you seeking?"

10. "Master, where dost thou dwell?" they answered, thus revealing the thirst for truth that consumed them. Our Lord replied, "Come and see," and led them to one of the huts, woven from the boughs of turpentine and palm trees, which then stood on the banks of the Jordan.

---

4. How did they receive this answer? 5. Repeat John's reply. 6. What did St. John testify by his words? 7. When did St. John again bear witness to Our Lord? 8. Repeat the Baptist's further testimony to the presence of Christ on earth. 9. What took place on the next day? 10. What did they answer?

11. According to the Jewish custom of reckoning the hours of the day from sunrise—six o'clock in the morning—it was the tenth hour of the day, or four o'clock in the afternoon, when the disciples entered the abode of Jesus, "and they passed the rest of the day with Him."

12. These first disciples of Our Lord were St. Andrew, the fisherman of Galilee, and St. John, the Evangelist. In his Gospel, the latter says nothing of this first intimate communion with Our Lord, but its effect was that both left Him with hearts full of joy and fervent faith.

13. St. Andrew at once sought his brother Simon, and said to him, "We have found the Messiah!" He then led him to the Saviour who saw in this Galilean the immovable Rock on which He would build His church.

14. "Thou art Simon, the son of Jō-na," said Our Lord to him, "but thou shall be called Kē'phas," that is Peter, which means a rock. Thus Our Lord showed from the very first His authority over His disciples, for the right of changing or altering a name was reserved to the rulers of Israel.

15. The next disciple who was brought in contact with Our Lord was Philip, a fellow-townsman of Peter and Andrew. On the following day when Our Lord was preparing to depart into Galilee, He met Philip and said to him, "Follow Me." And Philip abandoned himself to grace, and followed Jesus.

16. On the road to Galilee Our Lord and His companions were passing through the meadows near Bethel, which had once witnessed the Vision of Jacob, when they perceived a Jew seated under a fig-tree reading. It was Nathanael, destined to become the fifth disciple of Our Lord.

17. He was a friend of Philip, who went to him and said, "We have found Him Whom Moses in the Law, and the Prophets have announced—Jesus, the Son of Joseph of Nazareth."

---

11. What time of the day was this? 12. Who were these first disciples of Our Lord? 13. Whom did St. Andrew bring to Our Lord? 14. What did Our Lord say to Peter? 15. Who was the fourth disciple of Our Lord? 16. Where did they see Nathanael? 17. What did Philip say to him?

18. But Nathanael, who was deeply versed in sacred literature, knew that the Messiah was to be born in Bethlehem, and could place no faith in one hailing from an obscure village of ill repute in Galilee. "Of Nazareth," he answered, "Can any good come out of Nazareth?"

19. "Come and see," answered Philip. And he led his friend to the Saviour, who, as He saw Nathanael approaching, said, "Behold a true Israelite in whom there is no guile." Surprised, Nathanael said, "How knowest thou me?" The Saviour answered, "Before Philip called thee, when thou wast under the fig-tree, I saw thee."

20. Evidently Our Lord made allusion to something which Nathanael believed was known to himself alone, and thus revealed to him that he stood in the presence of One Who could read his heart. Filled with awe and wonder, he cried out, "Master, Thou art the Son of God, the King of Israel."

21. Jesus answered, "Because I have said to thee that I saw thee beneath the fig-tree, thou dost believe; thou shalt see things greater still. Amen, amen, I say unto thee, thou shalt see the heavens opened, and the angels of God ascending and descending upon the Son of Man."

Nathanael did not make use of the title, Son of God, as meaning that Jesus was the Son of God by nature, equal and consubstantial with His Father, but as meaning that He was the Son of God, the object of Israel's longing and its king. The Jews frequently used the title Son of God—bestowing it on angels, on princes of Israel, and on men distinguished for piety. But they meant only sonship by adoption. Their ignorance regarding the Trinity prevented most of them from seeing that the Messiah could be God, as is He Who sent Him, and when Jesus claimed to be the Son of God, equal to His Father, and One with Him, they looked on Him as a blasphemer, and in their frenzy would have liked to stone Him.

---

18. What objection did Nathanael make? 19. Did Philip lead Nathanael to Our Lord? 20. What did Our Lord's words reveal to Nathanael? 21. What did Our Lord answer?

CHAPTER IV.

THE MARRIAGE FEAST OF CANA.—OUR LORD FIXES HIS DWELLING AT CAPHARNAUM.

1. WITH His five disciples, Our Lord journeyed to Nazareth in Galilee, only to find that His mother had departed to a wedding in the village of Cana, (kă'na) a league to the north of Nazareth.

2. As Our Lord had also been invited, He went on thither that same evening with His five disciples and arrived just as the banquet was about to commence, on the evening of the third day, for the wedding festivities of the Jews lasted for several days, and sometimes even a week.

3. It is probable that the Blessed Virgin was a relative of the hosts, and had assisted in the preparations of the feast; at all events she knew that they had been able to provide only a small store of wine, and sympathized in their embarrassment at sight of the unexpected guests whom Our Lord had brought with Him, knowing that the wine would give out.

4. In her distress Our Blessed Lady betook herself to Jesus and said, "They have no wine." Our Lord answered, "Woman, what is it to me and to thee? Mine hour is not yet come." The title, woman, which here sounds harshly to our ears, was, among the Hebrews, a title of respect, consistent with the highest courtesy.

5. Whether Mary understood from her Son's words that the moment for supplying the want of wine had not yet arrived, or that but for her intercession, the beginning of miracles would not have taken place at that time, it is clear that she understood that her prayer was heard.

6. She therefore said to the waiters, "Whatsoever He shall say to you, do it." Now there were standing close at hand six

---

1. Whither did Our Lord now proceed? 2. Did Our Lord go to the marriage feast? 3. What want did Our Blessed Lady perceive? 4. Repeat her request to Our Lord and His answer. 5. What did Mary understand from her Son's words? 6. What did Mary say to the waiters?

great jars of stone, which, according to the custom of the Jews, were kept filled with water, for the frequent ablutions performed during the repast by the guests.

7. By the time the wine gave out, the urns were almost empty. At a word from Jesus, the servants filled them once more to the brim. Then He said, "Draw out now, and bear it to the Master of the Feast." This was one of the guests, selected to preside over the feasting, and see that there was nothing lacking.

8. When the waiters presented him with the cup, the Master of the Feast tasted the wine, not knowing whence it came, then said to the bridegroom, "Every man serves the good wine first, and when men have well drunk, that which is not so good, but thou hast kept the good wine till now."

9. Thus did Our Lord perform His first miracle, at the prayer of His Blessed Mother, and in order to sanctify the bond of marriage, which was to become in His Church a sacramental union.

10. For some reason Our Lord did not tarry long at Nazareth after returning to it from the marriage of Cana, but taking His mother, went with his disciples to the city of Ca phar'-na-um, which was situated on the western shore of the Lake of Ge nes' a-reth, and was about a day's journey from Nazareth. Here He made His home during His public life.

11. The Lake of Genesareth, or as it was more often called in the time of Our Lord, the Sea of Tiberias, lay in the midst of a plain which bloomed like a garden, and brought forth the product of every clime. Thousands of bright sails sparkled on its waters, Roman galleys, Herod's fine fleet, and numberless fisher-craft.

12. On the western shore lay a number of beautiful cities, chief of which was Tiberias, recently built by Herod Antipas, the ruler of Galilee, in honor of the Roman Emperor, Tiberius.

---

7. Continue. 8. What did the Master of the Feast say? 9. Why did Our Lord perform this miracle? 11. Where did Our Lord go soon after? 11. Describe the Lake of Genesareth. 12. Which was the most famous city of Genesareth?

THE FIRST MIRACLE.

As it was peopled mostly by foreigners, however, it is doubtful if Our Lord ever entered it.

13. North of Tiberias lay the cities made famous in the Gospel. Of Capharnaum, the "city of Jesus," it is difficult to discover even the exact site in our day, so terrible was the desolation which came upon it in consequence of having rejected the Word of God, and incurred His curse.

14. In the time of Our Lord, it was one of the most beautiful cities on the shores of Genesareth, shaded by myrtles, almond, apple, pomegranate, orange, date and citron trees, and so situated so as to be at the point of meeting for several great roads.

15. Thus it was a most advantageous spot for Our Lord's residence, for it brought Him in contact with such great numbers of men as are always to be found in great centres of commerce, and fulfilled the prophecy which had declared that Galilee of the Gentiles, which had been lying in the shadow of death, should be illuminated by the Sun of Justice.

CHAPTER V.

OUR LORD DRIVES THE SELLERS FROM THE TEMPLE—NICODEMUS.

1. SHORTLY after Our Lord had fixed His residence in Capharnaum, the Feast of the Pasch drew near, and He and His disciples took places in the caravan which was being formed by the pilgrims of Galilee to go up to Jerusalem, to celebrate it.

2. The Saviour entered the Holy City unknown and unnoticed amid the throng. His first act was to go up to the temple to pray, but as He was not a Levite, He had to remain with the other sons of Juda, in the lower courts, which were the scene of an unhallowed traffic.

---

13. What of Capharnaum? 14. Describe it in the time of Our Lord. 15. What did it thus prove for Our Lord, and what prophecy was fulfilled?

1. Whither did Our Lord go soon after? 2. Where did He at once go?

3. The Jews who were dispersed all over the world, went up every year to Jerusalem to celebrate the Passover. But as they could not bring with them from distant lands the animals necessary for the sacrifices, sellers began to edge their way into the courts of the temple to provide these.

4. In consequence these beautiful courts became a market, in which even the money-changers had a place, for each Jew had to offer a certain sum of money to the temple, and if he came from a heathen country, had to change its coin stamped with idolatrous images, for that of Israel.

5. Thus was the House of God profaned. True, the rites were always celebrated upon the topmost terrace, but the chanting and the prayers were no longer audible in the lower courts from the bellowing of cattle, the bleating of sheep, and the shrill cries of the money-changers.

6. The spectacle aroused the wrath of Our Lord; He seized a handful of the flexible rushes which the Orientals plait like cords and twisting them into a whip, advanced upon the throng with this uplifted, and drove both buyers and sellers, and money-changers out of the temple.

7. The sellers of doves He treated less severely, probably because they sold the offerings made by the poor. To them He said simply, "Take all these away from here, and do not make a house of traffic out of My Father's house." And the disciples remembered that it was written, "The zeal of Thy House hath eaten me up."

8. As for the throng of traders, they offered no resistance at all, but fled before Him. As their occupation was carried on with at least the tacit license of the authorities, there seems to have been no human reason for their terror, and we must only suppose that the hidden Godhead of Our Lord made itself felt in some unknown way.

---

3. What first brought sellers to approach the temple? 4. Who even had a place there? 5. What was the consequence? 6. How did Our Lord view this spectacle? 7. What did he say to the sellers of doves? 8. How is the absence of resistance on the traders' part ex-

9. The Pharisees, who were in authority, viewed this action on the part of Our Lord with jealousy, and demanded what sign He had to show as a warrant for His action. Our Lord answered, "Overthrow this Temple, and in three days I will raise it up again."

10. By these words Our Lord referred to His own Sacred Body, which they were to destroy, and which He was to raise up from the tomb in three days, thus giving the most conclusive sign of His Divine mission, which was to become the groundwork of the Christian faith, and convert thousands even of the Jews.

11. The blind Pharisees, however, understood merely that this obscure Galilean dared to speak of levelling the magnificent temple which had been forty-six years rebuilding, and erecting it again in three days. They never forgot His words, and in the last hours of His life, they repeated them in a distorted form, to procure his condemnation.

12. Still, even among the Pharisees, there were some whose hearts were turned to this new great Teacher. The first was a member of the Sanhedrin named Nic-o-dē'-mus, a man of great learning and noble birth, who had been one of the few of his sect to humble himself before John the Baptist, and receive his baptism.

13. Nicodemus was still too timid to seek Our Lord openly, so he stole to the house where Our Lord dwelt, by night, and said to Him, "Master, we know that thou art come from God, for no man can do the prodigies which Thou dost, if God be not with Him."

14. Our Lord knew that Nicodemus was eager to learn of the Kingdom of God,—His church—and answered, "Amen, amen, I say to thee, unless a man be born again of water and the Holy Ghost, he cannot enter into the Kingdom of God." This was hard for Nicodemus to understand till Our Lord

---

9. What did it rouse in the Pharisees? 10. What did Our Lord mean by these words? 11. What did the Pharisees understand Him to mean? 12. Who was Nicodemus? 13. When did he seek Our Lord? 14. What did Our Lord answer?

NICODEMUS WITH CHRIST.

explained that He meant a spiritual birth in the sacrament of baptism.

15. Jesus then went on to unfold to Nicodemus the Mystery of the Redemption by means of the Cross and the Passion, and in order to do so, took one of the most famous types of the Passion, which could hardly have been understood in any other way by the learned and devout among the Jews.

16. "As Moses," said Our Lord, "lifted up the Serpent in the desert, so must the Son of Man be lifted up, that whosoever believeth in Him shall not perish, but may have everlasting life. For God sent not His son into the world to judge the world, but that the world may be saved by Him. He that believeth in Him is not judged, but he that doth not believe is already judged."

17. Although Nicodemus firmly believed, he seems to have lacked the courage of his convictions. During the whole period of Our Lord's ministry we look in vain for Nicodemus among His disciples. Once only, we hear his voice timidly lifted in the Saviour's behalf before the Sanhedrin, then we meet him no more till amid the shadows of Calvary we find him beside the Cross.

CHAPTER VI.

IMPRISONMENT OF JOHN THE BAPTIST—THE SAMARITAN WOMAN.

1. OUR LORD did not tarry long in Jerusalem after the Passover, but went to the southern part of Judea, where He passed the greater part of the first year of His ministry—from April to December. As there were thus two centres of attraction, so to speak, for St. John the Baptist continued to preach, a dispute arose between the disciples of the two, in regard to the efficacy of the Baptism of John.

---

15. What did Our Lord then unfold to Nicodemus? 16. Repeat Our Lord's words. 17. Did Nicodemus become a disciple of Our Lord?
1. Did Our Lord remain in Jerusalem?

2. The Baptist's disciples finally appealed to himself. Then again the Precursor bore solemn witness to the Messiah, declaring that "Christ was the Bridegroom, and he himself but the friend of the Bridegroom." He added, "It is fitting that He should increase, and that I should diminish."

3. Shortly after, no doubt, in order to yield place to Our Lord, John quitted the Jordan, and ascended into Galilee. Herod Antipas, its ruler, the worthy son of Herod the Great, had some time before, repudiated his own wife, and espoused Herodias, the wife of his brother, who was still living.

4. This terrible transgression of the Law, which shocked all Galilee, was not suffered to pass unrebuked by the austere Baptist. Forcing his way into Herod's marble palace,—as of old Elias came before Achab—he sternly said to the wicked tetrarch, "It is not lawful for you to have your brother's wife."

5. In his rage the tyrant would have seized John then and there, but dared not for fear of the people. The hatred aroused in Herodias was still more bitter, for she knew that her crown was at stake, and she exerted all her influence with Herod, till he imprisoned John in a fortress on the coast of the Dead Sea.

6. As soon as Our Lord heard of the Baptist's imprisonment, He set out for Galilee by way of Samaria. Some hours traveling brought Him and His disciples to the lovely valley of Sĭ'chem in which was "Jacob's Well, which had been dug by that patriarch, and which was still in use, covered by an arcade, beneath which were a few stone seats.

7. Weary with His long journey, the Saviour seated Himself on one of these, while His disciples went into the neighboring town of Sichem, to buy food. It was a beautiful spring day, the barley-harvest was just past, and the fields of wheat were ripening in the balmy air.

8. Presently a Samaritan woman, with her slender water jar

---

2. To whom did John's disciples appeal? 3. Whither did John retire? 4. Did the Baptist rebuke Herod? 5. What was the consequence? 6. Whither did Our Lord go when he heard of John's imprisonment? 7. Where did our Saviour rest? 8. Who approached?

poised on her head, drew near the well. She saw there a stranger, whose apparel told that he was of the tribe of Juda. Between the Jews and the Samaritans, there were no dealings save those of commerce; great, therefore, was her surprise when the stranger said to her, "Give me to drink!"

9. "How," she said, "do you, a Jew, ask a drink of me who am a Samaritan? The Jews have no dealings with Samaritans."

10. To this rude answer, the Saviour replied gently, "If thou didst know the gift of God, and who it is that saith to thee, "Give me to drink, thou, perhaps, wouldst have asked of Him, and He would have given thee living water."

11. Unable to understand that the Saviour's words referred to grace, the Samaritan thought only of the limpid water in the depths of the ancient well. But the majesty of Our Lord had impressed her, and she now answered respectfully: "My Lord, thou hast no vessel, and the well is deep. Whence wilt thou draw this living water?"

12. Then she continued, "Art thou greater than our father Jacob, who gave us this well?" The Saviour answered, "He who drinks of this water shall thirst again, but he who drinks of the water which I will give him, shall never thirst. The water which I will give him, shall become in him a fountain springing up to eternal life."

13. The woman still understood His words literally. "Lord," she said, "Give me of this water, that I may no more thirst, and that I may be no more obliged to come hither to draw."

14. The woman's past life had been sinful, and in order that her heart might be purified for the reception of the truth, Our Lord recalled her with the utmost delicacy and gentleness, to a sense of her guilt. "Go," He said, "call thy husband, and come hither." She answered, "I have no husband."

---

9. Repeat her answer. 10. What did Our Saviour answer? 11. What did the Samaritan understand, and reply? 12. Continue the conversation. 13. How did she understand these words? 14. How did the Saviour recall her to a sense of sin?

15. The Saviour responded, "Thou art right in saying thou hast no husband." Her confession was good as far as it went, but what she withheld through shame or fear, Our Lord, with immense charity supplied. "Thou hast well said that thou hast no husband, for thou hast had five husbands."

16. The woman acknowledged the truth of his words by exclaiming, "Lord, I see that thou art a prophet." Her conscience was now aroused, and she sought from this Great Teacher, a solution of the religious difficulties between the Jews and the Samaritans, "Our fathers adored in this mountain and the Jews say that at Jerusalem is the place where men must adore."

17. She had pointed, as she spoke, to the mountain of Ger'i'zim which overhung the spot on which they were conversing, and whose summit was crowned with the ruins of the Samaritan temple, which had been destroyed by the Jews.

18. Our Lord answered, "Woman, believe me; the hour is coming when thou shalt no longer worship the Father either upon this mountain or in Jerusalem. You worship that which you do not know; as for Us, We worship that which We know, because salvation cometh of the Jews.

19. The hour cometh and now is, when the true adorer shall adore the Father in spirit and in truth. God is a spirit, and they that adore Him, must adore Him in spirit and truth."

20. The woman answered, "I know that the Messias, when He is come, will tell us all things. Jesus replied, "I am He Who am speaking with thee." Overjoyed, the woman left her jar and hastened back to the town, crying out to all whom she met, "Come and see a Man who has told me all my sins. Is He not the Christ?"

21. Meanwhile the disciples returned with the food and pressed the Saviour to eat. But He said to them, "I have food

---

15. What did He respond? 16. How did she acknowledge the truth of His words, and what did she further seek? 17. What had she pointed to as she spoke? 18. Repeat Our Lord's answer. 19. Continue. 20. Repeat the woman's words regarding the Messiah and the Saviour's reply. 21. Had the disciples returned?

to eat which you know not of. My food is to do the will of Him that sent me, and to accomplish His work."

22. While He was yet speaking the Samaritans came in crowds out of the city and besought him to enter it. So He did so and abode there two days, teaching and instructing them, and they declared that He was indeed the Saviour of the world.

CHAPTER VII.

OUR LORD HEALS THE NOBLEMAN'S SON.—PREACHES IN THE SYNAGOGUE AT NAZARETH, AND IS DRIVEN OUT.—A SABBATH DAY AT CAPHARNAUM.

1. AFTER tarrying two days at Sichar, Our Lord went on, teaching in the synagogues as He went, till He reached Galilee, where He was warmly welcomed, because his fame had spread throughout the whole country, "and he was extolled by all men."

2. He went first to Cana to rejoin His Blessed Mother, who, it is supposed, had passed the time of His absence with some relatives in that town. The news of His presence there spread rapidly until it reached the ears of a nobleman of the court of Herod Antipas, at Capharnaum, whose little son lay dangerously ill of a fever.

3. The poor father, seeing that all human aid was vain, determined to seek his son's cure from the Great Prophet, with the fame of Whose miracles the land was ringing. He at once set out for Cana, where he arrived after a journey of several hours, and poured out his entreaties at Our Lord's feet.

4. He at first received what seemed like a repulse, but this only made him redouble his entreaties. Then Our Lord said

---

22. Did the Samaritans beg Him to remain?
1. How was Our Lord received in Galilee? 2. Whither did the Saviour go first? 3. What did the father resolve? 4. Was his request granted?

to him, "Go, thy son liveth." Filled with joy, the nobleman hastened home to find that his son had indeed been restored to health at the self-same hour at which Our Lord had spoken, "and he believed, with all his household."

5. Soon after this great miracle, Our Lord went to Nazareth, His own city, and entered the synagogue on the Sabbath. It was the custom of the Jews to press any stranger distinguished for doctrine, to instruct the people, and this honor was now conferred on Our Lord.

6. After the prayers had been offered, and the benedictions given, therefore, Our Lord mounted the platform and received from the care-taker of the synagogue, a long scroll of papyrus rolled about a wand of ivory, containing the Oracles of Isaias, a portion of which was the lesson marked for the day, and read as follows:

7. "The Spirit of the Lord is upon me. He hath consecrated Me by Anointment; He hath sent Me to bring good tidings to the poor; to heal the afflicted hearts; to announce to the captives their deliverance, and to the blind, recovery of their sight, to bring back as free men those who be broken beneath their fetters, to publish forth the Year of Pardon of the Lord, and the Day of His Justice."

8. The reading finished, Our Lord rolled up the manuscript, handed it back to the server, and, according to the custom of the Jewish rabbis, seated Himself, and began to exhort the faithful. But what were His hearers' feelings when they heard Him declare, that "on this day, this same scripture is found to be fulfilled."

9. They were indeed the poor, the captives, the blind and sorrowful hearts, to whom He was bringing salvation; and for a moment, His language, so full of grace, appealed to them powerfully, and their wonder and delight found vent in acclamations of approval, mixed, however, with a certain patronizing

---

5. Whither did Our Lord go soon after this miracle? 6. What did Our Lord do therefore? 7. Repeat what Our Lord read. 8. How did He begin His exhortation? 9. How were His hearers affected?

pride for they said, "Is not this the son of Joseph the carpenter?"

10. They also required from Him some miraculous sign such as He had wrought at Cana and Capharnaum. The Gospel does not tell us whether they openly expressed this desire, but Our Lord answered it. "No doubt," He said, "you will say to Me this parable: 'Physician, heal thyself.'"

11. "But, Amen, I say to you, no prophet is accepted in His own country. There were many widows in the days of Elias in Israel, but to none of these was he sent, but to Sarepta of Sidon, to a widow woman there. And there were many lepers in Israel in the time of Eliseus the prophet, and none of them was healed but Naaman the Syrian."

12. At these words in which He dared to compare them, the children of Abraham, to pagan women and lepers, the insulted pride of his hearers filled them with a savage fury which was to have no parallel in Galilee, but only, some time later, among the proud and jealous priests at Jerusalem.

13. Rushing forward, they seized Our Lord, and swept Him along up to the summit of the mountain on which their town was built, thinking to cast Him headlong over the heights to the rocky hollows below. But when they reached the edge of the precipice a superhuman power rendered them helpless, and He passed through the midst of them, and went His way.

14. Quitting Nazareth at once, Our Lord went to Capharnaum, where He was warmly welcomed. Here, one Sabbath, He was preaching in the synagogue, to the admiring throng, when suddenly the air was rent by the shrill screams of a demoniac in the throes of frenzy.

15. "Let be," he screamed. "What is there between us and thee, Jesus of Nazareth? Art thou come to destroy us? I know who thou art—the Holy of God." Our Lord at once

---

10. What did they require from Him? 11. What reason did Our Lord give for this refusal to work miracles? 12. What did Our Lord's words rouse in the Nazarenes? 13. What did they do? 14. Whither did Our Lord now go? 15. What did the demoniac cry out?

A SABBATH DAY AT CAPHARNAUM. 241

hastened to the possessed, and stooping over him said, "Be silent, and depart from this man."

16. Satan obeyed; one last terrible cry escaped the breast of the demoniac; he was flung prone on the ground and writhed for some instants in fearful convulsions; then he rose up, before the eyes of all, free and sane.

17. But all the spectators were overwhelmed with awe, and they whispered to one another, "What new and all powerful doctrine is this? He commands the spirits and they obey." As yet, however, the carping spirit in which later, Our Lord's miracles were witnessed, was absent; they believed with a generous and simple faith.

18. Leaving the synagogue, Our Lord went to the dwelling of Peter, whose mother-in-law was fast sinking under a raging fever. He approached the bed of the dying woman, while all eyes were turned on Him, and every voice implored His aid. They did not beseech in vain, for in a voice of authority, He bade the disease depart.

19. He then took the hand of the weak and aged woman in His, and by that sacred contact so renewed her strength, that she rose up without a trace of weakness, and busied herself in preparing the noonday meal which was customary on the Sabbath, at which she then served the guests.

20. The news of this new prodigy flew through Capharnaum, and only the stern precepts of the Law enjoining unbroken quiet on the Sabbath, restrained the ardor of the multitude. But as soon as the setting sun sank beyond the distant hills, thus marking the close of the Holy Day, a long procession advanced through the streets bearing their sick to the Great Healer.

21. In the vast throng soon gathered about Simon Peter's door, every form of wretchedness known to poor human nature was to be seen. But not one was rejected; with infinite com-

---

16. Did Satan obey? 17. What feelings did this miracle arouse in the spectators? 18. What miracle did Our Lord work in the house of Simon Peter? 19. How did He restore her strength? 20. What was the result of this miracle in Capharnaun? 21. What was seen around

passion, Christ laid His hands on all and healed them. All through the night he ministered, and it was not till the dawn of the next day that the last sufferer quitted Him.

22. Without giving a moment to sleep, Our Lord rose, and passed through Capharnaum's deserted streets, till He reached a desert place. Here at length His disciples who had been eagerly seeking Him, found Him absorbed in prayer, and said to Him, "Every one is looking for you."

23. "Let us go elsewhere," replied Jesus, "into the neighboring towns and cities, and into the cities, so that I may preach there also, it is for this that I am come."

24. The inhabitants of Capharnaum who had now come up, would have stayed Him, but He repeated to them that His mission compelled Him to depart that He might carry unto others the Good Tidings of the Kingdom of God.

CHAPTER VIII.

THE MIRACULOUS DRAUGHT OF FISHES—THE HEALING OF THE LEPER—THE HEALING OF THE PARALYTIC—OUR LORD GOES UP TO JERUSALEM FOR THE SECOND PASCH—HEALS THE PARALYTIC AND DECLARES HIS DIVINITY TO THE PHARISEES.

1. ON leaving Capharnaum, Our Lord proceeded towards the north along the border of the Lake, and stopped at Bethsaida, the village home of His first disciples. Here the necessity of earning their bread, compelled the disciples to resume their occupation of fishing, while Our Lord preached to the multitude.

2. The best time for fishing is the hours before sunrise; they therefore launched their bark at night, but dredged and hauled in vain, till the sun rose and put an end to their

---

22. Whither did Our Lord then go? 23. What did Our Lord answer? 24. What did he tell the inhabitants of Capharnaum?
1. Whither did Our Lord go after leaving Capharnaum? 2. Was their fishing successful?

nopes, when greatly discouraged, they sought the shore, just as Our Lord approached it from the land, surrounded by eager crowds.

3. He at once perceived His disciples, who were washing their nets on the beach. At once He went on board Peter's bark, and desired him to draw a little away from the land; then from this first Chair of Peter, He began to instruct the people.

4. After He had finished His discourse, in His compassion for His disciples' disappointment, He said to Peter: "Push out now into the deeper water." And then to the other disciples: "Cast over your nets." Simon answered, "Master, we have labored all the night, without taking anything, but at Thy word, I will cast the net."

5. They dropped it over the side, and presently drew up such a great quantity of fish that the cords were breaking, and they had to signal their companions in the other boat to come to their aid. And the miraculous draught filled both boats to such a degree that they were almost submerged.

6. By this miracle Jesus revealed Himself as the Master of Nature. Peter, realizing that only her God could thus command her, yielded to the feeling of terror which was common to all Jews, who believed that to see God was to die, and fell at the feet of Christ, "Depart from me, O Lord," he said, "for I am a sinful man."

7. But Our Lord reassured him and all the other disciples, saying, "Be not afraid, hereafter you shall be fishers of men." These ardent simple hearts may not have fully understood His meaning, but it is possible some glimmering of their lofty destiny broke upon them, for they rowed their boats back to the shore, and forsook all things finally, to follow Him.

8. Surrounded by these companions, Christ traversed all Galilee, "teaching in the synogagues, preaching the Gospel of

---

3. What did Our Lord do when He perceived them? 4. What did He direct His disciples to do, after He had finished? 5. Were they successful? 6. What did Our Lord reveal Himself by this miracle? 7. How

the Kingdom, and healing all the infirm and the ill among the people." The very poorest villages, even those which had no synagogues, were not forgotten, He visited all, and departing, left behind Him the saving memory of His Presence.

9. While in one of these towns, a leper, hearing of His presence, in the energy of his despair, broke the rule which forbade all lepers to enter within the gates of the town, and threw himself at Our Lord's feet. "Lord," he cried in anguish, "if Thou wilt, Thou canst heal me."

10. Our Lord at once laid His divine hand on that wretched creature's body, "I will," He said, "be thou healed." He then commanded him to tell no one how his cure had been wrought, but to go and show himself to the priest, as the law commanded, and offer in return for his cure that which Moses had ordained.

11. But the leper did not keep the secret of his cure; it spread from town to town, and caused so intense an excitement that Our Lord was no longer able to enter any town publicly, but had to remain in the open country, whither the people flocked from all parts.

12. After a time, Our Lord returned to Capharnaum, where He found numbers of Scribes and Pharisees from Jerusalem and other parts of Judea, gathered, along with many of Galilee, in anticipation of His coming. As soon as He arrived, they hastened along with the people to the house where He was, and found Him teaching as usual.

13. Suddenly, in the midst of Our Lord's discourse, hands were seen making an opening in the ceiling, and then four men proceeded to let down at Our Saviour's feet, a pallet on which lay a sick man.

14. They had in vain tried to effect an entrance in the usual manner, owing to the immense crowds, so as a last resource, had lifted their burden to the low flat roof, which was only one

---

9. Who sought Him in a town of Galilee? 10. Did Our Lord hear his prayer? 11. Did the leper keep the secret of his cure? 12. Who were awaiting Our Lord's return at Capharnaum? 13. What was seen suddenly above? 14. Why did they effect an entrance in this way?

story in height, and made an opening in the earthen tiling of which it was composed.

10. This deed, more eloquent than any words, of their faith, touched Our Lord's heart, and He said to the sufferer, "My son, take courage; thy sins are forgiven thee." His speech scandalized the Scribes and Pharisees who were present, and they said, "What does this man mean to say? He is blaspheming. Who can forgive sins except God?"

11. Our Lord answered, "Why do you think evil things in your hearts? What is easier to say to a paralytic; 'Thy sins are forgiven thee,' or 'Rise up; take thy bed and go into thy house.'" But they returned no answer, for they were mistrustful as to the extent of His power, and feared to be brought to confusion.

12. But Our Lord replied to their thoughts, "Now that you may know the Son of Man has power to remit sins, 'I say to thee,' He said, turning to the paralytic, 'Arise, take up thy bed, and go into thy house.'"

13. The sick man at once arose, took up his pallet, threaded his way through the excited throngs and returned home, glorifying God. Those who had witnessed the miracle were at first dumb with amazement, but presently cried out, "We have seen marvellous things to-day."

14. Shortly after this miracle, Our Lord added another disciple to his little band. This was Lēvi, the publican, one of a class detested by the Jews, as the collectors of the Roman tax. He was seated as usual, in his toll office, in Capharnaum, when Our Lord said to him, "Follow me." He at once arose, left all and followed Christ, and took the name of Matthew.

15. The season of the Pasch again drew nigh, and Our Lord interrupted His Mission in Galilee, and, joining one of the caravans of pilgrims, ascended to Jerusalem, in order that He might once again offer to the ungrateful city the Salvation it had disdained.

---

10. Was Our Lord moved? 11. What did Our Lord answer? 12. Did He rebuke their thoughts? 13. Did it so happen? 14. What new disciple did Our Lord now choose? 15. Whither did He now go?

CHRIST HEALS THE PARALYTIC.

16. Now there was at Jerusalem, hard by the gate of the Flocks, a pool called Bĕ thes'da, or "the House of Mercy;" for at certain times an Angel of the Lord descended and stirred the waters, and the first to enter after he had moved them, was cured of whatsoever malady he was suffering from.

17. An immense number of stricken ones lay about the shore of the pool. Among them was a man who had waited for thirty-nine years to be dipped into the healing waters, but had been each time forestalled. He was now perceived by Our Lord Who had at once sought this scene of suffering.

18. "Dost thou wish to be cured?" Our Lord said to Him. He answered, "Lord, I have no one to carry me to the pool when the water is troubled, and the moment I reach there another goes down ahead of me." Our Lord answered, "Arise, take up thy bed and walk."

19. The poor man at once arose, took up his rug and walked. It was the Sabbath, a day on which it was not lawful to carry one's bed. The newly-cured man had not gone far, therefore, when he was met by some of the Pharisees who were horrified at his violation of the holy repose.

20. "He who cured me, told me Himself, 'Take up thy bed and walk,'" pleaded the poor man in excuse. "Who is the man?" they sternly demanded in answer, "who said to thee 'take up thy bed and walk?'" The man replied that he did not know his healer, but they felt sure that it was Christ, and at once sought Him to reproach Him for having broken the Sabbath.

21. But what was their astonishment when He openly declared to them that as He was the Son of God, He had all power over the Sabbath; and that, being God even as His Father, He could not know any surcease of activity. "My Father ceaseth not to work," He said, "and I work likewise."

22. He moreover, declared that He possessed three attri-

---

16. What was the pool of Bethesda? 17. Who lay about the pool? 18. Relate Our Lord's conversation with the cripple. 19. Did he obey? 20. Relate his conversation with the Pharisees. 21. What astonishing reply did Our Lord make? 22. What else did He declare?

butes of the Godhead—the power of remitting sin, the power of judging, and the power of raising up all flesh from the grave unto life at the last day.

23. In support of His Divinity, Our Lord appealed to three witnesses, His Miracles, the unmistakable sign of His Mission, the Voice of His Father, which at the Jordan, had proclaimed Him His Well-Beloved Son, and finally, the authority of the Scriptures.

24. "Search them," He said, "since you think you find eternal life therein; they themselves give testimony of Me, and you will not come to Me that you may have life!

25. "I know you; I know that you have not the love of God in you. I am come in the Name of My Father, and you receive Me not. Let another come in his own name, him you will receive."

CHAPTER IX.

OUR LORD CHOOSES THE APOSTLES.—THE SERMON ON THE MOUNT.

1. BY His positive declaration that He was the Son of God, equal to His Father, Our Lord had aroused the jealous fears of the members of the Sanhedrin, and they took counsel together, "as to what they might do to Jesus," who had quitted Judea, and gone back to Galilee, where their authority was more limited.

2. They resolved to appeal to the jealousy of Herod Antipas, and succeeded so well that Our Lord judged it prudent to cross to the other side of Lake of Genesareth, close to the domain of Philip. This was not Herod Philip, whose wife, Herodias, Herod Antipas had wedded, but another son of Herod the Great, and a just and humane prince.

---

23. What witnesses did He bring to prove His Divinity? 24. What did He say in regard to the Scriptures? 25. Continue.
1. What had Our Lord aroused in the Sanhedrin? 2. How did they effect their purpose?

3. Here Our Lord remained till the storm had blown over, and Herod had relapsed into his old indolence, and become too engrossed in the pursuit of pleasure to heed His movements. He then began to teach openly once more, and from a boat on the lake preached to vast crowds on the shore.

4. The time had now come when Our Lord was to choose the Twelve Apostles who were to be the base of His Great Work—that Church which was to be seen of all men, and to prevail over the gates of Hell. As was usual with Him before taking any important step, Our Lord retired and passed the night previous to it in prayer.

5. Tradition fixes as the scene of Our Lord's communing with His Heavenly Father, the lonely heights of a mountain, standing between the cities of Capharnaum and Tiberias. In the pale light of the dawn Christ arose, and going to where His disciples were slumbering, a short distance away, "He chose from among them twelve, to whom He gave the name of Apostles."

6. The Twelve Apostles were Peter, Andrew, James the Greater, John, Philip, Bartholomew, Thomas, Matthew, Leb'be-us or Thad'-de us, Simon the Zealot, James the Less, and Judas Is-kar'-i oth.

7. St. Peter, the head of the Apostolic College, and St. Andrew, were the sons of Jonas; St. James the Greater and St. John the Evangelist, were the sons of Zebedee, and on account of their great generous hearts and burning zeal, received from Our Lord the name of Boanerges (Bŏ-nerj'-es) or Sons of Thunder.

8. St. Bartholomew was Nathaniel, who had come from under the fig-tree to join Our Lord; St. Matthew was Levi the Publican; St. James the Less and St. Jude (Leb' beus or Thaddeus) were cousins of Our Lord; St. Thomas and St. Simon

---

3. Did He soon resume His ministry? 4. What great steps did Our Lord now take? 5. What spot is supposed to have been the scene of His prayer? 6. Name the twelve apostles. 7. Who were Sts. Peter, Andrew, James the Greater, and John the Evangelist? 8. Who were the others?

the Zealot, were Galileans. Judas, of the town of Kerioth, was the only one from Judea.

9. On the same mount where He had chosen the Apostles, Our Lord soon after delivered that wonderful sermon which is the completest expression of Christianity, and the summary of the Gospel. His hearers heard Him with the deepest surprise, for His words were opposed to every prejudice of the Jews.

10. They had always believed that the godly man is always blessed with temporal prosperity, and that sorrow and trouble were tokens of God's wrath. Hence, in spite of the spirit of charity breathed by the Law of Moses, they had scorned poverty, and demeaned themselves harshly to the sick and unfortunate, whom they regarded as sinners suffering under a just punishment.

11. How different from this was the teaching of Christ! And what joy must have filled those wretched and weary souls in the throng whose life had been a struggle, who had groaned under oppression, or panted under injustice, when they heard the Great Teacher utter the Beatitudes:

12. 1. "Blessed are the poor in spirit, because to them belongeth the Kingdom of God." That is, blessed are the rich who use wealth not for selfish ends, but to relieve suffering, and blessed are the poor who murmur not and envy not, but are resigned to God's will.

13. 2. "Blessed are those who weep, because they shall be comforted. 3. Blessed are the meek, because they shall possess the land. 4. Blessed are they that hunger and thirst after justice, because they shall have their fill. 5. Blessed are the merciful, because they shall obtain mercy. 6. Blessed are the peacemakers, because they shall be called the children of God. 7. Blessed are they who are pure of heart, because they shall

---

9. What did Our Lord deliver on this mount? 10. What had the Jews believed in regard to temporal prosperity? 11. How did the throng regard Christ's teaching? 12. What is the first Beatitude? 13. The second Beatitude? The third? The fourth? The fifth? The sixth? The seventh? The eighth?

see God. 8. Blessed are they who suffer persecution for justice's sake, for the Kingdom of Heaven is theirs."

14. In order to prevent the people from thinking that because He had swept away many of their illusions, He intended to revolutionize all Israel, Our Lord now went on to say that He had come, not to abolish the Law of Moses, but to elevate it to the point of perfection.

15. Moses had said, "Thou shalt not kill," Jesus would forbid even angry words and feelings of hatred. Moses denounced adultery; Christ condemned even an evil thought. Moses tolerated divorce, "because of the hardness of their hearts;" Christ restored marriage to its primitive sanctity.

16. Moses had forbidden perjury; Christ forbade swearing, saying, "Let your speech be, 'This is so,' 'That is not so,' 'Yes,' 'No.' Everything which is more than this comes from an evil source."

17. Moses had decreed the law of justice which demanded an eye for an eye, a tooth for a tooth. Christ preached the law of charity: "If any one strike you on the right cheek, turn to him the other." He did not mean that we should follow this precept literally, but merely inculcated a willingness to endure our wrongs for the love of God.

18. Our Lord next attacked the most deeply rooted Jewish prejudice of all. Knowing the weakness of his people, Moses had prohibited all intercourse with idolaters; the Jewish Doctors had turned this precaution into an odious precept to look upon every foreigner as an enemy, a teaching Our Lord now endeavored to supplant with that of charity.

19. "Love your enemies," He said, "do good to those that hate you; pray for those that maltreat and slander you, in order that you may be the children of your Heavenly Father, who makes His sun to rise upon the good and upon the bad, and sends down rain upon the just and the unjust.

---

14. What did Our Lord say in regard to the Law of Moses? 15. How did Our Lord perfect the Law in regard to murder and adultery? 16. In regard to perjury? 17. In regard to the stern law of Jewish justice? 18. What did Our Lord next attack? 19. Repeat His words.

20. "For if you love those that love you, what reward shall you have? Do not the publicans as much? And if you greet your brethren only, what more do you do? Do not Pagans the same? Be you therefore perfect, as your Heavenly Father is perfect."

21. Christ then denounced the proud and hypocritical Pharisees, who made a parade of their alms-giving, disfigured their faces that men might think they were fasting, and prayed with a loud voice in the synagogues and on the corners of the streets.

22. "Do not imitate them," said Our Lord, "for your Father knows of what you have need before you ask it of Him. Pray thus: Our Father, Who art in Heaven, hallowed be Thy Name; Thy Kingdom come; Thy Will be done on earth as it is in Heaven; give us this day our daily bread; forgive us our trespasses, as we forgive them that trespass against us; and lead us not into temptation, but deliver us from evil."

23. By this perfect prayer, Our Lord showed to what a height He would raise the carnal sons of Israel. Instead of looking for the reward of their virtue here below, they were to fix their thoughts on the things of eternity.

24. Their fasting and prayer were to be done in a humble, mortified spirit; their alms given in secret; they were no longer to share their thoughts between God and Mammon, but while they toiled for their daily bread, they were to feel no anxiety, no clinging to the treasures which rust corrodes, and thieves steal, but place all their trust in the Providence of their Father.

25. "Be not harassed about your life, what to eat and what to drink, nor for your body, as to how you shall be clothed. Is not the life more than the food, and the body more than the raiment? Behold the fowls of the air, for they sow not,

---

20. What did Our Lord say in regard to those who love only those that love them? 21. Did He denounce the Pharisees? 22. How did He teach them to pray? 23. What did Christ show by this prayer? 24. Continue. 25. Repeat Our Lord's words as to the needlessness of anxiety as to food and drink.

neither do they reap, nor gather into barns; yet your Heavenly Father feedeth them.

26. "Why are you solicitous as to your raiment? 'Consider the lilies of the field, how they grow; they labor not, neither do they spin. And I say to you that not even Solomon in all his glory was arrayed like one of these.'

27. "Now if God so clothe the grass of the field, which to-day is, and to-morrow will be cast into the oven, how much more shall He do unto you, O ye of little faith?

28. "Be not solicitous, therefore, saying, 'What shall we eat?' or 'What shall we drink?' or 'Wherewith shall we be clothed?' For after all these things do the heathens seek. For your Father knows you have need of all these things. Seek ye, therefore, first the Kingdom of God and His justice, and all these things shall be added unto you."

29. Our Lord also inculcated charity towards our neighbor: "Judge not and you shall not be judged, for with what judgment you have judged, you shall be judged, and with what measure you have measured, it shall be measured to you again.

30. "Why seest thou a mote in thy brother's eye, and seest not a beam in thy own eye? Hypocrite, cast out first the beam out of thine own eye, and then shalt thou see to cast out the mote out of thy brother's eye.

31. "All things, therefore, whatsoever you would that men should do to you, do you also to them; for this is the Law and the Prophets." Thus, in this single precept does Our Lord sum up our duty to our neighbor.

32. Our Lord now changes the tone of His discourse to that of warning. He tells His hearers of the difficulty of salvation; that the Kingdom of Heaven is taken only by violence; and warns them to look on it as a narrow gate through which it is not easy to enter and which it is very easy to miss.

---

26. As to raiment. 27. What did He tell them to conclude from this? 28. On what grounds did Our Lord again forbid all solicitude for earthly needs? 29. How did He inculcate charity towards our neighbor? 30. What of the mote and the beam? 31. How did Our Lord sum up our duty to our neighbor? 32. What tone did Christ's sermon now take?

33. "Enter ye in at the narrow gate," He says, "for wide is the gate and broad is the way that leadeth to destruction. Narrow is the gate and straight is the way that leadeth to eternal life, and few are those who find it."

34. Our Lord goes on to speak of the false teachers; the prophets who come in the clothing of sheep, but who are in reality wolves; and of His false disciples. "All those who say Lord! Lord! shall not for that reason enter into the kingdom," He says, "but he who doeth the will of My Father."

35. Our Lord concluded His marvellous discourse with a striking figure, which was given rise to by the practice which foolish men in the countries of the East are often betrayed into, of building in the dry bed of mountain torrents, where the stones are ready to the hand, instead of taking the trouble to dig the foundations deep and solid among the high rocks.

36. "Whosoever," said the Lord, "hears these, my words, and puts them in practice, I will show you to whom he is like. He is like to a man who builded a house, and having dug deep beforehand, sets its foundations upon the rock.

37. "And the rains fall, the floods come, the winds blow and beat about this house; but it has not fallen because it is founded on the rock.

38. "And he who hears these words which I speak, and does not put them in practice, is like the foolish man who has built his house on the sand. The rain falls, the floods come, the winds blow and beat about this house and it has fallen, and its ruin has been great."

---

33. Repeat the Saviour's words in reference to the narrow gate. 34. What does Our Lord say of the false prophets and of His false disciples? 35. How did Our Lord conclude His discourse? 36. Whom did Our Lord declare the man who heard His words and put them in practice to resemble? 37. What happened in time to this man's house? 38. Whom did Christ declare the man who heard his words and did not practice them, to resemble?

CHAPTER X.

JESUS HEALS THE ROMAN CENTURION'S SERVANT.—RESTORES THE WIDOW'S SON OF NAIM TO LIFE.—ANSWERS JOHN THE BAPTIST'S MESSENGERS.—FORGIVES THE SINS OF MARY MAGDALEN.

1. ACCOMPANIED by a great concourse, Jesus descended the mountain and returned to Capharnaum where He was to experience the joy of receiving the first Pagan or Gentile—one of the noblest souls of whom the Gospel makes mention.

2. He was one of Rome's centurions, in command of the legions which that empire kept stationed on the borders of the lake of Genesareth, for although Galilee was under Herod's rule, it was also under the vigilant overlordship of Rome, which was too well aware of Capharnaum's importance to leave it ungarrisoned.

3. This centurion was upright and pure of heart, and had been touched by the morality of the Jewish religion, to which he had borne witness by having a synagogue built in the town. He was also distinguished for sentiments of humanity rare in that age, for at the time of Our Lord's coming, he was mourning over an old servant who lay "sick unto death."

4. In his grief he learned of the entrance of Jesus into the city, but, not daring to hope that Israel's great prophet would listen to him, a Pagan, he went to the elders of Capharnaum and besought them to intercede for him.

5. Mindful of their debt of gratitude, they went to Our Lord and said to Him, "This man deserves that Thou shouldst assist him, for he loves our nation and he has built us a synagogue." Our Lord replied: "I will go and I will heal him."

6. The elders, therefore, departed and informed the cen-

---

1. What joy was awaiting Our Lord at Capharnaum? 2. Who was he? 3. What was the character of the centurion? 4. Did he seek the assistance of Christ? 5. Were the elders successful in their mission? 6. Continue.

turion that Our Lord was coming. The Roman's surprise was great, for he had never expected to receive Him in his house, knowing that in the eyes of the Pharisees the Jew who entered a heathen's dwelling was defiled.

7. Unwilling that the Great Prophet should incur such disgrace, the centurion hastened to meet Him and said to Him, "Lord, I am not worthy Thou shouldst enter under my roof, but say only one word and my servant shall be healed." His words filled Jesus with joy, and turning to the multitude that followed Him, He said, "Amen, I have not found so great faith even in Israel."

8. Such praise as this, which placed the heathen above the sons of Abraham, gave rise to bitter murmurings among the throng, who could not bear the thought of the Gentiles sharing in the reign of the Messiah. It may have been too, that Our Lord caught sight of some of the spies of the Sanhedrin; at all events, He uttered these terrible words:

9. "I say to you that many shall come from the East and the West, and shall sit down with Abraham, Isaac, and Jacob, in the Kingdom of Heaven. But the children of the kingdom shall be cast out into extreme darkness, where there shall be weeping and gnashing of teeth."

10. He then turned to the centurion, and said to him, "Go, and as thou hast believed, so be it done to thee." And the servant was healed at the same hour. The centurion serves all ages, as the model of Christians who seek the Lord, and the Church ordains that all who approach the Holy Table of the Eucharist, shall do so with his words on their lips.

11. On the day following this miracle, Our Lord went from Capharnaum to Na'im, which was about nine leagues distant, two miles south of Mount Tabor. It was the most glorious period of His ministry, and he was attended with an eager concourse of faithful souls.

---

7. What did the centurion do to avert this? 8. What effect had this praise? 9. Repeat Our Saviour's words. 10. What did He say to the centurion, and what does the latter serve as? 11. To what city did He go the next day?

THE DESCENT FROM THE CROSS.

12. As He was ascending the steep pathway which led to the gates of Naim, He met a funeral procession. According to the custom of the East, the body, anointed with perfumes, and swathed in linen bands, was borne on a litter; at its head marched the flute players, filling the air with plaintive notes; and it was followed by wailing hired mourners.

13. The chief mourner, however, was silent; her grief was too deep for tears. "For the dead man was his mother's only son, and she was a widow." The divine heart of Jesus was moved to compassion at the sight, and He said to her, "Weep not."

14. As He spoke, He touched the bier, and its bearers, understanding this gesture, stood still. The flutes were silent; the voices of the wailing women were still, a hush fell on the throng. Then in the silence Our Saviour's voice was heard, saying, "Young man, I say to thee, arise."

15. At this command from the Master of life and death, the dead man arose and began to speak. And the Saviour restored him to his mother. And the people glorified God, exclaiming, "A great prophet has risen up among us, and God hath visited His people."

16. John the Baptist had now been in prison for six months. He was permitted, however, to see his disciples, who kept him informed of the ministry of Christ. He now wished to make over these disciples to His Master, and to this end sent two of them formally to the Saviour, to ask, "Art Thou He that art to come, or are we to await another?"

17. Our Saviour permitted these envoys to witness several striking miracles which He performed, and then said, "Go, and report to John what you have seen. The blind see, the lame walk, the lepers are cleansed, the deaf hear, the dead rise again, and to the poor the gospel is preached, and blessed is he that shall not be scandalized in me."

18. During Our Lord's stay in Naim, a Pharisee named

---

12. What did He meet? 13. What of the chief mourner? 14. Describe the scene. 15. What took place? 16. What did John the Baptist do at this time? 17. What did Our Saviour answer? 18. Who invited Our Lord to a banquet in Naim?

Simon, influenced by curiosity, and the desire of entertaining a celebrated person, invited Him to a banquet. Pride, however, or the fear of his sect, prevented him from observing the usual ceremonies with which in the East, a guest is always received.

19. He therefore permitted the Saviour to enter his dwelling without seeing that His feet were bathed, or saluting Him with a kiss on the cheek, or offering Him perfumes for His hair. Our Lord took no notice of this neglect, however, but entered the banquet hall, and took His place at table.

20. According to the fashion introduced from Greece and Rome, the guests removed their sandals, and reclined on couches which were ranged about the table, with the feet extending to the outer circle. It was customary at these formal banquets for the hall to be thrown open, and for a crowd of onlookers to surround the guests with perfect freedom.

21. Among the crowd who thus gained access, was a woman who was well known for her sinful life. She had been drawn thither by a rumor of Christ's presence, and now stood with a vase of costly perfume in her hand, close to Him, eagerly drinking in His words.

22. Her feelings soon grew too great to be concealed; falling on her knees, she humbly bathed the Master's feet with her tears, then drying them with her beautiful hair, broke over them the fragile alabaster vase, and covered them with its precious, fragrant ointment.

23. Simon viewed her proceeding with haughty disgust. To him she was the vilest of vile creatures, against whom even to brush his garments, would be a defilement. He could only conclude that Jesus did not know her character, and argued to himself, "If this man were really a prophet, he would know that this woman is a sinner."

24. The Divine eyes of Jesus, on the contrary, saw in the poor outcast, torn by the first, fierce, saving pangs of repent-

---

19. How did Simon receive Our Lord? 20. How did the guests arrange themselves at table? 21. Who was among the crowd? 22. What effect had Our Lord's words on her? 23. What feeling did this rouse in Simon? 24. What did Our Lord see in her?

ance, a soul whom He had created, and whom He was to ransom with His blood. He read the thoughts of His proud, self-righteous host and answered them.

25. "Simon," He said, turning to him, "I have somewhat to say to thee." The Pharisee answered, "Master, say it." Our Lord then continued. "A creditor had two debtors; one owed him five hundred pence, and the other fifty. As they had not the wherewithal to pay him, he remitted each one's debt. Which of the two now loves him the most?"

26. Simon, not seeing what Our Lord desired to prove from this, answered, "Undoubtedly it would be he to whom he remitted the greater amount." "Thou hast judged rightly," answered Christ, then pointing to the sinner at his feet, He continued, "Simon, dost thou see this woman?"

27. "I entered thy dwelling; thou gavest Me no water for My Feet, but she has indeed washed My Feet with her tears, and has wiped them with her hair. Thou gavest me no kiss, while she, ever since I entered here, has not ceased to kiss My Feet.

28. "Thou hast not anointed My Head with oil, but she indeed has bathed My feet with ointments. And so, for this reason, I say to thee, many sins shall be remitted unto her, because she has loved much. But he to whom less is remitted, loves the less."

29. Then turning to the poor sinful woman at His Feet, who was shedding those bitter, burning tears which St. Augustine calls the heart's blood, He looked at her with infinite compassion, and uttered the consoling words, a proof of the miracle wrought by grace in her guilty soul; "Thy sins are forgiven thee. Thy faith hath made thee safe. Go in peace."

---

25. How did He illustrate this to Simon? 26. Relate Simon's answer and Our Lord's reply. 27. What did Our Lord say in regard to Simon's neglect of the duties of hospitality? 28. Continue. 29. What did he say to Magdalen?

CHAPTER XI.

OUR LORD RESTORES THE DEAF AND DUMB MAN.—RELATES THE PARABLES OF THE SOWER AND THE COCKLE.

1. THE public Life of Our Lord may be divided into two periods; one in which the Scribes and Pharisees did not openly attack Him; and a second, during which they exerted all their power to interfere with His mission.

2. The effect of their efforts became apparent, during a second journey which Our Lord began about this time, through the towns and hamlets of Galilee, when the simple, generous faith which had accepted His miracles, began to give place to the carping, suspicious spirit, to which their slanders gave rise.

3. One day, when He was preaching in Capharnaum, there was brought to Him a man, blind and dumb, who was possessed by a devil. Our Lord cured him, and the people, filled with admiration, cried out, "Is not this the Son of David?"

4. Some Scribes from Jerusalem, who were present, at once set to work to quench this ardor, and poison the minds of the beholders, by declaring that Our Lord cast out devils by Beelzebub, the prince of devils.

5. Our Lord answered, "How can Satan cast out Satan? If a kingdom be divided against itself, that kingdom cannot stand. But if Satan rise up against himself, he is divided and cannot stand, but hath an end. But if I, by the Spirit of God, cast out devils, then is the kingdom of God come upon you."

6. Our Lord concluded by calling His faithful followers about Him. "Whoever is not with me," He said, "is against me, and whoever gathereth not with me, scattereth."

7. His enemies, undaunted by this rebuke, proceeded to charge Our Lord with having "an unclean spirit." Whether

---

1. Into what may the public Life of Our Lord be divided? 2. When did the effect of their efforts become apparent? 3. What miracle did He perform at this time? 4. What did the Scribes suggest to the people? 5. Repeat Our Lord's answer. 6. How did He conclude? 7. What new charge did His enemies make?

this was because of His contempt for the Pharisaic ablutions, which He, on several occasions, dispensed with, or because of His tenderness for sinners, is not known, but it roused the Divine wrath, and called from Him a dreadful warning.

8. "I say unto you, every sin, every blasphemy, shall be forgiven men, but blasphemy against the Holy Spirit shall not be forgiven. And whosoever shall have spoken against the Son of Man, it shall be forgiven him; but the man who has spoken against the Holy Ghost, shall not be forgiven, either in this world, or in the other."

9. From this time Our Lord abandoned His former direct and simple style of teaching, and presented His doctrine in parables, according to the custom of the Scribes themselves. This form of instruction was peculiarly suited to the Oriental genius, which delights in allegory, and also served to baffle His enemies, and thus gain the time necessary for the establishment of His Church.

10. Accordingly, one day, when He sat in a boat on the Lake of Genesareth, teaching the crowds on the beach, the sight of the familiar harvest lands sloping up from the water's edge, no doubt, caused Him to make use of the well-known scene of the sowing of the seed, as a means of instruction.

11. "The sower," He said, "went out to sow, and while he was sowing, some grains fell into the roadway, and the birds of the air devoured them.

12. "Other seed fell on stony ground, where there was not much earth, and it sprang up at once, but when the sun was up, as it had no roots, it withered away. Still others fell among thistles, and the thistles grew up and choked them.

13. "Others, finally fell in good earth, and bore fruit, some a hundred, others sixty, and others thirty fold. He that hath ears to hear, let him hear!"

---

8. Repeat His warning. 9. Under what form did Our Lord henceforth impart His instructions? 10. What no doubt caused Him to use the figure of the sower? 11. What happened to the grains in the roadway? 12. What of those which fell in stony ground, and among thistles? 13. Of those which fell in good earth?

14. There Our Lord stopped, leaving his listeners to fathom the meaning hidden beneath the parable. But it remained a riddle, not only to the Jews, who were strangers to His doctrine, but even to the twelve apostles, who pressed about Him, asking why He spoke in this way.

15. Our Lord answered that if He concealed the mysteries of the Kingdom of God under the form of an allegory, it was only that His enemies might behold without perceiving, might hear without understanding, and thus gain Him the time necessary for the development of His doctrine. He then expanded His meaning in the Parable.

16. "The seed," He said, "is the Word of God. It falls upon the wayside—that is, upon hearts as cold and hard as those worn, beaten pathways, which afford it no nourishment.

17. "It falls upon the rock, that is, upon light superficial souls, who afford it no root, so that the first wind of temptation causes it to wither. It falls amid thorns—that is, upon worldly hearts, where it is choked by earthly cares, and the deceitfulness of riches."

18. Lastly, it falls on "good ground, on hearts who hearken to the Word and keep it, and bring forth fruit, bearing thirty, sixty, and one hundred fold."

19. Such was the first picture of the Church drawn by its creator; a field wherein the heavenly seed is sown with exceeding plentifulness, but yet will bear no fruit, if man's evil passions place an obstacle in its way. Our Lord made this still more clear by the Parable of the Cockle.

20. "The Kingdom of Heaven," He said, "is like to a man that sowed good seed in his field. But while men were asleep, his enemy came, and oversowed cockle among the wheat, and went his way."

21. And when the blade was sprung up, and brought forth fruit, then appeared also the cockle. And the servants of the

---

14. Did Our Lord explain? 15. Relate His answer. 16. What class does the wayside signify in the gospel? 17. The rocks and the thorns? 18. The good ground? 19. What was this parable? 20. What happened after the man sowed his field? 21. What appeared with the fruit?

master of the house came and said to him, "Master, didst thou not sow good seed in thy field? Whence then, is this cockle?" The master answered, "An enemy hath done this."

22. The servant said, "Wilt thou that we go and gather it up?" But He said, "No, lest while you gather up the cockle you root up the wheat, also, with it. Let both grow until the harvest, and then I will say to the reapers, 'Gather up first the cockle and bind it in bundles to burn, but the wheat gather into My barn.'"

When His disciples begged Him to explain this parable, He told them that He, the Son of God, sows the good seed, and Satan the cockle. The wheat represents the children of God and the cockle those of the devil. The harvest time is the end of the world, and the reapers are the angels.

CHAPTER XII.

CHRIST STILLS THE STORM.—ATTENDS MATTHEW'S BANQUET.—CURES THE POSSESSED MEN.—HEALS THE DAUGHTER OF JAIRUS.

1. OUR LORD returned to His dwelling in Capharnaum after this discourse, but, finding that the people flocked thither in such numbers as to prevent all repose, He determined to cross the lake to the lonely highlands of Perea.

2. Accompanied by His apostles, He therefore went on board a boat and steered for the opposite shore. It was now night, and, worn out by the toils of the day, Our Lord seated Himself in the stern, and resting His head on the pilot's pillow, fell asleep.

3. All at once, however, there sprung up one of those violent storms which burst with surprising suddenness on the Lake of Genesareth. Its placid waters, but lately scarcely stirred by the gentle night breeze, had become fierce, seething billows,

---

22. Repeat the servant's conversation with His Master.
1. Why did Our Lord quit Capharnaum? 2. What did He do after going on board the boat? 3. What sprang up while Christ slumbered?

CHRIST STILLS THE STORM.

lashed by wild winds to a fury that threatened to destroy the frail bark.

4. For some time the apostles refrained from waking Our Lord, but at last their fear grew so great that they forgot all else and cried out "Master! Master! save us, we perish!" Jesus awoke, but His first care was to calm their hearts. "Why are you fearful, O men of little faith?" He said.

5. Then He rebuked the winds and the sea, and there came a great calm. As the waves subsided, and the star-lit sky grew visible once more, the apostles saw how small indeed their faith had been to give way to terror when they bore Christ in their bark. But the sailors cried in awe, "What manner of man is this, for the winds and the sea obey Him?"

6. Our Lord did not find the repose He had hoped in Perea. Scarcely had He landed when piercing shrieks rent the air, as two frenzied creatures rushed to meet Him. They were possessed men who had taken refuge in the rock caverns among the cliffs on the shore which served as tombs.

7. Cowering in the dust before Him, they cried out, "What is there between us, Jesus, Son of the Most High? Art Thou come hither to torment us before the time?" Our Lord said to one of them, "Foul spirit, depart out of this man." It was loath to obey, and Our Lord added, "What is thy name?"

8. The fiend answered by the possessed man's mouth, "I am called Legion, because we are many." Then he besought Our Lord to permit them some refuge in the country-side and begged permission to enter into a herd of swine. Our Lord granted this and they at once took possession of the swine and bore ten thousand of them into the lake and drowned them.

9. Our Lord now entered into the territory of the Decapolis —that is ten cities which were Greek in origin and manners. Their inhabitants were devoted to earthly pleasures and had no desire to hear of the Kingdom of Heaven. They therefore

---

4. When did they awaken Our Lord? 5. What took place? 6. What happened when Our Lord landed in Perea? 7. What did they do? 8. What did the fiend answer? 9. What did the blinded inhabitants of the Decapolis request our Lord to do?

besought Jesus to depart from their coasts, and, yielding to their wishes, He re-embarked at once.

10. When He returned to Capharnaum, He was warmly received, and St. Matthew, the apostle, invited Him to a banquet which he gave in honor of his having been called by Our Saviour. As Matthew had been Levi, the Publican, his friends were, no doubt, also of this despised class, and it was soon noised about the town that Christ was feasting with Publicans.

11. Several of the Scribes and Pharisees at once hastened to the hall and were struck with horror at the sight. "How comes it," they said to the apostles, "that you and your master eat and drink with Publicans and sinners?" But Our Lord, Who heard their words, answered that He came to call, not the just, but sinners, to repentance.

12. While He was speaking, Jā'-i-rus, the chief of the synagogue in Capharnaum, rushed into the hall and fell at the feet of the Saviour in an agony of grief. "Lord," he said, "my little child, my only daughter, is dying,—but O come, lay Thy Hands upon her and she shall live."

13. Our Lord's compassionate Heart could not resist this appeal. He rose at once, and went with Jairus, followed by a surging crowd. In it was a woman who had been suffering from an issue of blood for twelve years and had spent all her fortune in fees to physicians, but vainly.

14. Her only hope was now in Jesus, but timidity prevented her from seeking His aid openly. But she thought to herself, "If I can but just touch His robe, I shall be healed." She therefore edged her way through the crowd, till she got close enough to Him to seize with her wasted fingers, the tassel of His mantle.

15. Her faith was instantly rewarded; she was healed. But Our Lord, who felt that power had gone out from Him turned round and asked, "Who touched my garment?"

---

10. Who gave a banquet after Our Lord's return to Capharnaum? 11. What did the Scribes and Pharisees say? 12. Who rushed into the room? 13. Did Our Lord go with him? 14. What kept her from seeking Our Lord's aid openly? 15. Was her faith rewarded?

16. The woman, seeing that He knew all, fell at His feet, and confessed the reason why she had touched Him, and the cure. Our Lord, who had merely required this acknowledgment, said gently, "Daughter, go in peace; thy faith hath made thee whole."

17. A messenger now came to Jairus to say, "Trouble the Master no longer. Thy daughter is dead." The father bent in speechless sorrow at the news, but Our Lord said to him, "Do not fear; only believe; she shall be saved." And He went on towards the house.

18. When He arrived there, He found the mourners already gathered within the darkened death-chamber, where the wails of the women mingled with the piercing music of the flutes. Our Lord said to them, "Weep not, the child is not dead, but sleepeth." He then bade all leave the room, save the child's parents, and Peter, James and John.

19. Then He approached the child, and taking her hand in His, said to her, "My child, arise!" And at once the little maid arose, and started to run, in high glee, for she was only twelve years old. The parents were beside themselves with joy, and Our Lord had to remind them to give her something to eat.

20. Our Lord endeavored to avoid the first outburst of excitement which the miracle aroused, by remaining in the house till the people without had dispersed; but "the fame of it was noised abroad throughout the whole country side."

---

16. Did the woman confess? 17. What news did a messenger bring Jairus? 18. Whom did Our Lord find there? 19. What did He then do? 20. Did the fame of this miracle spread?

CHAPTER XIII.

THE MISSION OF THE APOSTLES.—MARTYRDOM OF JOHN THE BAPTIST.—MIRACLE OF THE LOAVES AND FISHES.—CHRIST WALKS ON THE WATERS.

1. WHEN Our Lord left the mansion of Jairus, it was to begin His third and last mission in Galilee. Again He passed through every city and hamlet, preaching the Word of Life, and thus once again entered Nazareth, His old home.

2. But the blinded Nazarenes received Him no better now than at His first visit, and seeing that he could do them no good, Our Lord said farewell to the ungrateful city, and passed to more promising fields, where the harvest was great.

3. Our Lord, now taking compassion on the great multitude of the lost sheep of Israel, determined to associate His apostles with Himself in the preaching of the Word to them. So He called them about Him, and giving them the power to heal the sick, and cast out devils, sent them out, two by two, to preach the Kingdom of God.

4. A holy indifference to earthly cares was to be the peculiar feature of their ministry. Christ told them they must be ready to set out at all times, without making any preparations for the journey, or taking anything with them.

5. "When you go into a house," Our Lord said to them, "say, peace be to this house. And if the house be worthy, your peace shall come upon it; but if it be not worthy, your peace shall return to you.

6. "And whosoever shall not receive you, going forth out of house or city, shake off its dust from your feet. Amen, I say

---

1. Whither did Our Lord go after leaving the mansion of Jairus? 2. Did they receive Him any better? 3. Whom did Our Lord now send to preach the Word? 4. What did he tell them about their ministry? 5. What did Christ bid them do when they entered a house? 6. What dreadful doom did Christ pronounce on those who would not receive His apostles?

to you, it shall be more tolerable for the land of Sodom and Gomorrah in the day of judgment, than for that city.

7. "Behold I send you as sheep in the midst of wolves. Be you therefore, wise as serpents, and simple as doves. Beware of men, for they will deliver you up in councils, and they will scourge you in synagogues. And you shall be brought before governors, and before kings for My sake.

8. "The disciple is not above his Master, nor the servant above his lord. Fear not those that kill the body, and cannot kill the soul, but rather fear Him that can destroy body and soul in hell.

9. "Whosoever, therefore, shall confess me before men, I will also confess him before my Father, who is in Heaven. But whosoever shall deny me before men, I will also deny him before my Father, who is in Heaven.

10. "He that loveth father or mother more than Me, is not worthy of Me. And he that loveth son or daughter more than Me is not worthy of Me. And he that taketh not up his cross and followeth Me is not worthy of Me.

11. "He that findeth his life shall lose it, and he that loseth his life for My sake, shall find it. He that receiveth you, receiveth Me, and he that receiveth Me, Him that sent Me.

12. "And whosoever shall give to drink, to one of these little ones, only in the name of a disciple, Amen, I say to thee, he shall not lose his reward." The apostles then departed on their mission.

13. Our Lord continued to preach, as usual, in the cities of the lake country, until he heard of the death of John the Baptist. This had been brought to pass by Herodias, the wicked wife of Herod Antipas, while the latter was keeping high festival in honor of his birthday at Macheronte (mak-e-ron' tä) where the Precursor was imprisoned.

---

7. What persecutions did He predict for them? 8. What did He say of disciples and their master? 9. What promise did He make to them who confessed, and to those who denied Him? 10. Whom did He declare were not worthy of Him? 11. Of him who lost his life for His sake? 12. Of him who gave a cup of cold water in the name of even His disciple? 13. What did Our Lord hear of?

14. One of the features of the entertainment was a dance, in which Salome (sa-lōm'-ā), a daughter of Herodias by her former marriage, took part, and so charmed Herod Antipas with her grace and beauty, that he swore to give her whatever she should ask for, even to half of his kingdom.

15. Prompted by her wicked mother, the royal dancer demanded the head of John the Baptist. Her words struck Herod with consternation, but vanity made him abide by his oath. He gave the fatal order, and in a few moments the bleeding head of St. John the Baptist was brought to her on a large dish or charger.

16. But from that hour Herod knew no peace. Remorse made him suspicious and fearful, and when a short time later, new miracles of Jesus occasioned new outbursts of excitement among the people, the tyrant's shaken mind, forgetting all he had heard of the fame of Christ, conceived the idea that He was the Baptist, risen from the dead.

17. In vain those about the wretched tetrarch told him the truth; his frenzy of fear grew no less, and Our Lord therefore decided to retire to the domain of Philip, till the storm should pass. So He said to the Twelve Apostles who had by this time returned, "Let us go apart into some desert place and rest a little."

18. They therefore crossed the Lake of Genesareth and went to a wild and solitary place. But an immense multitude which was gathering to go up to Jerusalem for the Pasch, had caught sight of Christ as He landed, and now followed Him thither.

19. At the sight of these "sheep without a shepherd, Our Lord forgot His weariness and spoke to them of the Kingdom of God and healed all their sick." While He was still ministering to them the sun sank, and His disciples, fearing that the swiftly-following night of the Orient would surprise the throng in the wilderness, besought Him to dismiss them.

---

14. Who took part in the dance? 15. What did the princess ask for? 16. What did Herod's remorse lead him to imagine? 17. What did Our Lord decide to do? 18. Whom did they find on the other side of the lake? 19. How did Our Lord receive them?

CHRIST WALKS ON THE WATER.

20. "This place is a desert," they said, "and the hour is late; send away the people that they may find food and lodging in the nearest farm-houses and villages." But Our Lord answered, "They have no need to go, do you yourselves give them to eat."

21. He then inquired how much bread they had. Andrew replied that there were five loaves and two fishes. Our Lord said, "Bring them to me and bid the men sit down." Accordingly, the multitude, numbering five thousand, seated themselves on the grass.

22. Then Our Lord took the loaves and fishes, and, looking up to heaven, blessed them and gave to His apostles to distribute among the people. And when they were satisfied, Our Lord bade the apostles gather up the fragments lest they be wasted. They did so, and filled twelve baskets with them.

23. At this splendid miracle, the enthusiasm of the people rose to the highest pitch, and they began to plan to carry Him up to Jerusalem with them and make Him king. Our Lord therefore bade His apostles set sail at once for Capharnaum, then profited by the shades of night, to retire to the lonely heights of a mountain to pray.

24. Meanwhile, a tempest had burst over the lake. In vain the apostles rowed with all their strength, the fierce gale carried their boat out of its course and they made no progress. At length about the first watch of the night, their weary eyes beheld the Master walking towards them on the troubled waters.

25. At first they thought it was a phantom which they beheld and cried out in terror. But at once the calm voice which they knew so well said, "Fear not, it is I." And Peter, full of impetuous faith, cried out, "Lord, if it be Thee, bid me come to Thee upon the waters."

26. "Come," answered Our Lord. At once Peter sprang

---

20. Relate their speech to Our Lord and His reply. 21. Continue. 22. What did Christ do with the loaves and fishes? 23. What did this miracle rouse in the people? 24. How did it fare with the apostles, meanwhile? 25. What did they think at first? 26. What happened to Peter?

from the vessel's side, and, sustained by faith, trod the raging waters as firmly as if they had been the earth. But presently the fury of the tempest dismayed him; he gave way to terror and began to sink.

27. "Lord, save me," he cried. Our Lord held out His hand and sustained him, saying, "O thou of little faith, why hast thou doubted?" Then He entered the ship and at once the tempest stilled, and the little bark sped swiftly to the port of Capharnaum.

CHAPTER XIV.

CHRIST REVEALS THE MYSTERY OF THE EUCHARIST.—HEALS THE WOMAN OF CHANAAN'S DAUGHTER.—PETER PROCLAIMS THE DIVINITY OF CHRIST.

1. On the following morning great numbers of those who had been fed with the loaves and fishes returned to Capharnaum and sought Our Lord as He was teaching in the synagogue. But Jesus, who knew they were seeking Him for earthly goods, bade them, "toil not for the food that perisheth, but for that which is eternal life."

2. They answered, "Lord give us always this Bread." Christ answered, "It is I, I am the very Bread of life. He who comes to me shall never hunger, and he who believes in me shall never thirst. I am the living Bread which came down from heaven.

3. "If any man eat of this Bread, he shall live forever. The Bread which I give is My Flesh for the life of the world."

4. At these words an audible murmur of disapproval ran through the synagogue and the audience began to dispute among themselves, the majority arguing, "How can this man

---

27. Did Our Lord save him?
1. What took place the next morning? 2. What did they ask and what did Christ reply? 3. What did Our Lord declare of any one who should eat this Bread? 4. What followed these words of Our Lord?

give us His flesh to eat?" Far from correcting this literal interpretation of His words, however, Our Lord continued as follows:

5. "Amen, amen, I say to you, if you do not eat the Flesh of the Son of Man and drink His Blood, you shall not have life in you. Whoever eats My Flesh and drinks My Blood has life everlasting and I will raise him up on the last day."

6. Our Lord well knew how peculiarly revolting their religion made to the Jews, the idea of their consuming human flesh or blood, yet He did not hesitate to strike at this most deeply rooted of their beliefs, in order to establish firmly the great truth of the Eucharist.

7. Christ continued, "As the living Father hath sent Me and I live by the Father, so he that eateth Me, the same also shall live by Me. This is the Bread that comes down from Heaven. Not as your fathers did eat manna, and died. He that eateth this bread shall live forever."

8. A great number of His hearers found Our Lord's words too great a trial to their faith. "This is a hard saying," they protested, "who can bear it?" And after this many of his disciples drew away from His company, and walked no more with Him.

9. When Our Lord saw Himself thus deserted, He said sadly to His Apostles, "Will you too go away?" And Peter impetuously answered in the name of all: "Lord, to whom should we go? Thou hast the words of Eternal Life. We believe, we know that thou art the Holy of God."

10. Our Lord now quitted Galilee, and passed to the pagan lands to the northward, to the home of the race of Chanaan, where He abode for almost six months, devoting all His time and attention to the Apostles, completing His instructions to them, and tracing before their eyes the plan of His Church.

---

5. Repeat Our Lord's words in regard to the Holy Eucharist. 6. What is to be observed in regard to this? 7. What else did Our Lord say on this great point? 8. What effect had the announcement of this mystery on His followers? 9. What did He then say to his apostles? 10. Whither did our Lord now go?

11. Though He sought to remain unknown, the news of the presence of Israel's great prophet spread among the inhabitants of the country, and as He was passing along a road not far from the great city of Tyre, a woman ran out of her house and besought Him to cure her daughter, who was a violent maniac.

12. "Have mercy on me, my Lord, thou son of David," she entreated. Our Lord took no notice of her, and passed on, but she followed Him pleading for mercy, till He entered a house. As she continued to cry without, His apostles begged Him to grant her request and send her away. But He answered, "I am not sent save to the lost sheep of the house of Israel."

13. At length the woman gained admission, and fell at Our Lord's feet, crying, "Lord, help me." But He answered, "It is not good to take the bread of the children, and cast it to the dogs."

14. But the woman's faith and humility were proof against even this bitter rebuff. "It is true, my Lord," she answered, "but even the little whelps eat the crumbs of the children's bread which fall beneath the table."

15. At these words Our Lord who had only resisted so long, in order to strengthen the faith which He saw burning within her soul, uttered a cry of joy. "Ah, woman, thy faith is great," He said, "be it done to thee as thou wilt." At the same hour her daughter was cured.

16. From the borderland of Tyre, Our Lord went to the Decapolis, whose inhabitants had before refused His ministry. This time He did not preach the Word of Life to them, but His presence was soon known and there was brought to him a deaf and dumb man to be cured.

17. Our Lord took him aside and put His fingers into the deaf ears and touched the dumb lips with His saliva, then said in

---

11. Who sought His help? 12. How did Our Lord treat her? 13. Did she gain admission? 14. Did this repulse her? 15. What did this draw from Our Lord? 16. Whither did Our Lord go from Tyre? 17. How did He cure him?

the Aramean tongue, which was the language then spoken by the Jews: "Ephphetha," which means, "Be thou opened." And at once the man heard and spoke.

18. Shortly afterwards, Our Lord passed up the bank of the Jordan into the domain of Philip till He came to Ces'-a-rē-a Phi-lip'-pī, the stately city built on the ruins of ancient Dan, by that tetrarch, and named in honor of his patron, Tiberius Cæsar, the Roman Emperor, as well as of himself.

19. Our Lord did not enter the city, but passed on to the forest country about Mount Hermon. During His sojourn here He one day arose from prayer and said to His apostles, "Who do they say that I am?"

20. Sorrowful to the ears of the Master must have been the answer. Some thought He must be the Baptist, or the prophet Jeremias, risen again, others that He was a new prophet. But no one in carnal Israel held Him to be the Messiah.

21. Jesus answered, "Who do you say I am?" Put at a time when many had rejected Him, and the malice of His powerful enemies had made Him seek an asylum in a strange land, the question was a decisive test of the apostles' faith. But Peter answered firmly, "Thou art Christ, the son of the Living God."

22. Our Lord answered, "Blessed art thou, Simon son of Jonas, because flesh and blood have not revealed this unto thee, but my Father, who is in heaven. And I say to thee, that thou art Peter, and on this rock I will build my Church and the gates of hell shall not prevail against it.

23. "And I will give to thee the keys of the kingdom of heaven, and whatsoever thou shalt bind upon earth, it shall be bound also in heaven, and whatsoever thou shalt loose upon earth, it shall be loosed also in heaven."

---

18. Whither did Our Lord now proceed? 19. What question did Our Lord ask the apostles at Mount Hermon? 20. What was the answer? 21. What did Our Lord answer? 22. Repeat Our Lord's answer to Peter. 23. What power did he confer on Peter?

CHAPTER XV.

OUR LORD TRANSFIGURED ON MOUNT TABOR.—PAYS THE TAX BY A MIRACLE.—BLESSES LITTLE CHILDREN.—PARABLE OF THE UNFORGIVING SERVANT.

Didrachma (di-drak'-ma). An ancient Jewish coin equal to about thirty cents of our money.

Sta'ter. An ancient Jewish coin worth about sixty cents of our money.

1. A FEW days later, Our Lord descended the Valley of the Jordan, into Galilee, and proceeded to Mount Tabor. Leaving nine of His apostles at the foot, He ascended the steep sides with Peter, James and John, "the sons of the Thunder."

2. It was twilight when they began the ascent, and when they at length reached the summit, and saw the Master rapt in prayer, according to His nightly custom, they wearily stretched themselves on the ground, and were soon asleep.

3. But lo! while praying, Christ is transfigured; through the veil of flesh His Divinity shines forth; whiter than the snow grow his garments, more radiant than the sun, His face. Amid this shining effulgence of the God-Head two other figures appear; Moses on one side, representing the Law, Elias, on the other, representing the Prophets, adore the Divinity of Christ.

4. The glory of the Vision made itself felt even through the closed lids of the Apostles; their eyes opened upon its heart-piercing splendor; and they heard Moses and Elias speak with Christ of His Passion and Resurrection.

5. In an ecstasy of joy, Peter cried out, "Master, it is good for us to be here; if thou wilt, let us make here three tabernacles: one for Thee, one for Moses, and one for Elias." But even while he spoke, a radiant cloud enveloped them, and from the silvery mist, a Voice said, "This is My Beloved Son in whom I am well pleased; hear ye Him."

---

1. To what mountain did Our Lord now go? 2. What did the apostles do on reaching the top? 3. Describe the transfiguration of Our Lord. 4. Did it awaken the Apostles? 5. What did Peter cry out, and what took place?

6. Filled with awe, the apostles fell prostrate on the ground; and so remained, till the Saviour touched them, saying, "Arise, and fear not." They did so, and beheld Jesus alone, and bearing His usual aspect. As they descended the mountain Our Lord charged them not to reveal what they had seen till the Son of Man had risen from the dead.

7. Our Lord returned to Capharnaum, but no eager throngs greeted Him as He passed through its streets. Only the collector of the didrachma which every Jew had to pay annually for the support of the Temple, came to Peter and said, "Doth not thy Master pay the didrachma?"

8. When Peter gave Our Lord this message, Christ said to him: "Of whom do the kings of earth exact tribute? Of their own children or of foreigners?" "Of foreigners." answered Peter. "Then the children are free," replied Our Lord, thus reminding the apostle, that as God, He was above all human laws.

9. "Nevertheless," He added, "that we may not give scandal, go to the lake, and cast a hook. The first fish which thou shalt draw from the water, take it and open its mouth. In it thou wilt find a stater; this thou wilt take and give it to him for me, and for thee."

10. Thus Jesus as man, respected the law, and paid the tribute, but paid as God,—by a miracle. He then continued His way to the dwelling of some faithful disciple, where He dwelt with His apostles while in Capharnaum.

11. Some little children gathered about Him as He was instructing His apostles. They would have sent them away, thinking they disturbed Him, but He said: "Suffer little children to come unto Me, and forbid them not, for of such is the Kingdom of Heaven."

12. He then caressed the little ones, and blessed them; then

---

6. How were the apostles affected? 7. What happened when Our Lord returned to Capharnaum? 8. What did Our Lord say to Peter's message? 9. Continue. 10. What is to be remarked of Our Lord's action? 11. What did Our Lord say of the little children? 12. What did He show one of the children to the apostles as?

folding one in His arms, told the apostles that it was to be their model. "Amen, I say to you, unless you become as little children, you cannot enter into the Kingdom of Heaven."

13. "If any one," He continued, "shall scandalize one of these children who believe in Me, it were better for him that a mill-stone were hung about his neck, and that he were cast into the depths of the sea.

14. "Whoever receives a little child like this in My Name, receiveth Me, and he who entertaineth Me, receiveth not Me but Him that sent Me."

15. Jesus then proceeded to speak of the law of Christian forgiveness; and Peter asked, "Lord, if my brother sin against me, how many times shall I forgive him? As much as seven times?" "I do not say seven times," answered Christ, "but until seventy times seven times."

16. The Jewish doctors taught that to pardon three times was the height of perfection, but Christ required that forgiveness be accorded as often as one was sinned against. To make this clear, He pictured to them the court of one of those absolute Oriental monarchs, whose lightest breath can make or mar the most splendid fortunes.

17. "The kingdom of heaven," said Our Lord, "is like to a king who would take account of his servants. And one was brought to him that owed him ten thousand talents. (That is, more than eighteen million dollars).

18. "As he had not wherewith to pay it, his lord commanded that he should be sold, and his wife and children and all that he had, and payment to be made. But the servant, falling down besought him, saying; 'Have patience with me, and I will pay thee all."

19. "Now the king, being moved with compassion, let him

---

13. What terrible doom did He predict for those who brought scandals on His church? 14. What did he say of those who receive one in His name? 15. What law of forgiveness did Christ lay down? 16. How did He make clear the difference between His teaching and the Jewish Doctors? 17. To what did Christ liken the Kingdom of Heaven? 18. What did the king command? 19. Did he pardon him?

go, and forgave him the debt. But when the servant had gone out he found one of his fellow-servants who owed him a hundred pence and laying hold of him, he throttled him, saying, 'Pay what thou owest.'

20. "Then his fellow-servant, falling down, besought him, saying, 'Have patience with me and I will pay thee all.' Yet he would not and cast him into prison till he should pay the debt.

21. "Now his fellow-servants, seeing what was done, were very much grieved, and they told the king, who called him and said to him, 'Thou wicked servant, I forgave thee all the debt because thou besoughtest me. Shouldst thou not then have had compassion on thy fellow-servant, as I had compassion on thee?'

22. "And then the king being angry, delivered him to the torturers, until he should pay all the debt. So also" concluded Our Lord, "shall my Heavenly Father do to you, if you forgive not every one his brother, from your hearts."

23. Our Lord then laid down the following rule, of fraternal correction. "If thy brother offend thee, go and reprove him between thee and him alone. If he will hear thee, thou shalt gain thy brother.

24. "If he will not hear thee, try again, taking with thee one or two more. If he will not hear them, tell the church, and if he will not hear the church, let him be to thee as the heathen and the publican."

---

20. Did the debtor pray for mercy? 21. What did the king say to the unforgiving servant when he heard this? 22. How did the king punish him? 23. What rule did Our Lord lay down for fraternal correction? 24. What is to be done if he will not hear one?

CHAPTER XVI.

OUR LORD GOES UP TO JERUSALEM.—REPULSES THE SCRIBE —CALLS THE YOUNG MAN FROM THE HOUSE OF MOURNING.—THE SANHEDRIN SEND GUARDS TO SEIZE HIM.— NICODEMUS DEFENDS HIM.—CHRIST RESTORES SIGHT TO THE MAN BORN BLIND.

1. AUTUMN was now upon the land, the harvest was gathered, and in all parts caravans were forming for the journey to Jerusalem, to celebrate the Feast of Tabernacles, the gladdest of all Israel's solemnities, in which was commemorated the entrance of the nation into a land flowing with milk and honey.

2. As it was also a memorial of their sojourn in the desert, the people were accustomed to leave their houses during the seven days devoted to its celebration, and dwell in tents, as their forefathers had done during their wanderings.

3. Leafy pavilions, woven of the boughs of the olive, pine, myrtle and palm trees, therefore filled during the season, the streets, squares, and low flat housetops of Jerusalem, giving the city the appearance of a forest of verdure from which rose songs of joy answering the blare of trumpets from the temple.

4. Our Lord resolved to go up to Jerusalem to this Feast, and set out accordingly, with His apostles. As they walked along the highway, a Scribe who had been touched by hearing some of Our Lord's conversation, said to him, "Master, I will follow thee whithersoever thou goest."

5. Our Lord knew that the Scribe's heart held an overmastering attachment to the things of this world. He therefore answered, "The foxes have their holes, the birds of the air have their nests, but the Son of Man hath not where to lay his Head." Such poverty was too great for the Scribe; he disappeared.

---

1. What did Israel celebrate in the Autumn? 2. What custom did they observe at this time? 3. Describe the scene. 4. What did the Scribe say to Our Lord? 5. Repeat Our Lord's answer and its result

6. On the same day, and on the same road, Our Lord passed a house where a son was weeping for the death of his father. The young man felt himself drawn to leave all and follow the Master, and our Lord, as ready to help the weak, as to rebuke the presumptuous, said to him, "Follow Me."

7. The young man hesitated, and begged leave to first bury his father. But Our Lord, who doubtless knew that delay would be fatal to that wavering soul, answered him in these words, which so many saints have repeated since, when breaking the dearest ties, "Leave the dead to bury their dead, do thou go and announce the Kingdom of God."

8. On entering Jerusalem, Our Lord went at once to the temple, where He taught the people. In vain the Scribes and Pharisees endeavored to puzzle Him with their questions, His answers, marked by Divine clearness and power, discomfited them, while His scathing rebukes of their hypocrisy stung them to such fury that they resolved to seize Him.

9. The Sanhedrin therefore sent guards to arrest Him, but they were afraid to attempt it, on account of the enthusiasm of the people for Him. Only one voice protested against this action, it was that of Nicodemus, the Doctor who had sought Him by night.

10. He ventured to ask, "Does our law allow us to condemn a man without having heard him and without knowing what he has done?" Even this timid defence enraged the Sanhedrin; they exclaimed "Ah, thou, too! art thou a Galilean? Search the scriptures, and learn that no prophet has come out of Galilee." Their blind rage made them forget that Elias, Jonas, and Osee had come from Galilee.

11. As Our Lord was passing through the streets of Jerusalem on the Sabbath, He saw a beggar who had been born blind, and the disciples asked whether he was so afflicted because of his par-

---

6. What did he say to the young man? 7. Did the young man obey? 8. What did Jesus do on entering Jerusalem? 9. What did the Sanhedrin do? 10. What did Nicodemus say, and what did the Sanhedrin answer? 11. What did His disciples ask Our Lord in regard to the blind man?

ents' sins or because of his own? Our Lord answered, because of neither, "but that the works of God might be made manifest in Him."

12. Our Lord then spat on the ground, and mixing a little clay with His saliva, anointed the man's eyes with it. He then told him to go and wash in the pool of Siloe. Full of faith, the beggar departed and returned, cured.

13. His neighbors could not believe it was the same man, until they questioned him, whereupon, some of them hastened off to inform the Sanhedrin. They at once sent for the man, and after he had related his marvellous cure, said to him, "What sayest thou of Him who hath opened thine eyes?"

14. "He is a prophet," answered the man. From this firm avowal, the Sanhedrin saw their only hope was to convince the people that the man was an impostor. They therefore sent for his parents, and when they declared that he had been born blind, asked how it was he now saw?

15. The parents, who stood in terror of the Sanhedrin, which had publicly decreed that any one who confessed Jesus to be the Messiah, should be excommunicated from the synagogue, cautiously replied, "We know that this is our son, and that he was born blind. But how he now seeth, we know not. Ask himself; he is of age: let him speak for himself."

16. The Sanhedrin therefore attempted to work on the man's feelings. "Give glory to God," they urged, "we know that this man is a sinner." "If He is a sinner," answered the man, "I know not, all I know is, that I was blind and now I see."

17. The Sanhedrin saw that they had to do with a steadfast soul, whom they would not be able to browbeat. So they began to re-examine him, in the hope of picking a flaw in his evidence. "What was it He did to thee?" they asked, "how did He open thy eyes?"

18. The man, weary of the useless repetitions of his story,

---

12. How did he cure him? 13. What was the consequence? 14. What did they see from his answer? 15. What did his parents testify? 16. What attempt did the Sanhedrin then make? 17. What did they try next? 18. What did the man answer?

answered, "I have told you already. Why would you hear it again? Would you also become His disciples?"

19. They answered haughtily, "Thou thyself may be His disciple, but for us, we are the disciples of Moses. We know that God spoke to Moses. But as for this man we know not whence he is."

20. Far from being terrified, the man answered boldly, "It is wonderful that you should not know whence he comes, and nevertheless, he has opened my eyes. From the beginning of the world, it hath not been heard that any one opened the eyes of the blind. If this man were not from God he could do nothing."

21. At these words the Sanhedrin rose in indignation, and cried, "Thou art nothing but a mass of sins, and dare thou teach us?" And they put him out of the synagogue. But the Master did not forget this first Confessor of the faith.

22. He sought him out, and said to him, "Believest thou in the Son of God?" "Who is He, Lord, that I may believe in Him?" answered the man. "Thou hast seen Him," answered Christ, "and it is He Who is speaking to thee." "I believe, Lord," answered the beggar, and falling down he adored Him.

CHAPTER XVII.

OUR LORD SENDS THE SEVENTY-TWO DISCIPLES—PARABLE OF THE GOOD SAMARITAN—MARY AND MARTHA.

1. OUR LORD soon after quitted Jerusalem, and returned to Galilee. Here He sent out seventy-two of His disciples, " to go into every town, and every place whither He was to come," to recall men to repentance, to heal the sick, to prepare the ways of the Lord, and to publish the Kingdom of God.

---

19. Relate the Sanhedrin's reply. 20. Relate the man's resolute answer. 21. What was the consequence? 22. Relate Our Lord's conversation with the man. 1. Whither did Our Lord go from Jerusalem?

2. After their departure, Our Lord remained for some time among the lake cities. But His Words were no longer heeded, and He Himself was slighted and neglected by the people whom He had loaded with His favors.

3. So at last He turned away from the lake cities with the terrible words on His lips: "Woe to thee! Woe to thee! for if Tyre and Sidon had seen the miracles which have been wrought in you, they would long ago have done penance. And thou Capharnaum, which are exalted unto Heaven, thou shalt be thrust down even unto Hell."

4. Thirty years later, the words of Our Lord were terribly fulfilled. The Roman legions overran Galilee, massacred the Jews, and destroyed the lake cities which have since been left a heap of silent ruins.

5. Leaving Galilee, Our Lord went towards Perea, beyond the Jordan. On the road, He met His disciples returning to Him with great joy. "Master," they cried, "even the devils are subject to us in thy Name." But Our Lord reminded them how Satan had fallen from Heaven, and bade them, "rejoice, rather, that their names were written in the Book of Life."

6. Then He prayed as follows, "I give thanks to Thee, O Father, Lord of Heaven and Earth, that Thou hast hidden these things from the wise and prudent, and hast revealed them to little ones."

7. While Our Lord was conversing with His disciples, a Pharisee whom they encountered on the road, said to Him, "Master, what shall I do to possess eternal life?" The Lord, Who saw that his design was to tempt Him, referred him to the Law of Moses, asking, "What dost thou read there?"

8. Long before, Moses had revealed the two great precepts of Christian life which from century to century, had been taught by Israel's Prophets and Doctors of the Law to her people.

---

2. Did the cities of Galilee heed Him now? 3. What terrible doom did He pronounce on the lake cities? 4. When were His words fulfilled? 5. Where did He meet His disciples? 6. Repeat the prayer of Our Lord. 7. What did the Pharisee ask Our Lord? 8. What of the two great precepts of Christian life?

"Thou shalt love the Lord, thy God, with thy whole soul, with thy whole heart, with all thy strength, with all thy mind, and thy neighbor as thyself."

9. Therefore when the lawyer answered thus, Jesus said, "Thou hast answered aright. This do, and thou shalt live." But the Pharisee raised another question. "Who is my neighbor?" he asked.

10. It was the custom of Our Lord to make use of the scenes and objects most familiar to His hearers in order to convey to them the meaning of His great truths. He therefore now made use of the road on which they were journeying, to impress on the proud Pharisee, the fact that all man's fellow-beings are his neighbors.

11. They were passing through the mountainous stretch of country which extends between Jericho and Jerusalem, following a track which bore the name of the "Highway of Blood" because of the fierce robbers which infested it. Our Lord therefore pictured the common incident of a traveller, wounded and plundered by these brigands and left to die.

12. The first to pass by was a priest, on his way from Jerusalem; he continued on his journey, without noticing the wounded man. A Levite followed, and showed no more concern. Then came a Samaritan—the offspring of a race held accursed by Israel; he went to the wounded man and bound up his wounds, pouring in oil and wine.

13. Then the Good Samaritan put him on his horse and took him to an inn, where he tended him. The next morning, he gave the innkeeper two denarii (de nar' ē ī—equal to about forty cents) and said: "Take care of him; and whatever thou dost spend beside, I on my return, will repay thee."

14. "Which one of these three," Jesus asked, "would seem to you to be the neighbor of the man who fell into the robbers' hands?" There was no room for hesitation; and the scribe,

---

9. What did Our Lord reply? 10. What custom did Our Lord observe? 11. Where were they journeying? 12. Who passed him by? 13. What did he do then? 14. What did Our Lord make the Pharisee confess?

who could not bring himself to say the hated word Samaritan, answered, "He who took compassion on him." Our Lord answered, "Go then, and do likewise."

15. Our Lord had turned back towards Jerusalem when He met His disciples, but He did not go as far as the Holy City. Pausing at Bethany, which was separated from Jerusalem by the Mount of Olives, He rested in the house of Lazarus.

16. Lazarus was a man of high station, perhaps like Nicodemus, even a Doctor of the Law, and a friend of Jesus, and blessed in being permitted to offer Him hospitality. He had two sisters, Martha, who seems to have always dwelt in retirement within his house; and Mary, whom many sacred writers believe to be the Magdalen.

17. It would appear that on this day, the Master had not been expected at Bethany, for His arrival evidently created a stir in the household. Martha especially made great efforts to provide suitably for the occasion, but Mary, forgetful of all earthly cares in the presence of the Master, seated herself at His feet, and eagerly drank in the Word of Life.

18. Mary's conduct displeased Martha so much that she at length complained to Jesus; "Lord, dost thou not see that my sister leaves me to serve alone? Bid her, then help me." But the Master answered, "Martha, Martha, thou art careful and troubled about many things; there is only one thing necessary. Mary has chosen the better part; it shall not be taken from her."

---

15. Where did Our Lord rest? 16. Who was Lazarus? 17. Was Our Lord expected? 18. What did Martha do?

CHAPTER XVIII.

OUR LORD TEACHES HIS DISCIPLES TO PRAY.—DECLARES MARY BLESSED.—PARABLES OF THE FOOLISH RICH MAN, AND THE BARREN FIG-TREE.—CHRIST DECLARES HIS DIVINITY.

1. AFTER leaving Bethany, Our Lord went to Perea the second time, where there were many of the disciples of John the Baptist. And after He had finished praying one day in a secluded place, one of these, who had joined his band, approached Him and said, "Lord, teach us to pray, just as John did for His disciples."

2. Our Lord answered his wish by teaching him the Our Father. He then impressed on His disciples the vital necessity of prayer, charging them to pray unceasingly even though God should seem to be deaf to their petitions.

3. To put this duty before them in all its importance, Our Lord related the Parable of a man at whose house a guest arrived in the middle of the night when he has nothing to offer him. The host therefore hurries off to a friend's house, and implores him to get up and give him three loaves.

4. The friend who has retired to rest, is deaf to his pleading for a long time, but at last worn out with his importunities, he rises and gives him the three loaves. "And in like manner, I say to you," concluded Our Lord, "Ask, and it shall be given you; seek, and you shall find; knock, and it shall be opened to you."

5. About this same time, as Our Lord was entering a dwelling where He was to rest, two blind men called out, "Son of David, have pity on us!" Their faith moved the Saviour; He said to them, "Do you believe that I am able to do this for you?"

6. "Yes, Lord," they answered. Then He touched their

---

1. Whither did Our Lord go after leaving Bethany? 2. Did Our Lord comply? 3. How did he make them understand the duty of prayer? 4. How does he gain his request? 5. Who begged Him to cure them?

eyes, saying, "Let it be done unto you according to your faith." And at once their sight was restored.

7. As they were going away, a man was brought to Jesus, who had a dumb devil. Our Lord cured him, and a woman gave voice to the awe and delight which filled the crowd who beheld the miracle by exclaiming: "Blessed the womb which bore Thee, and the breasts which gave Thee suck."

8. "Ay, doubtless," answered Our Lord, "but blesseder still are those who hear the Word of God, and keep it." Thus He proclaimed that Mary had attained a blessedness still more exalted than that conferred by her Divine Motherhood, by conceiving Jesus Christ by faith, and bearing Him before man, by the fulfilment of His will.

9. Drawn by the report of the great miracles, a dense throng now surged about Our Lord, and some among them now demanded of Him a still more extraordinary miracle as a sign of His Mission. Our Lord knew that they had been incited to ask this by the Pharisees, and it was to these therefore, that He addressed the following stern rebuke.

10. "An adulterous generation seeketh a sign," He said, "and a sign shall not be given it, but the sign of Jonas the prophet. For as Jonas was in the whale's belly three days and three nights, so shall the Son of Man be in the heart of the earth three days and three nights.

11. The men of Nineveh shall rise in this generation, and shall condemn it, because they did penance at the preaching of Jonas. The queen of the south shall rise in judgment with this generation, and shall condemn it, because she came from the ends of the earth to hear the wisdom of Solomon, and behold, a greater than Solomon is here."

12. As Our Lord was another day discoursing to the people, a man in the crowd, desirous to turn His commanding power to

---

7. What did the woman cry out in the crowd at this new miracle? 8. Relate Our Lord's answer and its meaning. 9. What was demanded of Our Lord as a sign of His Mission? 10. Repeat this rebuke. 11. What of the men of Nineveh, and the Queen of Saba? 12. What did the man in the crowd ask him?

his own private ends, called out; "Master, speak to my brother that he may divide his inheritance with me." Christ answered, "Man, who hath made me a judge, or a divider over you?"

13. Then turning to the people, He bade them beware of covetousness, for that "a man's life doth not consist in the abundance of things." Then He related a parable of a certain rich man whose fields yielded such rich harvests that his barns could not hold them.

14. Then he said to himself, "I will tear down my barns, and I will build greater ones, and then I will gather all my crops and all my goods. And I will say; My soul, thou hast great store of things for many years; take thine ease, eat, drink, and have good cheer."

15. But God said to him, "Foolish man, this night shall thy soul be required of thee, and whose shall be that great wealth which thou hast acquired?" So Our Lord added, "So is he that layeth up treasure for himself and is not rich towards God."

16. While Our Lord was thus preaching the word in Perea, a report reached there of a fresh attempt on the part of the Jews of Jerusalem to throw off the yoke of Rome. A band of Galileans had led the insurrection, but had been surprised and massacred in the temple by Pontius Pilate's soldiers.

17. To Jewish eyes, such an event seemed to be permitted by God only in atonement for some previous crime, and some of Christ's disciples hastened to ask of Jesus the reason of the massacre. But Our Lord told them that misfortune is not always a punishment for crime, and bade them refrain from attempting to sound the depths of God's mysteries.

18. He then went on to relate the parable of the fig-tree which for three years bore no fruit, so that the vintager resolved to cut it down. But the vine-dresser implored him to grant it another year, during which he would dig about its roots and apply nourishment to them.

---

13. What did Our Lord warn the people in regard to covetousness? 14. What did the rich man say to himself? 15. What did God say to him? 16. What report reached Perea? 17. How did the Jews regard such an event? 18. What parable did Our Lord then relate?

19. "Then if it bear fruit," said the vintager, "it shall be kept; if not, you shall cut it down." By the fig-tree Our Lord meant Jerusalem which for three years had resisted Him; and which now was to have, through his intercession, another period of grace—that from the time of His Death to its destruction.

20. Our Lord now quitted Perea and went up to Jerusalem to the Feast of the Dedication, or the Feast of Lights, which commemorated the Purification of the temple by Judas Machabeus. For one week the Jews surged through the temple bearing palms in their hands and singing sacred songs, while every evening Jerusalem was brilliantly illuminated.

21. Leaving His disciples to take part in the feast making, Our Lord repaired to Solomon's portico, which in winter furnished a walk warmed by the rays of the sun. Here some members of the Sanhedrin gathered about Him. "Until when," they said, "do Thou mean to keep us in suspense? If Thou art the Christ, say so openly."

22. Our Lord answered, "I speak to you and you believe not. The works that I do in the name of My Father, they give testimony of Me, I and the Father are one."

23. At this second unmistakable declaration that He was their God, the Jews were roused to such fury that they snatched up stones to stone Him. But Jesus quelled their madness. "I have done in your presence," He said, "many good works from My Father; for which one are you now about to stone me?"

24. "It is not for any good works we intend to stone thee; but for blasphemy, because that Thou, being a man, makest Thyself God," answered the would-be deicides.

25. Our Lord answered, "If I do not the works of My Father, believe Me not. But if I do, though you will not be-

---

19. What did the vintager declare and what was the meaning of this parable? 20. For what did Our Lord go to Jerusalem? 21. Where did the members of the Sanhedrin find Him? 22. Relate Our Lord's reply. 23. What was its effect on the Jews? 24. What did they answer? 25. What did Our Lord answer?

lieve Me, believe the works, that you may know and believe the Father is in Me and I in the Father." At these words they again tried to seize Him, but He passed from the midst of them, out of the temple.

CHAPTER XIX.

OUR LORD RAISES LAZARUS FROM THE DEAD.

1. AFTER quitting Jerusalem Our Lord returned to Perea, where He continued His ministry. The Pharisees reproached Him with associating with sinners, whereupon He answered them in these beautiful parables of the Good Shepherd seeking his lost sheep, and The Prodigal Son, which show so clearly the infinite depth of Divine Love.

2. There He was ministering, when He received news from the sisters of Lazarus that the latter was dangerously ill. Our Lord's answer to the message was as follows: "This sickness is not unto death, but for the glory of God, in order that the Son of God may be glorified thereby."

3. Two days later He set out for Bethany, but when He arrived, He found that His friend was dead and that his body had already been placed in the tomb. On the news of His arrival, Martha hastened out to meet Him and said, "Lord, if Thou hadst been here my brother would not have died."

4. Our Lord answered, "Thy brother shall rise again." "I know," Martha replied, "he shall rise again in the Resurrection, on the last day." But Our Lord gently reminded her of Who He was, in these life-giving words which the Church still uses to console us in the hour of our bereavement. "I am the Resurrection and the Life; he that believeth in Me, although he be dead he shall live. Believest thou this?"

5. Martha answered, "Yea, Lord, I believe that Thou art

---

1. Why did Our Lord relate the parables of the Lost Sheep and the Prodigal Son? 2. What news reached Our Lord in Perea? 3. Did He return to Bethany? 4. What did Our Lord answer? 5. What did Martha answer?

the Christ, the Son of the Living God, Who art come into this world." Martha then sped into the house and said to Mary, who was absorbed in grief, "The Master is here; He is asking for thee."

6. Mary rose and hurried away, followed by the mourning friends who supposed she was going to weep at the tomb. Like Martha, she too fell at Jesus' feet, sobbing out, "Lord, if Thou hadst been here my brother had not died."

7. Our Lord, whose human sympathies were exquisitely tender, was deeply troubled at the sight of Mary's sorrow, which was shared by her friends. "Where have you laid him?" He asked. Mary answered, "Come and see." And Jesus wept.

8. At the sight of His tears the mourners whispered to one another, "See how He loved him!" And they followed Him to the tomb; which, according to the custom of the wealthy Jews, was a cavern hewn out of a rock, and sealed with a stone.

9. "Take away the stone," commanded Jesus. But Martha, who had now arrived, objected, "Master, he is already corrupt; it is four days since he died." Our Lord answered, "Did I not say to thee that if thou wilt believe thou shalt see the glory of God?"

10. The stone was accordingly rolled away and the body of Lazarus disclosed to view. Then, lifting His eyes to Heaven, Jesus prayed. "Father, I give Thee thanks that Thou hast heard Me. For Myself, I know that Thou hearest Me always, but for the sake of these people who stand about Me, I have said it, in order that they may believe that Thou hast sent Me."

11. Then He cried out with a loud voice, "Lazarus, come forth!" And at once the dead man emerged from the grave with his feet and hands wrapped in the winding sheet, and his

---

6. What did Mary say to Our Lord when she met Him? 7. What effect had her sorrow on Our Lord? 8. What did the mourners say at the sight of His grief? 9. What did Jesus command? 10. Repeat the prayer of Our Lord. 11. Continue.

face shrouded in the cere-cloth, while the spectators stood pale and speechless with terror.

12. "Loose his bonds," said Jesus, "and let him go." And at once the hideous shroud fell from him, and Lazarus was restored to his family. Many of the Jews who witnessed this miracle believed in Christ, but others made haste to inform the Sanhedrin.

13. In deep perplexity as to their course, all its members at once assembled, and took counsel. "What are we doing?" said some. "This man is working many miracles. If we let Him go on acting thus, all will believe in Him, and the Romans will come and destroy our city and our nation."

14. At length the High-Priest, Caiphas (ka yä'fas) rose to address the assembly. Although a mere creature of Rome, his station gave great weight to his words. "You neither understand anything of all this," he said, "nor do you consider that it is far better that one man should die for the people, than that the whole nation perish."

15. In this cruel speech the haughty and unscrupulous high-priest was the unconscious mouth-piece of the Almighty. As St. John says: "Caiphas said this, not of Himself, but being Pontiff for that year, he prophesied that Jesus should die for his nation, and not only for his nation, but that he might gather together in one, God's children who are scattered abroad."

16. Our Lord was probably made aware of their evil designs, for He withdrew from Jerusalem to Eph'rem, a town on the borders of Samaria, where He consecrated a few of the last weeks of His Life to intimate converse with His disciples.

17. When He left this retreat, a few weeks before the Paschal-tide, He passed northward for the last time across Samaria and Galilee. On the borders of Galilee He restored ten lepers to health. Of these only one, a Samaritan,

---

12. What did Jesus command, and what was the effect of this miracle? 13. What did some of the members of the Sanhedrin declare? 14. What did Caiphas say? 15. As what did Caiphas serve? 16. What did Our Lord do? 17. Whither did He go from Ephrem?

returned to give Him thanks, after having obeyed His command and shown himself to the priest.

18. This sole grateful one merited that Jesus now complete in his heart the work He had already begun. "Arise," He said, "and go thy way; thy faith hath saved thee."

19. In order to rebuke the self-conceit of some of His disciples, Our Lord related about this time, the parable of how two men went up into the temple to pray. One was a Pharisee who sang his own praises as follows:

20. "My God, I give thee thanks for that I am not like the rest of men, violent, unjust, unclean, as is also yonder publican. I fast twice a week; I pay tithes upon all I possess."

21. But the other, who was a publican, stood afar off, and dared not so much as to lift up his eyes to Heaven; with bowed head he smote his, breast saying, "O Lord, have pity on me, who am a sinner."

22. "And," Our Lord added, "I tell you this man went down to his house justified, and not the other, for he who exalts himself shall be humbled, and he that humbleth himself shall be exalted."

CHAPTER XX.

CHRIST'S TEACHING IN REGARD TO DIVORCE.

1. This lesson was the last which Galilee was to hear from the Great Teacher. Bidding His native land a last farewell, Our Lord now crossed the Jordan and descended its eastern bank. He soon reached Perea, where as before, the Pharisees soon pressed about Him with subtle questions.

2. Among those on which they asked His opinion was that of divorce. This was a vexed subject in Israel, for while the Law

---

18. Who was this one? 19. How did Our Lord rebuke the self-conceit some of His disciples? 20. Repeat the Pharisee's prayer. 21. What did the other pray? 22. What did Our Lord conclude?

1. Whither did Our Lord now go? 2. On what did they ask His opinion?

of Moses permitted divorce, the more austere Doctors of the Law contended that it was only for scandalous disorders, thus opposing another school led by the great Rabbi Hil'lel, which insisted that a slight pretext sufficed for the severance of the marriage bond.

3. The answer which they received must have sounded strange indeed, in their ears. Far from pronouncing either School of Hebrew Doctors right, Our Lord solemnly declared that marriage was an eternal bond. "Let no man put asunder," He said, "what God hath joined together."

4. The Pharisees replied by asking why Moses had permitted it then. But Our Lord showed them that they had transformed the bare toleration of an act into a positive precept. "It was because of the hardness of your hearts," He calmly answered, "but at the beginning it was not thus."

5. Then in plain unmistakable words, Jesus Christ dowered the holy sacrament of marriage with its full perfection by pronouncing it indissoluble.

6. The discomfited Pharisees withdrew, and then Our Lord, for the first time, drew aside the veil, and permitted His apostles to glance at the loveliness of Christian virginity, which was to be so prized in His Holy Church.

7. "Whosoever is able to understand, let him understand," said Our Lord. But their minds were not spiritual enough to comprehend; the Holy Ghost would have to descend on them before their ears could be opened "to the hymning of Virgins who follow the Lamb whithersoever He goeth," which St. John heard in his Vision of Heaven.

8. As Our Lord was proceeding along the road after this instruction, a rich and distinguished young man who dwelt in those parts, come running after Him, and falling on his knees before Him, asked, "Master, what shall I do that I may have eternal life?"

---

3. How were they answered? 4. What did the Pharisees reply? 5. What did Our Lord then say regarding marriage? 6. What did Our Lord permit the Apostles? 7. Did they comprehend? 8. What did the young man ask Him?

9. Our Lord answered by bidding him keep the commandments. The young man fervently answered that he had done so from his youth; what did he lack yet? Our Lord then pointed out the narrow road of perfection. "Go," He said, "sell all thou hast and give it to the poor; then come and follow me."

10. Our Lord's words had struck at the young man's passion of love of wealth, which, sincere as he was, he could not bring himself to conquer. He fell back with a sad face, and went away.

11. Our Lord followed him with His eyes, and spoke of how difficult it was for the rich to enter into God's kingdom, declaring that it was easier for a camel to pass through the eye of a needle, than for a rich man to enter God's kingdom.

12. He enforced this teaching of the evil consequences of the possession of riches by the Parable of the Unjust Steward, and of Dives and Lazarus.

13. When we reflect, however, that it is the rich Abraham whom the tortured Dives implored to send Lazarus down to him with a drop of water, we perceive that it is not the mere possession of riches which Our Lord condemns, but that unholy love of wealth which prevents its possessors from devoting it to good works.

14. When the Apostles heard Jesus thus condemn all attachment to earthly goods, Peter eagerly asked: "Lord, we have left all to follow thee, what shall there be for us?"

15. Glorious, indeed, was the Saviour's answer. To all who had left aught for His sake, were it home, parents, children, spouse, or lands; a hundred-fold should be given; a foretaste of Heaven on earth, even in the midst of persecution, and "life everlasting."

16. To the apostles, along with all this it should be granted

---

9. What did Our Lord answer? 10. Did He obey? 11. What did Our Lord say about riches? 12. How did He express this teaching? 13. What do we perceive in this parable of Dives? 14. What did Peter ask? 15. What was Our Lord's answer? 16. What was granted besides to the Apostles?

to sit on twelve Thrones whence they shall judge the Tribes of Israel on the day when the Son of Man shall take possession of the Throne of His Majesty.

17. Lest they should become puffed up, with these glorious prerogatives and imagine that they were their rightful inheritance, Our Lord went on to say that they were purely the gifts of grace, and that though Israel was the first to be called, yet the Gentiles should precede them, and share with them the celestial kingdom.

18. To make them realize this truth, He related the Parable of the Lord of the Vineyard. Under this guise, He represents the Heavenly Father, hiring laborers at different hours of the day, and when night comes, rewarding the latest comers with the denarius promised to those who have toiled since daybreak.

19. To the latter who question the justice of this action, and who represent the Jews grudging the Gentiles a portion in the Heavenly Kingdom, the Lord of the Vineyard answered: " My friend, I do thee no wrong; didst thou not agree with Me for a denarius? "

20. " Then take what is thine, and go. If notwithstanding, I wish to give unto this last as much as to thee, is it not lawful for me to do what I will with mine own? Must thy eye be evil, because I am just? "

21. Our Lord concluded by uttering one of those maxims with which He so often rent the haughty hearts of the Jews: " The first shall be last, and the last first! Many are called, but few are chosen! "

---

17. What did Our Lord warn His Apostles? 18. How did He make them realize this truth? 19. What did the Lord of the Vineyard answer these fault-finders? 20. Continue His answer. 21. How did Our Lord conclude?

CHAPTER XXI.

OUR LORD CALLS ZACHEUS.—BANQUET AT BETHANY, AT WHICH MAGDALEN ANOINTS HIM.

Spike′nard. A fragrant essential oil, highly prized by the ancients.

De-nar′i us,—de nar-i-i. A Roman coin equal to about eighteen cents in our money.

1. PREACHING and blessing the people, Our Lord descended the Jordan to Jericho. When He came to where the road veered off in the direction of Jerusalem, the apostles were terrified to see Him take the direction of the Holy City.

2. Then the Saviour paused and said to them: "Behold, we go to Jerusalem, and soon all things which the Prophets have written concerning the Son of Man shall be accomplished. He shall be delivered to the Princes of the Priesthood and to the Scribes, and they shall condemn Him to death.

3. "And they shall deliver Him to the Gentiles. He shall be mocked and reviled: they shall spit upon His face; after they have scourged Him, they shall crucify Him, and the third day He shall rise again."

4. But the apostles, whose minds were still absorbed in dreams of a great earthly kingdom, did not comprehend their Master even when He thus plainly told them of the bitter suffering and humiliation which were to inaugurate His reign. And they continued their journey to the beautiful city of Jericho.

5. As Our Lord drew near, a blind man on the wayside called out: "Jesus, Son of David, have mercy on me!" Touched by his faith, Our Lord cured him, and then entered the city to pass the night. Such dense crowds surged about Him, that a man named Zacheus, who was anxious to see Him, had to climb a fig-tree to do so.

---

1. Did Our Lord turn toward Jerusalem? 2. How did He announce His passion to them? 3. Continue. 4. Did they comprehend? 5. What miracle did He work?

6. Now Zacheus was chief of the publicans, a tax-collector, and specially detested by the citizens of Jericho, because of the large fortune which he had made in the exercise of his office. Nevertheless, he was an upright and generous man, and much nearer the Kingdom of God than his enemies.

7. When, therefore, Our Lord saw him in the fig-tree, He said to him: "Zacheus, make haste and come down, for to-day I must lodge in thy house." Murmurs of disapproval arose from the Jews, who were incensed that Christ should prefer this outcast to the nobility of Jericho.

8. But the happy host had small heed for their sneers; he conducted the Lord to his house, and threw open, not only it, but his heart as well to Him; for on the morrow when the Lord was departing, he said as follows:

9. "Lord, behold now I give the half of my goods to the poor; and for every wrong that I have done, I now return fourfold." Christ answered: "To-day this household has found salvation, for the Son of Man is come to seek and to save that which is lost."

10. Our Lord now went into Bethany, "where there was a great feast made for Him at the house of Simon the leper." Some sacred writers suppose Simon to have been the dead father of Lazarus, whose mansion was still known by that name; however this may be, Lazarus was present at the entertainment.

11. While Our Lord was at table, Mary Magdalen entered the banqueting-hall, as she had done at that other memorable feast when He had forgiven her sins, and broke over His feet a frail alabaster vase containing spikenard of exquisite purity, with which she also anointed His head.

12. The Master graciously accepted Magdalen's homage, but as the fragrance of the costly perfume spread through the hall, it roused the passion of avarice which consumed the heart of one of the apostles—Judas, and he demanded: "Could not

---

6. Who was Zacheus? 7. What did Our Lord say to him? 8. What effect had this on Zacheus? 9. Repeat Zacheus' words and Our Lord's answer. 10. Where was there a feast made for Our Lord? 11. What did Magdalen do? 12. What did it rouse in Judas?

this perfume have been sold for three hundred denarii, (about $54.00) and given to the poor?"

13. The other apostles taking pattern by him, began to murmur also, "To what purpose is this waste?" But Jesus reproved them: "Why do you molest this woman?" He asked. "You will always have the poor with you; but Me you have not always.

14. "For she, in pouring this ointment on My body, hath done it for my burial. Amen, I say to you, wherever the Gospel shall be preached in the whole world, that which she has now done, shall be told in memory of her."

---

13. Did the other apostles murmur also? 14. Continue.

III.—HOLY WEEK.

CHAPTER I.

PALM SUNDAY.—JESUS ENTERS JERUSALEM IN TRIUMPH.

1. As the Festival of the Pasch approached, the members of the Sanhedrin congratulated themselves on having driven Our Lord from Jerusalem, for among the vast throngs of Jews who were daily arriving there from all parts of the world, to celebrate the Feast, there was the greatest eagerness to see the Great Prophet.

2. Their disappointment was great in learning that He was no longer to be seen in the Holy City, and in the streets and porches of the Temple, His absence, and the chances of His coming up for the Pasch, were the only topics of discussion.

3. The excitement rose to its height when, six days before the Pasch, the news reached Jerusalem that Our Saviour had advanced as far as Bethany, on His way thither. As it was the Sabbath, the people were forced to remain inactive till the sunset marked the end of the hallowed repose, when they streamed out towards Bethany.

4. The following day Our Lord proceeded towards Jerusalem attended by a vast concourse. When He reached the village known as Bethpage (beth'-fa-gē) or The House of Figs, because it stood amid plentiful fig vineyards, He gave the following directions to two of His disciples:

5. "Go into yonder village lying before us," He said. "Upon

---

1. What was the feeling towards Our Lord in Jerusalem? 2. Were they disappointed? 3. When did they hear of The Saviour's approach? 4. When did Our Lord move towards Jerusalem? 5. Repeat Our Lord's words.

your entrance you shall find an ass tied, and a colt with her, on which no man has ever yet mounted. Take them and bring them to Me. And if any one say to you, 'What are you doing?' say 'The Lord has need of them, and straightway he will let them go.'"

6. The disciples obeyed, and soon returned with the animals Christ designated. Then Our Lord seated Himself on the ass which walked quietly beside her foal. Thus the procession advanced; the Apostles, believing that at last the earthly reign of the Messiah was to begin, were in a transport of joy which was shared by the multitude.

7. Some of these stripped the fig and palm trees of their leafy boughs, and covered the road with their branches, while others paid Him the greatest token of Oriental respect, by casting their garments in the way.

8. Thus they ascended the crest of the Mount of Olives to its summit, where they came in view of the beautiful city of Jerusalem, girt with its towers and battlements, and with the snowy marble, and gleaming gold of the Temple in its midst.

9. At once the Apostles burst into a song of triumph, "Hosanna to the Son of David; Blessed be the King of Israel, Who Cometh in the Name of the Lord." But Our Lord did not share their gladness. He saw the city which was soon to put Her Redeemer to death, and He wept aloud.

10. "If thou hadst known," He mourned, "if only in this day which is still granted thee—that which might bring thee Peace. But now all this is hidden from thine eyes. There will come a time when thine enemies shall compass thee about with trenches and shut thee up, and straiten thee on every side.

11. "And they shall destroy thee and thy children, all beaten down to the ground in thy midst, and shall not leave in thee one stone upon another, because thou hast not known the time wherein God hath visited thee."

---

6. What took place? 7. What did some of the multitude do? 8. At what point did they come in sight of Jerusalem? 9. What did the Apostles cry out? 10. Repeat Our Lord's prophecy in regard to Jerusalem. 11. How did He predict its utter destruction?

JESUS ENTERS JERUSALEM IN TRIUMPH. 305

12. Meanwhile another great multitude surged forth from Jerusalem to greet the Son of David, waving palm-branches and filling the air with their joyous cries of "Hosanna." When they met Him, and saw Him with His friend Lazarus, whom He had raised from the tomb, by His side, they turned and led the way into the Holy City.

13. The sight of the vast concourse, the sound of the songs of triumph, filled the Pharisees with alarm. How would the Roman governor view such a demonstration? Some of them forced their way through the crowd to Jesus and said to Him, "Master, restrain your disciples."

14. Our Lord answered, "If they hold their peace, the very stones will cry out." And thus was fulfilled the prophecy of Zachary: "Rejoice greatly, thou daughter of Sion! Behold thy King cometh to thee; lowly and gentle, He bringeth thee salvation; poor, He rideth upon an ass, and upon an ass's colt."

15. In this royal state the Saviour was conducted through Jerusalem as far as the Temple. There the procession dispersed, for Jewish custom did not permit pilgrims to approach the sanctuary in travelling attire, their feet stained with dust.

16. That night Jesus again quitted Jerusalem, for He did not wish to leave Himself in the power of the Sanhedrin until the time when He chose to deliver Himself into their hands. He probably passed it in prayer in the neighborhood of Bethany, for in the morning when He and His Apostles were returning to Jerusalem, we read that they were hungry.

17. The road along which they were passing was bordered with fig-trees. Although it was not yet quite the season for figs, the rich foliage of one tree seemed to promise a premature crop. On examining it, however, no fruit was found on its branches, and Our Lord said, "Henceforth may never fruit be found on thee."

18. This, the only ruin wrought by the merciful Saviour,

---

12. Who came out to meet them? 13. What did the sight arouse in the Pharisees? 14. What did Our Lord answer and what was fulfilled? 15. Where did the people conduct Our Lord? 16. When did Christ quit

was a terrible judgment for the Jews, of whom it was the figure, who, while boasting of their laws and ceremonies, used these outward signs only to hide the insincerity of their righteousness.

19. Our Lord hastened on to Jerusalem and went at once to the temple which He a second time cleared of the hucksters who were trading in its holy courts. "It is written, 'My house is a house of prayer,'" He cried, "but you have made it a den of thieves."

20. When they had fled, trembling, before Him, a stillness fell upon the holy place, through which His Sacred Voice could now be clearly heard as He taught the people, who flocked about Him bringing their blind and crippled to be healed.

21. Angrily the High-Priests, Scribes and Chief Magistrates watched Him as He thus ministered, but remained silent until the children who were brought up in the Temple for the service of the Almighty began to rehearse the triumph of the previous day, as they played about the courts.

22. "Hosanna," sang the clear childish voices, "Hosanna to the Son of David." Unable to control themselves any longer, the Pharisees approached the Saviour, and said to Him: "Do you hear what these are saying?" "Ay," He replied, "Have you never read, 'Out of the mouths of babes and sucklings Thou hast brought forth perfect praise?'"

CHAPTER II.

THE LAST DAY IN THE MINISTRY OF JESUS.

1. THE following morning, after spending this night, like the preceding one, outside of the city walls, Our Lord returned to Jerusalem, and entered the Temple, where He again taught

---

19. Where did Our Lord go on entering Jerusalem? 20. What did He do after they had fled? 21. What roused the Pharisees as they watched Him? 22. What did the Pharisees say of the children's singing, and what did Our Lord answer?

1. Did Our Lord appear in the temple the following day?

the people. The Pharisees watched Him as closely as ever, and thus were forced to hear what would be the result of their plottings against Him.

2. To this end He related the Parable of the Marriage-Feast. A king is about to celebrate the nuptials of his son, and sends messengers to bid the guests to the entertainment. But the latter maltreat the king's servants, and put them to death. Then the king sends His armies, destroys the murderers, and sets fire to the city.

3. Our Lord then represented the king as telling his servants to gather in all they should find, good or evil, to fill up the banquet-hall. But these were not to sit down to the feast in their tatters or dirt; according to Oriental usage, the king had provided sumptuous robes for them to wear.

4. One of the guests, however, neglected to don the robe provided for him, and appeared at the banquet in his own mean dress. And when the king went in to see his guests, and perceived this man without a wedding-garment, he said to him: "Friend, how didst thou enter here without having put on marriage-raiment?"

5. The shame-stricken guest had nothing to answer, and the king commanded his servants to bind him hand and foot, and cast him into the outer darkness; "there shall be weeping and gnashing of teeth. For many are called, but few are chosen."

6. In these guests, gathered in from the highway, are pre-figured those whom the Apostles were soon to gather into the Church, as the wedding-garment is the emblem of those virtues with which Christian souls must adorn themselves to be true members of It.

7. After hearing this parable, the Pharisees retired, and in despair of entrapping the Saviour by their own efforts, resolved to seek the assistance of some courtiers of Herod, who were in

---

2. What Parable did He therefore relate? 3. What did the king do in consequence? 4. What did one of the guests neglect to do? 5. What did the guest answer? 6. Whom do these latter guests prefigure? 7. What did the Pharisees do?

Jerusalem. They usually held these supporters of the Roman power in the utmost aversion, but this was forgotten in their desire to ruin Our Lord.

8. Their plan was to make some of these Herodians act the part of honest, upright men, perplexed as to how far their allegiance to Rome could be maintained with loyalty to their own country and observance of the Law of Moses.

9. They soon succeeded in persuading the Herodians to act with them, and at an opportune moment, a party of them approached the Saviour with every appearance of sincerity, and begged Him to arbitrate between them.

10. "Master," they reverently said, "we know that Thou art a true speaker, and that Thou dost not put Thyself out for any one, whoever he may be; that Thou hast no respect for the person of man, but teach the way of God in all sincerity. Is it lawful for us to pay tribute to Cæsar or not?"

11. It was a cunningly-laid snare, and one which it seemed impossible for Jesus to escape. To condemn the tribute would be to incur the displeasure of Rome: to declare it lawful would be to infuriate the Jews, who would view it as flattery addressed to their foreign masters.

12. Clearly perceiving the ambush, the Saviour turned to some of the disciples of the Pharisees who had accompanied the Herodians; "Ye hypocrites," He said, "Why do you tempt Me? Bring Me the coin with which you pay the tribute."

13. They brought Him a Roman denarius. He took it, and displaying to them the figure of the Roman emperor, with the inscription, "TIBERIUS CÆSAR, SON OF THE DIVINE AUGUSTUS," asked, "Whose image and inscription is this?" They answered, "Cæsar's." Our Lord replied: "Render to Cæsar that which is Cæsar's; and to God that which is God's."

14. Our Lord then descended into the Gentiles' Porch, where

---

8. What was their plan? 9. Did they effect this? 10. Repeat their address to Our Lord. 11. What is to be observed of this snare? 12. What did Our Lord answer? 13. What did He say when He received the denarius? 14. Where did He then descend?

stood the great coffers in which all offerings for the Temple were deposited. A knot of wealthy Jews were casting into them their large gifts, when a poor widow stole up and dropped in ten small coins, less than one of our cents in value.

15. Our Lord pointed out this humble soul to His disciples, and said to them: "In truth this poor widow has given more than all the others; for they indeed, have put but a portion from their abundance into the treasury, while she out of her poverty has given all she had, even her whole living."

16. Our Lord then arose and traversed the length of the porch. His disciples followed, admiring the splendors of the Temple, and calling His attention to the rich materials of which it was composed. Our Lord answered, "Of all these great buildings, truly I tell you, there shall not remain a stone upon a stone."

17. This awful prophecy was the Saviour's farewell to the Temple. He now quitted it, never to enter it again, and with His apostles, crossed the brook of Kedron, and ascended the Mount of Olives.

CHAPTER III.

OUR LORD FORETELLS THE DESTRUCTION OF JERUSALEM, AND OF THE WORLD.—THE LAST JUDGMENT.

1. On reaching the summit of the Mount of Olives, Our Lord seated Himself, and James, John and Andrew, drawing near, asked Him when the Temple should be destroyed, and what signs should precede the end of the world.

2. Our Lord answered as One who sees all things eternally present, to Whom one thousand years are but as one day. He linked the catastrophes which were to precede the end of the Jewish world, and the still more terrible ones which shall pre-

---

15. What did Our Lord say of the latter? 16. What did Our Lord say regarding the Temple? 17. What was the prophecy?
1. What did the apostles now ask Our Lord? 2. What is to be observed of Our Lord's answer?

cede the end of the universe, so that at first sight it seems hard to distinguish between them.

3. Our Lord revealed first what was to precede the fall of Jerusalem; false prophets seducing Judea; a thousand scourges falling on her, wars, plagues, famine, great earthquakes; then "the beginning of sorrows," that is to say the persecution of the new-born Church."

4. "Thereupon," continued Our Lord, "the end shall come. When you shall see the hosts encompassing Jerusalem, know that its ruin is nigh. Then let those that are in Judea flee to the mountains. Let not him who is in the field return to his dwelling in quest of his garment.

5. "For there shall be then great tribulation, such as hath not been from the beginning of the world till now, nor ever shall be aught like unto it. There shall be wrath upon this people. They shall fall by the edge of the sword, and shall be led away captives unto all nations."

6. Our Lord then foretold that Jerusalem should be trampled under foot by the Gentiles, even until the time of the nations be accomplished—that is until all people shall successively enter the Church; and then only, when the salvation of the Gentiles is consummated, shall the remnant of Israel be saved in their turn.

7. Thereafter shall come the end of the world, heralded by signs which shall proclaim its coming as plainly as the fig-tree's leafage marks the coming of summer. Many will come, saying, "I am the Christ," and they shall seduce many.

8. At that dread time too, the stars shall be veiled from sight, the souls of men filled with anguish at the roaring of the sea, and the powers of heaven shall be shaken from their spheres. Then the Cross, the sign of the Son of Man, shall appear in the sky, and Christ shall descend upon the clouds in great power and majesty.

---

3. What did Christ reveal first? 4. By what sign were they to know when to leave Jerusalem? 5. What did He say of its tribulation? 6. How long shall Jerusalem be trampled underfoot? 7. Shall the end of the world be heralded? 8. Continue.

CHRIST FORETELLS THE END OF THE WORLD. 311

9. Then all human-kind shall rise from their graves, awakened by the Angel's trumpeting, while dark hosts of eagles, the avengers of God, shall fall upon the old, dead world as upon an abandoned carass. Such shall be the last scene of the earth's existence, the day and hour which remain a secret with God.

10. Christ therefore charged all Christians to "watch and pray; for ye know not when the Master will come—if it shall be at even, or at midnight, whether at cockcrow, or in the morning"—for fear lest coming suddenly, He surprise them.

11. He illustrated this truth by the Parable of the Five Wise and Five Foolish Virgins. According to Oriental custom, these ten maidens go to the house of the bride to attend her at the marriage. Five take only the oil that is in their lamps, but the other five take a store of oil with them.

12. At midnight the cry is heard, "Behold the bridegroom cometh, go ye forth to meet him!" Then the foolish virgins, fearing that their lamps would go out for want of oil during the marriage-festival, hurried off to buy some.

13. But when they returned they found the door shut. In vain they cried: "Lord, Lord! open to us!" He answered, "Of a truth, I say unto you, I know you not." "Watch then," ordered Our Lord; "for you know neither the day nor the hour."

14. Our Lord then went on to set before all Christians the necessity of making the most of the time and talents bestowed on them, by relating the Parable of the Talents. A man who was about to go into a distant country, called his servants and delivered to them his goods.

15. To one he gave five talents, to another two, to another one. Then he took his departure. Then the one who had received the five talents traded with it so that he made five more; and the one who had received the two did likewise, and gained

---

9. What shall be the last scene of the earth? 10. What did Christ charge all Christians? 11. By what parable did Our Lord impress the need for eternal vigilance in Christians? 12. What is heard at midnight? 13. What did they find on their return? 14. Why did He relate the Parable of the Talents? 15. Continue.

two more. But he that had received the one hid it in the earth.

16. After a long time the Lord returned and reckoned with these servants. And when He heard how the first had made his five talents ten, He said to him: "Well done, thou good and faithful servant; because thou hast been faithful over a few things, I will set thee over many things; enter thou into the joy of thy Lord." And to the second servant, who had made his two talents into five, he said the same.

17. But the servant who had received one talent said: "Lord, I know that thou art a hard man, and, being afraid, I went and hid thy talent in the earth; behold, here thou hast that which is thine." Then the Lord said, "Take ye away, therefore, the talent from him and give it to him that hath ten talents.

18. "For to every one that hath shall be given and he shall abound; but from him that hath not, that also which he seemeth to have shall be taken away. And the unprofitable servant cast ye out into exterior darkness."

19. Our Lord then returned to His Prophecy of the end of the world and completed it by setting before His apostles the scene of the Last Judgment. In presence of the celestial King, seated upon the throne of His majesty, all the nations of the earth shall be assembled together.

20. Then He shall separate them, one from the other, even as a shepherd separates the sheep from the goats. Then shall the sheep be gladdened by His loving words: "Come ye blessed of My Father, come hither and possess the Kingdom which hath been prepared for you from the foundation of the world.

21. "For I was hungry and you gave me to eat, I was thirsty and you gave Me to drink; I was a stranger and you took Me

---

16. What did He say to the first and the second servants? 17. What did He say to the servant with the one talent? 18. Continue. 19. What scene did Our Lord then portray to His apostles? 20. How will they be separated and how shall the elect be greeted? 21. What will He tell them they have done to Him?

in; I was naked and you clothed Me, I was sick and you visited Me; in prison and you came to Me."

22. Overwhelmed by such praises, the righteous, in their humility, will exclaim: "Lord, when have we done these things to thee?" And the King shall answer: "Amen, I say to you, as long as you did it to one of these, my least brethren, you did it unto Me."

23. Then shall He say to those on his left hand: "Depart from Me, ye cursed, into everlasting fire which was prepared for the devil and his angels.

24. "For I was hungry and you gave Me not to eat; I was thirsty and you gave Me not to drink; I was a stranger and you took Me not in; sick, and in prison and you did not visit Me."

25. Then they shall ask Him: "When did we see Thee thus, Lord, and not minister to Thee?" And the Lord shall answer: "Amen, I say to you, as long as you did it not to one of these, my least ones, neither did you do it to Me."

26. Then Jesus brought his discourse to a close. "You know," He said, "that the Passover takes place in two days, and that the Son of Man shall be delivered up to be crucified."

CHAPTER IV.

THE LAST SUPPER.

1. ON the following day, Wednesday, Our Lord did not appear either in the Temple or in Jerusalem. On the morning of Thursday the apostles inquired of Him where they were to eat the Paschal Supper, for they were now in the First Day of Asymes (ăz' īmes) or the time of eating unleavened bread.

---

22. What will they answer in their humility? 23. What will He say to those on His left hand? 24. What reproach will He make to them? 25. What will they ask and what will He answer? 26. How did the Saviour conclude His discourse?

2. Leaving Judas unnoticed, though he was the one usually entrusted with the care of providing for their material wants, Our Lord said to Peter and John, "Go and prepare what is necessary." Knowing how dangerous Jerusalem was for them, they inquired, "Master, where wilt thou that we prepare for thee to eat the Pasch?"

3. Our Lord answered: "Go into the city; as you are entering you shall meet a man carrying a jar of water; follow him, and, on reaching the house which he shall enter, say to the master of the dwelling: 'The Master saith, "Mine hour is close at hand, and I am to keep the Pasch with My disciples at thine abode.'

4. "'Where is the room where I may eat the Passover?' Then he himself shall show you a large upper chamber furnished with couches and arranged beforehand. There do you prepare all things needful."

5. Peter and John obeyed and found the householder, who was probably some disciple of Our Lord, hitherto unknown to them. Tradition still fixes the site of this Upper Chamber, so dear to the Christian heart, where the first Eucharistic sacrifice was offered and where the new-born Church found a first shelter; where the Risen Saviour appeared to His Apostles, and the Holy Ghost descended upon them.

6. It was a room with white walls; in the centre stood a low table, with one side free for the servers, while along the other couches were arranged. When Our Lord came at evening with the rest of His apostles, the board was spread with the dishes which comprised the Paschal supper.

7. The principal dish was the Lamb, which had to be penetrated in the form of a Cross, by two branches of pomegranate wood, without having any of its bones broken, and then baked in the furnace. At one side of it were set bitter herbs, such as cresses and parsley, in remembrance of the sorrows of Egypt.

---

2. What did He answer and what did they ask? 3. What did He direct them to do? 4. Continue. 5. Did they obey? 6. Describe the Upper Chamber. 7. What was the principal dish?

THE LAST SUPPER. 315

8. The two other prescribed dishes were the Azyme bread, thin and tasteless, like the paste which the yeast had not time to leaven before the hurried flight of Israel from Egypt, and the Char'o seth—a compound of figs, apples, and citron, cooked in vinegar, and colored by means of cinnamon or other spices, the hue of red bricks, to symbolize the mortar-pits in which they had labored during their cruel bondage.

9. When Our Lord had taken His place at the table, He said to them: "With great desire I have desired to eat this Passover with you before I suffer."

10. Then to make His apostles understand that He meant the accomplishment of a real sacrifice in the Eucharist, He added, "Of a truth, I say unto you: I will nevermore eat this Pasch, until the mystery thereof be fulfilled in the Kingdom of God."

11. The cup of wine mingled with a little water, with the drinking of which the Supper began, was then prepared. Taking it from the hands of His Apostle, Our Lord pronounced over it the accustomed blessing, and afterwards moistened His lips with it, as the master of the household was wont to do.

12. Then he gave it to His Apostles, saying: "Take it, and divide it among you: but as for Me, I will no more drink of the fruit of the vine, until the Kingdom of God cometh."

13. After all had drunk of it, a basin full of water and a towel were passed around that all might purify their hands. Then Jesus rose from the table, and having laid aside His garment, and girded Himself with a towel, poured out water into a basin, and prepared to wash the feet of His Apostles.

14. Peter was the first to see the Master kneel down before him. "What, Lord," he exclaimed, "wouldst thou wash my feet?" Our Lord answered, "Thou knowest not at this time what I wish to do, but thou shalt know shortly."

---

8. What were the other two dishes? 9. What did Our Lord say on taking His place at table? 10. Repeat Our Lord's words in regard to the real sacrifice in the Eucharist. 11. What was then passed around the board? 12. What did He say to His apostles? 13. What took place then? 14. Whom did Our Lord kneel before first?

15. Thus He gave Peter to understand that this ablution was only a symbol,—a figure of the Redemption which washes away our sins. But Peter refused to see anything but the humiliation of his Master. "Never, no, never," he repeated, "shalt Thou wash my feet."

16. To overcome his resistance, Our Lord said, "If I do not wash thee, thou shalt have no part with Me." At once Peter comprehended all that this threat implied and with his usual fervor cried out, " Lord, not only my feet, but my hands and my head."

17. After Our Lord had washed the feet of the Twelve, He resumed His garment, and again took His place on the couch, and told them that they should do to one another as He had done to them. That is, they were not so much to copy the mere action of Jesus, as His self-renunciation, and make self-denial the law of their lives.

18. The Paschal Supper then proceeded. When it was drawing to a close, and whilst they were still eating, Jesus took one of the loaves of unleavened bread, and having given thanks, He blessed it.

19. Then He broke it and offered each of His apostles a portion, saying: "Take ye and eat, This is My Body which is given for you."

20. In like manner, taking the chalice, He gave thanks and blessed it saying: " Drink ye all of this; for This is My Blood of the New Testament, which shall be shed for many for the remission of sins."

21. After the institution of the Sacrament of the Eucharist, Our Lord revealed to His apostles the terrible crime of Judas. "Amen, I say to you, that one of you shall betray me, and even

---

15. What did He give Peter to understand? 16. What did Our Lord say? 17. What did Our Lord tell His apostles to learn from the lesson of humility which He had given them? 18. What did Jesus do when the meal was drawing to a close? 19. How did He institute the Sacrament of the Eucharist? 20. Continue. 21. What did he then reveal to them?

now he eateth with Me." Deeply troubled, they asked with one voice, "Is it I, Lord?"

22. Jesus answered: "It is one of the Twelve; he that dippeth his hand in the dish with Me; that man shall betray Me."

23. As several of the Apostles had no doubt touched the dish at that very moment, this distinction on the part of the Saviour only conveyed to Judas the knowledge that Jesus knew of his crime. It was the appeal of Infinite Mercy to the sinner to repent while there was yet time.

24. Seeing that Judas remained insensible to His tenderness, Our Lord appealed to his fears. "The Son of Man indeed goeth," He said, "according to that which is written of Him, but woe to that man by whom the Son of Man shall be betrayed. It were better for that man never to have been born."

25. Terrified by His menacing words, each of the apostles again asked if it were he? At last the traitor said, "Is it I, Lord?" "Thou hast said it;" answered Jesus, "thou art he." This reply, spoken in a low tone, reached the ears of Judas alone. But it did not move him.

26. Our Lord then said to him. "That which thou dost, do quickly." Judas at once rose up, and leaving the upper chamber, went forth into the night, to consummate his crime by betraying the Master whose Sacred Body he had just profaned in the Sacrament of the Eucharist.

27. So soon as Judas had departed, Jesus had no further thought save for the salvation of the world, and His soul exulted in the prospect of the perfected work of Redemption. "Now is the Son of Man glorified," He said, "and God is glorified in Him; nor will He any longer delay to glorify Himself."

28. Then He comforted His apostles who were overwhelmed with sorrow. He told them that he was soon to leave them, and said to them: "I give you a new commandment, that

---

22. What did he answer? 23. Did this enlighten them? 24. How did Our Lord again appeal to him? 25. Did Judas ask if it were he? 26. What did Our Lord tell him? 27. What joy now filled the Saviour's soul? 28. How did He comfort His apostles?

you love one another as I have loved you. By this shall all men know that you are My Disciples."

29. But Peter said: "Lord, whither art Thou going?" "Whither I go," answered Jesus, "thou canst not follow Me now; later on thou shalt follow Me." "Why cannot I follow Thee now?" answered Peter, "I will lay down my life for Thee."

30. "Thou wilt lay down thy life for Me!" answered Jesus. "Of a truth, yea, of a truth, I tell thee, the cock shall not crow till thou deny Me thrice."

31. Peter was overwhelmed with sadness at this prediction. Jesus therefore said to him: "Simon, Simon, behold Satan hath desired to sift you as wheat. But I have prayed for thee that thy faith fail not; and thou being once converted, confirm thy brethren.

32. "All of you shall be scandalized in Me this night. For it is written: 'I will strike the shepherd, and the sheep of the flock shall be dispersed!'"

33. Our Lord then bade them feel no alarm nor trouble, but believe in Him, for He was going to leave them now only to prepare a place for them among the many mansions in His Father's House.

34. "I will return," He added, "and will take you to Myself that where I am you also may be. And where I go you know, and the way you know."

35. But Thomas said, "Lord, we know not whither Thou goest, and how can we know the way?" Jesus answered: "I am the Way, the Truth, the Life. No man cometh to the Father but by Me.

36. "And I will ask the Father, and He will give you another Paraclete, that He may abide with you forever—the Spirit of Truth, the Comforter—the Holy Ghost, whom the

---

29. What did Peter ask? 30. What did Jesus reveal to Peter? 31. How did Our Lord console Him? 32. What did He foretell to all of the apostles? 33. How did he disarm their fears? 34. What promise did He make them? 35. What did Thomas ask and what did Jesus answer? 36. What did Jesus promise would come upon them?

Father will send in My Name—He will teach you all things, and bring all things to your mind, whatsoever I shall have said to you."

37. I leave you My Peace. Nor do I give you Peace like that which the world giveth. "Let not your heart be troubled, neither let it be afraid." You have heard that which I said to you: I go away, but it is only that I may return to you.

38. If you loved Me, you would rejoice for Me that I go unto My Father. I have but a little longer wherein I may speak with you, for the Prince of this world draweth nigh; and notwithstanding, he hath no power over Me.

39. Yet this must be, that so the world may know I love My Father, and that I do that which He commandeth Me. Then He said to the Apostles, "Arise, let us go hence."

40. The final hymns which closed the Paschal Supper were chanted, and then Our Lord left the upper chamber, and followed by His apostles, went out towards the city gates.

CHAPTER V.

THE PASSION OF OUR DIVINE LORD.—THE AGONY IN THE GARDEN.

1. CROSSING the brook of Kedron, Our Lord ascended the Mount of Olives till He came to a garden called Geth-sem'-a-ne (The Olive Press) on account of one of those instruments which stood there. It was a familiar spot to the Apostles, for the Master often spent there His nights of prayer.

2. "Sit you here," He said to His Apostles, at the gateway of the garden, "while I go yonder and pray." And taking with Him, Peter, James and John, He led them into the blackest shadows of the olive orchard. His soul was filled with

---

37. What did He leave to them? 38. Why did He tell them they should rejoice? 39. Why did He say His Passion must be? 40. What was done?

1. Whither did Our Lord go? 2. What did He say at the gateway?

anguish, and He groaned aloud: "My soul is sorrowful even unto death! wait here, watch and pray!"

3. Then withdrawing from them about a stone's throw, He fell on His knees, His head bowed down till His face pressed the ground, and prayed that if it were possible this hour might pass from Him. "Nevertheless," He said, with resignation, "not My Will, but Thine be done!"

4. Then He returned to His Apostles, craving for human sympathy in His sorrow. But alas! Peter, the intrepid champion of a few hours before, James, even John the Well-Beloved, all slept while He was racked with anguish almost before their eyes.

5. "Simon," He said, with gentle reproach, "couldst thou not watch one hour with Me? Watch ye and pray that ye enter not into temptation; the spirit is willing, but the flesh is weak."

6. Then He withdrew from them again, and once more cast Himself down in the throes of that fierce agony, while His lips still murmured the same prayer as before, "Father, if this chalice cannot pass except I drink it, Thy Will be done."

7. Presently He arose and returned to His Apostles, only to find that weariness had again weighed down their eyelids in slumber. "And they knew not what to answer Him," says St. Mark. Then He left them again, to endure the most awful hour of all that awful agony.

8. Unspeakable was the suffering of the meek Lamb of God, crushed by the weight of the empire of evil throughout the long procession of the ages. No human heart shared that lonely vigil, no human eyes saw the sweat of blood which that nameless agony caused to flow from His sacred Body.

9. Only the Father heard His prayer: "Father, if this chalice may not pass except I drink it, Thy Will be done,"

---

3. What did Our Lord then do? 4. How did He find His Apostles when He returned? 5. What did He say to Peter? 6. Did He leave them again? 7. How did He find them the second time? 8. What fearful anguish seized Our Lord now? 9. Did the Father hear His prayer and console Him?

THE AGONY IN THE GARDEN.

and sent an Angel to console and strengthen Him. And then Jesus rose up "stronger than His sorrow," and prepared for "all that was to come upon Him."

10. Going once more to His Apostles, He said to them: "Sleep on now, and take your rest! Behold the hour is at hand when the Son of Man shall be delivered into the hands of sinners; rise up, come; lo! he that will betray Me is at hand."

11. Our Lord was still speaking when at the foot of the garden appeared a Roman tribune with his soldiers, accompanied by the officers of the Sanhedrin, Temple-guards, and some of the servants of the High-Priest. They were led by Judas.

12. They had paused in consultation, when suddenly He whom they came to seek, appeared before them. "Whom do you seek?" He said to them. Judas was dumfounded, but the rest thinking He was some stranger, answered, "Jesus of Nazareth."

13. Jesus answered, "I am He." In terror they recoiled and fell at His feet. When they had gathered strength to rise again, Our Lord again asked: "Whom seek ye?" They answered again "Jesus of Nazareth." "Then if you are seeking Me," Christ answered, "let these go their way." Thus even in the hour of His foes' triumph, He decrees how far their violence shall extend.

14. Judas now approached Our Lord to give the signal agreed upon for His capture. "Master, Master, hail," he said, and touched with his traitorous lips the cheek of Jesus, who answered; "Judas, friend, is it for this that thou art here? to betray the Son of Man with a kiss?"

15. The soldiers then came up and seized Our Lord. At the sight, the Apostles cried out, "Master, shall we strike at them?" In his wrath Peter waited for no permission but struck off the ear of Malchus, a servant of the High-Priest.

---

10. What did He say to His Apostles? 11. Who came while He was still speaking? 12. When did He appear before them? 13. What did He answer? 14. What did Judas now do? 15. What did the soldiers do and to what rash act was Peter roused?

16. But Our Lord rebuked Peter for thus disturbing His Passion; "Return thy sword to thy sheath," he said, "for whosoever taketh the sword, shall perish by the sword."

17. "Thinkest thou that I cannot ask My Father, and presently He will send hither unto me, twelve legions of angels? Yet how then shall the Scriptures be fulfilled wherein it says that even so it must needs be?"

18. So saying He touched the ear of Malchus and healed him. Then the Apostles all fled, and Our Lord turned his face towards Jerusalem, and began to tread for our sakes the weary steps of the Via Dolorosa.

CHAPTER VI.

THE PASSION OF OUR DIVINE LORD.—THE VIA DOLOROSA.

1. At the time of Our Lord, there were two High-Priests in Jerusalem. Annas who had held the office, had been deposed by Rome and his son-in-law Caiphas appointed to fill his place. In spite of this fact, the Jews continued to regard Annas as their only legitimate Pontiff.

2. On entering Jerusalem therefore, Our Divine Lord was conducted to the palace where dwelt both Annas and Caiphas, but taken first before Annas, who questioned Him at some length "as to His disciples and concerning His doctrine." He thus endeavored to show Him as a conspirer against the power of Rome.

3. But the Saviour firmly vindicated Himself of all earthly ambitions. "I have taught always in the synagogues and the Temple, whither the Jews resort, and I have said nothing in private. Why question Me? Ask those who have heard Me, as to what I have said to them."

---

16. How did Our Lord rebuke Peter? 17. Continue Our Lord's words. 18. What miracle did He then perform, and what took place afterwards?

1. Who were Annas and Caiphas? 2. Before whom was Our Lord conducted? 3. What answer did the Saviour make?

4. At these words, one of the servants of Annas' suite, gave the Saviour a blow, saying, "Is that the way thou answerest the High-Priest?" Our Lord replied: "If I have spoken evil, give testimony of the evil; but if well, why strikest thou Me?"

5. Finding himself unable to criminate Our Lord, Annas sent Him to Caiphas, who had by this time hastily assembled the Sanhedrin, and presided over its night session himself. Before this High Court of Justice, Our blessed Redeemer was now led.

6. The Jewish law required that in capital offences, all evidence for the accused must be heard first. This rule was now utterly broken; in derisive answer to Our Lord's request that they interrogate His hearers, they brought forward a number of false witnesses to testify that they had heard Him utter scandalous sayings.

7. In the end two men testified that they had heard Our Lord say that he was able to destroy the Temple of God, and in three days rebuild it. But they contradicted each other as to what His words had really been on the subject, while Our Lord remained silent.

8. Then Caiphas descended from his seat and advanced to where Our Lord stood. "Answerest Thou nothing to the things which these witness against Thee?" he asked Him. Still the Saviour remained silent. Then Caiphas said, "I adjure Thee, by the Living God, tell us if Thou be the Son of God."

9. The Saviour answered, "I am He. Moreover, I say unto you, hereafter you shall see the Son of Man seated at the right hand of the Majesty of God, and coming in the clouds of heaven."

10. The High-Priest's answer was to rend his garments, and cry out, "What further need have we of witnesses? You have

---

4. What insult was now offered Our Lord, and what did He answer? 5. To whom did Annas send Christ? 6. What did the Jewish law require? 7. What did two men at last testify? 8. What did Caiphas then ask Christ? 9. Repeat Our Saviour's answer. 10. How did the High-Priest receive it?

PASSION OF OUR DIVINE LORD.—THE VIA DOLOROSA. 325

heard the blasphemy. How seems this matter unto you?" The assembly answered "He is worthy of death."

11. The Sanhedrin then adjourned, and handed Our Lord over to their guards for the rest of the night. Aided by the understrappers and hangers on of the court, these subjected the meek Lamb of God to the most unspeakable indignities, until daybreak.

12. After recovering from the first terror, Peter and John had followed Our Lord to Jerusalem. The Well-Beloved Disciple's love made him brave all peril, and kept him in sight of Jesus till the end. The two apostles managed to gain access to the courtyard of the High-Priest's palace whither the guards had conducted Jesus.

13. As the nights of Judea even at this season of the year are extremely chilly, a fire of thorny brushwood, such as grows about Jerusalem, had been lit in the courtyard. Peter now approached it to warm his hands. As he did so, the portress scanned him closely and exclaimed "Art not thou one of this man's disciples?"

14. "No, I am not," Peter answered. A little while after a man approached Peter and said to him; "Thou also art one of them;" Peter answered, "O man, I am not." And then the cock crew.

15. An hour passed, and then one of the servants who heard Peter speak, said to him: "Surely thou art one of this man's disciples, for even thy speech doth betray thee. Thou art a Galilean." But Peter swore that he knew not the man. And then the cock crew a second time.

16. Then Jesus turned and looked at Peter. And at once Peter remembered His words: "Before the cock crows thou shalt have denied Me thrice." Overwhelmed with grief at the thought of his faithlessness, he rushed out of the palace and wept bitterly.

---

11. What did the Sanhedrin then do? 12. Who followed Our Lord? 13. What was in the courtyard? 14. What did Peter answer? 15. How did Peter come to deny Jesus the third time? 16. What did Our Lord do, and what did it arouse in Peter?

17. Early in the morning, Our Lord was brought once more before the Sanhedrin. Again they asked Him if He was the Messiah, again He answered that He was. They then declared Him guilty of death.

18. But as since the exile of Archelaus, the Roman governor alone had power to put prisoners to death, they conducted Him to the Antonia, a fortress north of the Temple, where Pontius Pilate resided during the Jewish Passover.

19. Among those who saw Jesus led away thither was Judas. The sight of His Redeemer's sufferings had aroused in the wretched man all the horrors of remorse unmingled with repentance. "Satan who had entered into him" kept him from seeking peace and salvation from Jesus, and drove him to despair.

20. Rushing into the presence of the priests and ancients in the temple, he held out to them the thirty shekels (about $18.60) for which he had sold his Master. "I have sinned," he cried; "I have betrayed the blood of the Just One." They answered with disdain: "What is that to us? That is thy affair!"

21. In a frenzy of despair, Judas rushed from the Temple, flinging as he went the price of his treachery on the threshhold, and hurried to a wild and lonely stretch of land beyond the brook of Kedron, where he hanged himself in a clay-field belonging to a potter.

---

17. What took place in the morning? 18. Who could alone punish unto death? 19. What emotions did the sufferings of Jesus arouse in Judas? 20. What did he say to the priests and ancients? 21. What was his terrible end?

CHAPTER VII.

THE PASSION OF OUR LORD.—THE VIA DOLOROSA.—(CONTINUED.)

1. The priests had not been able to accompany Our Lord to Pilate, because their presence was necessary at the Temple for the morning sacrifice; it was for this reason Judas had sought them there. But the rest of the assembly conducted Him to the Pre-tor'-i-um, as the residence of the Roman governor was called.

2. On arriving at the entrance, the members of the Sanhedrin paused; they dared not cross the threshold of a heathen, for they would thus have been contaminated and rendered unfit to take part in the Paschal rites. Pilate, respecting their scruples, came to meet them in the outer court.

3. "What accusation do you bring against this man?" asked the judicial Roman. The Sanhedrin knew that their true reason for wishing the death of Jesus—that He called Himself the Son of God, equal to the Father—would have little weight with Rome. They therefore resolved to effect His ruin on political grounds.

4. "We have found Him," they said, "exciting the people, forbidding to pay tribute to Cæsar, and calling Himself the Christ King." But Pilate knew the Jews too well to be duped by their sudden zeal to avenge the wrongs of Rome.

5. Determined to sift the matter, he re-entered the pretorium and had Our Lord brought to him. When they were alone, Pilate said to Jesus, "Art Thou truly King of the Jews?" Our Lord answered: "My Kingdom is not of this world." "Then Thou art a King!" said Pilate. Christ answered: "Thou hast said it."

---

1. Who conducted Our Lord to Pilate? 2. Where were the Jews obliged to pause? 3. What question did Pilate ask, and what ground did they take? 4. Relate their reply and what Pilate thought of it.

6. Our Lord then added: "I was born and I came into the world in order to render homage to the Truth. Whosoever is of the Truth, heareth My Voice." Stirred by doubt, Pilate answered, "What is truth?" and then went back to the Jews, and told them he saw no ground for condemning Jesus.

7. At his words, their fury grew intense and they made all sorts of charges against the Saviour who had now been conducted once more before them. Pilate turned to Him and said: "Dost Thou not hear of how many things they accuse Thee?" But Our Lord remained silent.

8. "He stirs up the people," urged the members of the Sanhedrin fiercely; "teaching throughout all Judea, beginning from Galilee to this place." The word Galilee suggested to the perplexed Pilate an expedient—if Our Lord were a Galilean, the proper person to judge Him was Herod, who was even then in Jerusalem.

9. Pilate therefore bade his guards conduct Our Lord to the residence of that prince. Herod, who was full of curiosity concerning Him, was pleased to see Him, hoping that He would perform some miracle in order to gain His liberty. He therefore received Him with some show of respect, and pressed Him to show His supernatural powers.

10. But Our Lord, who had only words of tender mercy for the weak Pilate, deigned not so much as a word in reply to the mocking Herod. Disconcerted by His silence, and perhaps dreading such terrors as had haunted him after the death of John the Baptist, the indolent prince sent Him back to Pilate.

11. In token however, of derision for Christ, Herod had Him clothed in a white robe. As this garment was also assumed by Jews acquitted of capital offences, Pilate argued with the Sanhedrin, that Herod had found nothing in Him worthy of death, and that He therefore should be acquitted.

---

6. For what did Our Lord tell Pilate He came into the world? 7. What was the result of Pilate's declaration? 8. What did they charge Our Lord with and what did it suggest to Pilate? 9. Did Pilate send Our Lord to Herod? 10. What resulted? 11. How did Herod act to show his scorn for Christ?

12. So terrible a storm of opposition greeted his words, that Pilate was silenced, until the sight of the immense crowds of people ascending the approaches to the fortress, suggested a new expedient to him in behalf of Our Lord.

13. It was the custom at the Jewish Pasch, for the Roman governor, in order to heighten the solemnity of the festival, to grant a pardon to some prisoner designated by the people. Among those who now lay under sentence of death, was a notorious robber named Barabbas.

14. Pilate therefore exclaimed to the people: "Whom do you wish me to release to you, Barabbas, or Jesus who is called the Messiah?" And so speaking, he ascended his tribunal which was set before the Pretorium.

15. While they were discussing his offer, a servant brought the following message to him from his wife: "Let there be nothing between you and that just man, for I have been greatly distressed in a dream this day because of him."

16. Alone against all these wicked judges, these false witnesses and inhuman wretches, a pagan woman had courage and tenderness to plead the cause of Jesus. But it was useless, for the priests and magistrates had by this time prevailed on the multitude to choose Barabbas in preference to Christ.

17. And so when Pilate asked whom they decided to release, the populace cried out: "Away with this man! Release Barabbas." "What shall I do then with Him whom you call King of the Jews?" asked Pilate. "Crucify Him! crucify Him," they answered.

18. "But what evil has He done?" persisted Pilate. "As for me, I find no cause of death in Him. I will chastise Him therefore, and let Him go." Our Lord was therefore bound to a pillar in the presence of the people, His garment was stripped

---

12. Was Pilate silenced? 13. What custom prevailed at the Jewish Pasch? 14. What did Pilate ask the people? 15. What message did his wife send to him? 16. Was this intercession of this good pagan woman of any avail? 17. For whose release did they ask? 18. What iniquitous concession did Pilate make in the hope of saving Our Lord?

from His shoulders, and He was scourged with a horrible scourge of many lashes.

19. He was then led into the palace, and covered with a red soldier's cloak, while in mockery of regal state, a crown of long deep thorns was placed on His head, and a reed thrust into His hand for a sceptre.

20. Then the soldiery bent the knee before Him in mockery, crying, "Hail, King of the Jews!" Others spat upon Him, and snatching the reed from His hand, struck Him in the Head, driving the thorns still deeper into His sacred flesh. At last they blindfolded Him, and mockingly asked Him to prophesy who struck Him.

21. When at length, Our Lord was led back to Pilate, His condition was so pitable, that the governor thought the sight of Him must move even His enemies to compassion. So he led Him out before them, and said to them "Ecce Homo!" (Behold the Man!). But their hearts were steeled against pity: their only answer was the awful cry, "Crucify Him! Crucify Him."

22. Pilate answered: "Take Him you and crucify Him: for I find no cause in Him." He spoke only in irony, for the Sanhedrin had no power to put any one to death, and in despair of making him yield to their wishes, they at last unmasked the true reason of their savage hatred of Christ.

23. "We have a law," they cried, "and according to that law He ought to die; because He made Himself the Son of God." These words increased the uneasiness of Pilate; the idea that the meek, blood-stained, thorn-crowned Victim might indeed be God, smote him with a vague terror.

24. Re-entering the Pretorium once more with Our Lord, he said to Him, "Whence art Thou?" Our Lord remained silent, and Pilate went on; "Speakest Thou not to me?

---

19. How was Our Lord then attired? 20. What did the soldiery do to Him? 21. What did Pilate do when Our Lord was led back to him? 22. What did Pilate answer? 23. What did the Sanhedrin now reveal, and what effect had it on Pilate? 24. What did he ask Our Lord?

Knowest Thou not that I have power to crucify Thee, and power to release Thee?"

25. Our Lord answered, "Thou shouldst not have any power against Me, if it were not given thee from above. And this is why the crime of him who delivers Me into thy hands is greater than thine."

26. Pilate's conscience was now aroused; he went out once more to argue with the Jews in defence of Jesus, but was soon overwhelmed with cries of "If thou dost release this man, thou art no friend of Cæsar."

27. This was a terrible threat, for Tiberius, the Cæsar, or Roman emperor, of that day, was a tyrant whose lightest susspicions had only to be aroused against the most powerful or favored of his subjects, to insure their ruin.

28. Inspired by their savage hatred of Christ, the cunning Jews had struck the right chord in Pilate's timid heart, and awakened a fear for himself which mastered his compassion for Our Lord.

29. Ascending the tribunal, he caused Jesus to be brought before him. But before giving Him up, he caused water to be brought, and washed his hands before all the people saying: "I am innocent of the blood of this Just Man; look you to it."

30. The deicides answered "His blood be upon us, and upon our children." Then Pilate, utterly vanquished, released Barabbas, and delivered Jesus into their hands to be crucified.

CHAPTER VIII.

THE PASSION OF OUR LORD.—THE VIA DOLOROSA.—(CONCLUDED.)

1. A ROMAN centurion with a band of soldiers, acted as the executioner of the sentence pronounced on Our Lord by Pilate.

---

25. What did Our Lord answer? 26. Did Pilate strive again to save Our Lord? 27. Did Pilate fear Cæsar? 28. Did this conquer Pilate? 29. What did Pilate do before condemning Jesus? 30. What did the deicides answer?
1. Who carried out the sentence?

They took from His bruised Body the red cloak, and clothing Him in His own garments, laid on His shoulders the cross on which He was to be crucified.

2. Attended by the members of the Sandedrin, and followed by the populace, Our Divine Lord was then led westward through the most hilly streets of Jerusalem, to the gate of Ephraim. But as He toiled up the ascent which led to it, His strength, exhausted by the agony of Gethsemane, and the terrible scourging, failed Him, and He sank to the ground.

3. The soldiers thereupon compelled a countryman named Simon of Cyrene, who was just entering the gate, to carry the cross with Our Saviour to the place of execution.

4. At the sight of the Man of Sorrows thus led to die, some pious women shed tears of compassion. But Christ, turning towards them, said: "Daughters of Jerusalem, weep not over Me; but weep for yourselves and your children.

5. "For behold the days shall come when they shall say to the mountains: 'Fall upon us,' and to the hills, 'Cover us,' for if men deal thus with the green wood, what shall be done in the dry?"

6. This solemn exhortation to penance on the part of the suffering Lamb of God, referred to the impending destruction of Jerusalem which, forty years later, perhaps these very same women or their children were to witness. He warned them how great was their need of it, when they saw Him, the Just, the Perfect One, thus suffering.

7. Bereft of His strength, Our Lord at last reached the summit of the hill of Calvary outside the gates of Jerusalem. According to Jewish custom, He was here offered wine mingled with myrrh and poppy, to deaden His sensibility to suffering. But Our Lord refused to drink of it.

8. The Saviour was then stripped of His garments, and His

---

2. Whither was Our Lord then led? 3. Whom did the soldiers compel to assist Our Lord? 4. Who were moved to compassion? 5. Continue. 6. What did this reply of Our Lord mean? 7. What happened when Our Lord reached Calvary? 8. What was then done to Our Saviour?

hands and feet nailed to the Cross. Two thieves were crucified with Him, one on the right, and one on the left.

9. The soldiers then placed above the head of Christ, the inscription dictated by Pilate in Hebrew, Greek, and Latin: "Jesus of Nazareth, King of the Jews." Pilate thus showed his contempt for the Jews.

10. The High-Priests at once went back to Pilate to inform Him that the people desired the title changed to: "Behold him who called himself the King of the Jews," but Pilate answered: "That which is written, is written."

11. It was not even granted to Our Lord to have His agony respected. Calvary lay just at the gates of Jerusalem, and during the three long hours during which, for our sake, He hung naked, bruised, and thorn-crowned on the bitter cross, a mocking, blaspheming crowd surged at its foot.

12. The first thought of Our Divine Lord when He was thus raised between heaven and earth, was to pray for his executioners. It was in their behalf He uttered His first words on the Cross: "Father, forgive them, for they know not what they do."

13. Unmindful of these touching words, the soldiers were busy dividing His garments among them. For His seamless tunic, probably spun and woven by the loving hands of Mary, they cast lots, thus fulfilling the prophecy, "They have parted My garments among them, upon My robe they have cast lots."

14. The rabble cried out to Our Lord: "Thou that destroyest the Temple of God, and in three days buildest it up, save thyself. If thou be the Son of God, come down from the cross."

15. The members of the Sanhedrin cried out: "He saved others, himself He cannot save." The two crucified thieves

---

9. What inscription was placed above His head? 10. What did the High-Priests do? 11. What took place beneath the cross? 12. For whom did Our Lord first pray? 13. What did the soldiers do? 14. How did the rabble insult Our Lord? 15. How did the members of the Sanhedrin insult Him?

caught the words, and one of them echoed the blasphemy, crying out: "If Thou be Christ, save Thyself and us."

16. But the other thief rebuked him, saying: "Thou hast no fear of God, though thou art condemned to the same sentence! Yet for us, this is only justice, since we suffer the just reward of our deeds; but this man hath done no evil."

17. Then filled with faith he turned to Jesus, and implored: "Lord when thou shalt come into Thy Kingdom, remember me!" Then Our Lord spoke for the second time, and said to the penitent who had recognized his Saviour in the hour of His humiliation: "Amen, I say to thee, this day shalt thou be with Me in Paradise."

18. The storm of passion about the cross gradually stilled, for a darkness which had been gathering over the whole earth, for some hours, now began to mount upward to the cross, and hide the Crucified One from human gaze. The crowds fell back and thus permitted the Blessed Virgin, with John the Beloved disciple, and Mary Magdalen, to approach it.

19. Looking down upon His Mother, whose heart He now saw pierced with the sword which the aged Simeon had foretold should transfix it, Jesus spoke for the third time and said to her, "Woman, behold thy Son." Then turning to John, He said, "Behold thy mother!" And from that moment, the disciple regarded Mary as his mother.

20. Deeper and deeper grew the darkness which clouded the awful agony of Jesus. Again, as in His first agony, the unspeakable suffering of Jesus was caused by the wickedness of mankind, whose sins from the beginning to the end of time all stood forth before His dying eyes.

21. Terrible also to His merciful heart was the thought that so many would refuse to profit by His Passion. The multitude of the damned were all visible to His eyes, and He

---

16. What did the penitent thief exclaim? 17. What did he beg of Jesus? 18. What enabled the Blessed Virgin to approach the cross? 19. What did Our Lord say to His mother and to John? 20. What caused the terrible suffering of Jesus? 21. What also caused our Lord's suffering?

mourned that for so vast a number, His sweat, His toils and His death should be in vain.

22. That He might drink this chalice of sorrow even to the dregs, Jesus was abandoned in this awful desolation by His Father. This was the crown of His suffering, whose intensity was only revealed by the bitter cry which went up through the gloom, when Our Lord spoke for the fourth time: "My God, My God, why hast Thou forsaken Me?"

23. The darkness now lifted, the end was drawing near. In a few moments Jesus spoke for the fifth time, saying: "I thirst." Then one of the soldiers took a sponge, and, steeping it in vinegar and gall, put it on the end of a reed and presented it to Our Lord's lips.

24. And when Jesus had tasted it He spoke for the sixth time, saying, "It is consummated!" His work was now finished, and He spoke for the seventh and last time: "Father," He cried with a loud voice, "into Thy Hands I commend My Spirit."

25. Then bowing down His sacred head, Our Lord expired. "And immediately the veil of the Temple was rent from the top to the bottom and torn in twain; the earth trembled, rocks were cloven asunder, graves opened and many bodies of the Saints who had slept rose from their tombs."

26. These prodigies caused the Roman centurion to cry out: "This was indeed the Son of God." His soldiers echoed the cry, and the Jews withdrew from Calvary, "striking their breasts."

27. The High-Priests besought Pilate to have the bodies of the crucified removed before the Sabbath. He therefore sent a band of soldiers with heavy clubs to break their bones if they were still living, in order to kill them before taking them down from the cross.

---

22. What was the crown of Our Lord's suffering? 23. What did Our Lord say when He spoke the fifth time? 24. What were the sixth and seventh words on the cross? 25. What prodigies attended Our Lord's death? 26. What effect had they on the Roman centurion? 27. What did the High-Priests beseech Pilate?

28. After killing the two thieves in this manner, the soldiers came to Our Lord but found Him already dead. In order to make sure that life was altogether extinct, however, one of them buried his lance in the Saviour's side and caused a stream of blood and water to gush forth.

29. As evening drew nigh, a rich and powerful Jew named Joseph of Arimathea, presented himself on Calvary. He was a member of the Sanhedrin, but, far from taking any part in condemning Jesus, had long been one of His secret disciples.

30. He had obtained from Pilate permission to bury the body of Our Lord and had purchased a linen shroud and a winding-sheet. Another prince of Israel, Nicodemus, the timid Scribe, who had gone by night to converse with Jesus, assisted him in his holy work.

31. Reverently they took down the sacred Body, and, wrapping it in the linen shroud with costly perfumes and spices, swathed it in the winding-sheet. Then they hastened—for the Sabbath was almost upon them—to a garden near Calvary, owned by Joseph, where there was a yet unused tomb hewn out of the side of a cliff.

32. In this death-chamber they tenderly laid the Sacred Body on a stone couch, according to Jewish custom. Then, after closing the mouth of the grave with a great stone, they returned to Jerusalem, just as the stars which announced the Great Sabbath of the Pasch, shone out in the evening sky.

33. On the following day, the chief priests went to Pilate and said: "Sir, we have remembered that that seducer said when He was yet alive: "After three days, I will rise again." Command therefore the sepulchre to be guarded till the third day, lest His disciples come and steal Him away, and say to the people: "He is risen from the dead."

---

28. What did they do to Our Lord? 29. Who came to Calvary near evening? 30. What had Joseph obtained from Pilate? 31. Where did they bear the Sacred Body of Our Lord after taking it down from the Cross? 32. Continue. 33. What did the chief priests ask Pilate?

CHRIST RESTORES THE WIDOW'S SON TO LIFE.

34. Pilate answered: "Take some of the guards; go guard it as well as you know how." So they went to the tomb, and, after sealing the great stone which closed the entrance, placed a guard of Roman soldiers before it.

---

34. What did Pilate answer?

IV.—FORTY DAYS OF OUR LORD ON EARTH AFTER HIS RESURRECTION.

CHAPTER I.

RESURRECTION OF OUR DIVINE LORD.

1. EARLY on the morning of the third day, there was a mighty earthquake, and Jesus rose from the tomb, glorious and immortal. An Angel of the Lord descended from Heaven, and His face shone brighter than lightning, and His garments were as white as snow.

2. So terrified were the guards at His appearance that they fell senseless to the ground. When they regained consciousness, they rose and fled back to the city.

3. They at once told the High-Priest what had occurred. The latter gave them a sum of money and bade them say that Christ's disciples stole away His Body while they were asleep; a story which is believed by the Jews till the present day.

4. While this was taking place, Mary Magdalen, Sa'lō'mē, and Mary the mother of James, were hastening towards the tomb with perfumes and sweet spices, to anoint the Body of Our Lord.

5. As they came, they said to one another: "Who will help us to remove the stone from the door of the sepulchre?" But when they arrived there, they found it already rolled away. At once Mary Magdalen became convinced that Our Lord's

---

1. Describe the Resurrection of Our Divine Lord. 2. How were the guards affected? 3. How did the High-Priests bid them account for the removal of the Body of Jesus? 4. Who were hastening to the

enemies had stolen His Body, and hurried back to Jerusalem to tell the apostles.

6. The other two pious women entered the sepulchre. A young man, clothed in shining white garments, was seated on the right hand side of the dark death chamber. At sight of him they trembled but he said: "Do not fear, you seek Jesus of Nazareth, who was crucified. He is risen. He is no longer here.

7. "Go quickly and announce to Peter and the disciples that He is risen from the dead. He will go before you into Galilee; there you shall see Him, according as He foretold you." Filled with joy, the women departed.

8. At the words of Magdalen, Peter and John had hastened to the tomb. Entering, they found the linen cloths which had enfolded Our Lord's Body, and the napkin which had enwrapt His sacred head, carefully folded. At this token, "they comprehended that Christ was risen indeed."

9. According to Christian tradition, the first to whom the Risen Lord appeared on that first Easter Sunday morning was His Blessed Mother, although the first that the Gospel tells us had the privilege of beholding Him, was Mary Magdalen.

10. After relating to the Apostles what she had seen, Magdalen had returned to the tomb. There she saw two Angels, one of whom said to her: "Woman, why weepest thou?" She sorrowfully answered: "Because they have taken away My Lord, and I know not where they have laid Him."

11. Then turning, she saw a Man, who said to her: "Whom seekest thou?" Supposing Him to be the gardener, Mary answered; "Sir, if Thou hast taken Him, tell me where Thou hast laid Him, and I will take Him away.

12. Our Lord for it was He, spoke but one word in answer:

---

6. Whom did the other pious women find within the tomb? 7. What else did the Angel say? 8. Which of the apostles now entered the tomb? 9. To whom did Christ first appear? 10. Whom did Magdalen find in the tomb when she returned? 11. Whom did she see when she

RESURRECTION OF OUR DIVINE LORD.

"Mary!" Instantly recognizing Him, Mary fell at His feet, crying, "Master!"

13. But Our Lord said to her. "Touch Me not! Go to My Brethren and say to them; I ascend to My Father and your Father, to My God, and your God." And Mary Magdalen rose up and hastened to carry the Lord's message to the disciples.

14. The day wore on, and save Peter and John, none of the disciples believed that the Lord had risen. Towards evening two of them started towards Emmaus, a village distant about two hours walk from Jerusalem.

15. They were discussing on the road, the late events in Jerusalem, when Jesus joined them under the guise of a stranger, and asked of what events they were speaking, and why they were so sad.

16. One of them, named Cleophas, answered; "Stranger, art thou then the only one in Jerusalem ignorant of the things which have happened there in these days?" Our Lord asked: "What things?"

17. Cleophas answered: "Concerning Jesus of Nazareth, who was a prophet, and concerning our chief priests and rulers who crucified Him. Now to-day, it is the third day since these things were done. Yea, some women, also of our company, who have been at the sepulchre, say He is alive."

18. Our Lord answered; "O foolish, and slow of heart to believe all the things which the prophets have spoken. Ought not Christ to have suffered these things, and so enter into His glory?"

19. Then, beginning with Moses and the prophets, He explained to them all that had been foretold of Him. When they reached the hamlet of Emmaus, Our Lord made as if He would go further, but they begged Him to stay with them, as the day was far spent.

---

13. What did Our Lord say to her? 14. What occurred towards the close of the day? 15. When did Our Lord join them? 16. What did Cleophas answer? 17. What reply did Cleophas make? 18. What did Our Lord answer? 19. What did Our Lord explain to them?

20. He yielded to their entreaties and remained; and when they sat down to table, He took bread, blessed, brake it, and gave it to them. And at once their eyes were opened and they knew Him.

21. Then He vanished, and they said to one another: "Were not our hearts burning within us, whilst He was speaking in the way, and revealed to us the meaning of the Scriptures?"

22. That same evening they returned to Jerusalem, where they found the eleven gathered together, in that same upper chamber which had served as a supper-room. They were greeted with the words: "The Lord has truly risen. He has appeared to Simon."

CHAPTER II.

OUR LORD APPEARS TO HIS APOSTLES.—INSTITUTES THE SACRAMENT OF PENANCE.—MAKES PETER THE HEAD OF THE CHURCH.—THE ASCENSION.

1. THE apostles were still at supper, when all at once Jesus stood in the midst of them and said: "Peace be unto you."

2. They trembled with fear, thinking it was a spirit, but He said: "It is I; fear nothing! Why are you troubled? Behold my hands and feet; a spirit hath not flesh and bones as you see I have."

3. Then He showed them His pierced hands and His feet, and His wounded side. But they were still overcome with awe. Then Jesus, in order to show them that His Risen Body had kept its nature unchanged, said: "Have you here anything to eat?"

4. A portion of roasted fish and some honeycomb were on the

---

20. How did they recognize Him? 21. What did they say to each other after He had disappeared? 22. What did they hear when they returned to Jerusalem?

1. When did Jesus appear to the apostles? 2. How did they regard Him? 3. How did Our Lord convince them? 4. Did Our Lord partake of food?

table. Our Lord ate of these and gave the remainder to the apostles, saying: "Peace be to you! As the Father hath sent Me, I also send you."

5. Then He breathed upon them and said, "Receive ye the Holy Ghost; whose sins you shall forgive, they are forgiven; whose sins you shall retain, they are retained."

6. Thus did Our Lord institute the Sacrament of Penance; and confer on mortals the power of disposing of eternal treasures, the right of opening and shutting the gates of Heaven.

7. It happened that Thomas, one of the Twelve Apostles, was not in the supper-room when Our Lord appeared, and when the apostles told him that they had seen Him, he declared that he would not believe that Christ had risen unless he put his hands in the print of the nails and into the wound in His side.

8. Eight days after, the apostles were again assembled and Thomas with them. Suddenly Jesus appeared in the midst of them, saying, "Peace be to you!" Then, turning to Thomas, He bade him put his fingers in the print of the nails in His hands and feet and into His wounded side.

9. Thomas did so and exclaimed with fervor: "My Lord and My God!" Jesus gently rebuked his incredulity by contrasting his tardy faith with the happiness of those many souls who should believe in Him without having seen Him. "Thomas," He said, "thou hast believed because thou hast seen Me. Blessed are they that without seeing have believed!"

10. When the Paschal-tide was over, many of Our Lord's disciples returned to Galilee, whither Jesus had promised to precede them. Here, one dawn, as seven of the apostles were returning to the shore of the Lake of Genesareth, after a fruitless night of fishing, they saw Jesus standing on the shore.

11. At first they did not recognize Him, but He told them to cast their nets on the right side of the boat. The vast quan-

---

5. What did He say to the apostles? 6. What did Our Lord thus institute? 7. What did Thomas say? 8. Did Jesus appear to Thomas? 9. How did Our Lord rebuke Thomas after he had done so? 10. Whither did many of the disciples go? 11. Did they recognize Him?

tity of fish which filled their nets when they did so made John exclaim: "It is the Lord."

12. When they reached the beach Our Lord ate with them. When the meal was finished Jesus said to Peter: "Simon, son of John, lovest thou Me more than these?" "Lord," answered Peter, "Thou knowest that I love Thee."

13. Jesus answered: "Feed My lambs." Then Our Lord said to him again: "Simon, son of John, lovest thou Me?" Peter again answered: "Yes, Lord, Thou knowest that I love Thee." Christ answered: "Feed My Lambs."

14. Then for the third time Jesus asked him: "Simon, son of John, lovest thou Me?" Grieved to hear Our Lord thus questioning him, Peter answered, "Lord, Thou knowest all things. Thou knowest that I love Thee."

15. The humility of Peter was now proven beyond doubt, and made his love accounted worthy of God's highest favors. Our Lord answered, "Feed my sheep," thus making him once for all the infallible Teacher, the Judge from whom there is no appeal, the supreme Shepherd of the Church.

16. During Our Lord's stay on earth, He frequently appeared to His apostles, and confided to them the things that were necessary for them to know for the organization and government of His Church.

17. At last the Saviour's mission was fulfilled, and all that remained for Him to do was to fulfil His promise to manifest Himself to all His disciples assembled together. He therefore did so on a certain day, on a mountain which He designated.

18. On the fortieth day after His resurrection, Jesus brought His apostles to Mount Olivet, and said to them: "All power is given to Me in Heaven and on earth. Go, therefore, and teach all nations; baptizing them in the name of the Father, and of the Son, and of the Holy Ghost.

---

12. What did Our Lord do? 13. What did Jesus answer? 14. Did He ask for the third time? 15. What dignity was now conferred on Peter? 16. Did Our Lord often appear to His Apostles? 17. Was Our Saviour's mission now fulfilled? 18. Whither did Our Lord take his apostles on the fortieth day after His Resurrection?

OUR LORD APPEARS TO HIS APOSTLES.

19. "Teach them to keep all things that I have commanded you; and behold I am with you all days even to the consummation of the world."

20. Then, lifting up His hands, He blessed them. And even as He did so, He rose slowly from the earth, until a cloud hid Him from their sight.

21. The apostles remained gazing up into heaven, when two angels stood by them and said to them: "Men of Galilee, why stand you thus gazing up into heaven? This Jesus who is taken up from you into Heaven, shall so come as you have seen Him go into Heaven." And the apostles fell prostrate, adoring God.

---

19. What injunction did He give them? 20. Describe the Ascension. 21. Who spoke to the apostles?

THE ASCENSION.

V.—ACTS OF THE APOSTLES.

CHAPTER I.

ELECTION OF MATTHIAS.—DESCENT OF THE HOLY GHOST.—THE APOSTLES PREACH THE GOSPEL.—ANANIAS AND SAPHIRA. PHIRA.

1. DESCENDING from Mount Olivet, the apostles repaired to the upper chamber or supper-room, where they remained in prayer for ten days, with Our Blessed Lady and other holy women, and a great number of disciples.

2. During this time, Peter arose and said that it was expedient that a new apostle should be chosen in the place of the traitor Judas. After praying for light, they therefore cast lots, and the choice fell on Matthias, who was thenceforth one of the twelve.

3. At the end of the ten days, the Jews celebrated the Feast of Pentecost. The apostles were assembled in prayer, when suddenly there came a sound from heaven as of a mighty, rushing wind, and it filled the whole house where they were sitting.

4. Then there appeared to them cloven tongues, as it were, and sat upon every one of them. And they were filled with the Holy Ghost, and began to speak in divers tongues.

5. The report of these marvels spread through Jerusalem, where Jews from every country in the world were gathered for the celebration of the Feast. Many of them hastened to the house where the apostles were assembled, and each one was astonished to hear them speak in his own tongue.

---

1. Whither did the apostles go from Olivet? 2. What did Peter advise? 3. What took place on the Feast of Pentecost? 4. What appeared to them? 5. Who sought the Apostles?

6. Some mocked the apostles, declaring they were intoxicated, but Peter going out into the street, rebuked them, declaring that what they did was done by the power of Jesus of Nazareth, Whom they had put to death.

7. He therefore bade them do penance and be baptized. His words had a divine power which penetrated many hearts, and caused them to believe and be baptized, to the number of three thousand.

8. One day, shortly after, as Peter and John were entering the Temple, by the Gate called the Beautiful, they passed a beggar who had been lame from his birth, who begged them for an alms.

9. Peter answered: "Silver and gold I have none, but what I have I give to thee; in the name of Jesus Christ of Nazareth, rise up and walk!" Then Peter took the cripple by his right hand, and at once the man arose cured, and entered the Temple.

10. The people were filled with amazement at this sight, but Peter again told them not to wonder, for the miracle had been wrought by Jesus of Nazareth, whom they had put to death, and exhorted them to do penance.

11. Many of those who heard him were converted, but while he was still speaking, the chief priests and officers of the temple came and arrested them, and cast them into prison, where they remained till the following day.

12. Then the Sanhedrin had the apostles brought before them, and asked, "By what power, or in whose name have you done this?" Peter answered that it was in the Name of His Lord, Jesus Christ of Nazareth.

13. Then the Sanhedrin had them removed, and deliberated as to the best means of preventing the influence of the miracle

---

6. What did Peter answer those who mocked them? 7. Were many baptized? 8. Whom did Peter and John meet before the Temple? 9. What did Peter answer? 10. What did Peter again say to the people? 11. What did the chief priests do to the apostles? 12. What did the Sanhedrin demand? 13. What did the Sanhedrin deliberate upon and decide?

from spreading among the people, and finally decided to forbid the apostles to work any more miracles.

14. They therefore had the apostles brought in once more, and commanded them to speak no more in the Name of Jesus. But they answered: "If it be just in the sight of God to hear you rather than God, judge ye, for we cannot but speak the things which we have seen and heard."

15. When the other apostles and the disciples of Jesus heard what had taken place, they were moved to great fervor, and prayed that God might strengthen them in the faith and work signs and wonders by their hands.

16. And as they prayed, the house in which they were was shaken, and the Holy Ghost descended upon them, and imparted to them the gift of courage and the spirit of concord.

17. This beginning of the Church of Christ was marked by all the features which might be expected in a community which was the purest and freshest outburst of the seed sown in Our Lord's Human life—unity in the Apostolic doctrine, in the reception of the Blessed Sacrament, and common ownership of earthly possessions.

18. Even among these first Christians, unhappily, there were unworthy members. There was a certain man called An-a-nī' as who with his wife Saphira (Sa-fī' ra), had become a Christian. The pair sold a field, but gave only a part of the price which they received for it, to Peter.

19. But when Ananias brought him the money, Peter said to him: "Ananias, why hast thou let Satan tempt thee to lie to the Holy Ghost? Why hast thou kept back a part of the price of the field? Thou hast not lied to men, but to God." And at once Ananias fell dead at Peter's feet.

20. Three hours later, Saphira came and repeated the same

---

14. What did they command the apostles? 15. For what did the disciples pray? 16. What did the Holy Ghost impart to them? 17. What marked the beginning of the Church? 18. Who were Ananias and Saphira? 19. What did Peter say to him, and what terrible punishment befell him? 20. What happened to Saphira?

story, when she also fell dead. And when the faithful heard of this terrible punishment of falsehood, fear and terror came upon them.

CHAPTER II.

THE SANHEDRIN ARRESTS THE APOSTLES.—THE RABBI GAMALIEL'S COUNSEL TO THE SANHEDRIN.—ST. STEPHEN, THE FIRST MARTYR.—PHILIP BAPTIZES THE OFFICER OF QUEEN CANDACE.—CONVERSION OF SAUL.

1. THE apostles wrought so many signs and wonders among the people, that the number of the faithful rapidly increased. The Sanhedrin therefore caused the twelve Apostles to be imprisoned.

2. But an angel of the Lord came by night, and opened the doors of the prison, and said to them: "Go, and standing, speak in the Temple to the people, the words of life." They did so, and when the Sanhedrin heard of it, they had them arrested again and brought before them.

3. Then its members said to them: "We commanded you that you should not teach in this name. Behold, you have filled Jerusalem with your doctrine."

4. The apostles answered: "We ought to obey God rather than men. The God of our fathers hath raised up Jesus, Whom you put to death, hanging Him upon a tree. This Prince and Saviour, God hath exalted with His right hand, to give penitence to Israel, and remission of sins."

5. These words aroused the Sanhedrin to such anger that they thought of putting the apostles to death. But its head, the Rabbi Ga-ma'li-el, caused the prisoners to be removed from the hall, and then addressed the assembly as follows:

6. "Ye men of Israel, consider with yourselves what you are

---

1. What did the Sanhedrin do to the apostles? 2. What did the angel tell them to do? 3. What did its members say to them? 4. Relate their answer. 5. What effect had their words? 6. Repeat Gamaliel's words.

about to do with these men. If this work be of men, it will fall to nothing. But if it be of God, you are not able to destroy it, lest, perhaps, you be found to oppose God."

7. Gamaliel's words so far impressed the assembly that they contented themselves with scourging the apostles, and then set them free, with an injunction to speak no more in the name of Jesus. But far from heeding this, the apostles continued to proclaim everywhere, the glory and power of the Crucified Saviour.

8. As the Christians grew in numbers, the apostles chose certain holy men, called deacons, to attend to the temporal concerns of the Church. Among these was Stephen, who was the first to shed his blood for Christ, being stoned to death by order of the Sanhedrin.

9. While he was being put to death, a young man named Saul, held the garments of his murderers. With his dying breath, Stephen prayed to God to forgive all who had part in his death, and so pleasing was his prayer to God, that many sacred writers believe it obtained Saul's conversion.

10. Stephen's death only began a fierce persecution of all who believed in Christ. The most ardent of the persecutors was Saul, who went from house to house, seeking out all who professed to be followers of Jesus, and casting them into prison.

11. In consequence of this fierce persecution, many of the disciples left Jerusalem, and went from place to place throughout Judea and Samaria, preaching the word of God. Philip, one of the deacons, made many converts in Samaria, and later, Peter and John went thither and confirmed them.

12. After Peter and John had preached the gospel in Samaria, they returned to Jerusalem, but an angel appeared to Philip, and told him to go to the south by the road that led from Jerusalem to Gaza.

---

7. How did the Sanhedrin treat the apostles in consequence? 8. Whom did the apostles choose to attend to temporal concerns? 9. Who held the garments of Stephen's murderers? 10. Of what was Stephen's death the beginning? 11. What did many of the disciples do in consequence? 12. Whither was Philip told to proceed?

13. Philip set out at once, and was overtaken on the road by the treasurer of Queen Candace of Ethiopia, who was returning from Jerusalem, whither he had gone to worship. As he rode along, sitting in his chariot, he read aloud the prophecy of Isaias.

14. Moved by the Holy Ghost, Philip went up to him, and heard him read: "As a sheep, He was led to the slaughter, and like a lamb, without a voice, before His shearers, so He opened not His mouth."

15. Then Philip asked him: "Thinkest thou that thou understandest what thou readest?" The treasurer replied: "How can I, unless some one show me?" Philip then entered the chariot, and explained to him all the Scriptures relating to Jesus Christ.

16. After a time, they came to a stream, and the treasurer said to Philip: "See, here is water, what hindereth me from being baptized?" Philip answered: "If thou believest with thy whole heart, thou mayest!"

17. The treasurer replied: "I believe that Jesus Christ is the Son of God." He then stopped the chariot, and they both went down into the stream, in which Philip baptized him.

18. But when they came up out of the water, the Spirit of the Lord took away Philip, and the officer saw him no more. But he went on his way rejoicing.

19. Meanwhile, Saul, after conducting the persecution of the Christians in Jerusalem with the greatest ardor, went to the High-Priest, and asked for letters to the authorities in Damascus, giving him permission to arrest all the disciples of Christ in that city, and bring them prisoners to Jerusalem.

20. He obtained the letters and set out, but on the road, a bright light shone about him and he was thrown to the ground.

---

13. Who overtook him on the way? 14. What did Philip hear him read? 15. What did Philip ask him? 16. When did he ask to be baptized? 17. Continue. 18. What took place when they came out of the water? 19. What did Saul ask for? 20. What happened to him on the road?

CONVERSION OF SAUL.

At the same moment, a voice asked: "Saul, Saul, why persecutest thou Me?"

21. Saul answered: "Who art Thou, Lord?" The Voice replied; "I am Jesus, Whom thou dost persecute." Trembling with awe, Saul asked: "Lord what wilt thou have me to do?" The Lord answered: "Arise, and go into the city, and there it shall be told thee what thou must do."

22. Saul rose, but found that he was blind. His companions led him to Damascus, where he remained for three days without eating or drinking.

23. At the end of that time, Our Lord appeared to one of His disciples in Damascus, named Ananias, and said: "Arise, and go into the street that is called Strait, and seek in the house of Judas, Saul of Tarsus, for behold, he prayeth."

24. Ananias answered: "Lord, I have heard from many of this man, how great evils he hath done to thy saints at Jerusalem."

25. The Lord replied: "Go, for this man is a vessel of election to Me, to carry My Name before the Gentiles and kings, and the children of Israel. For I will show him how great things he must suffer for my Name."

26. So Ananias went to Saul, and laying his hands on him, said to him: "Saul, brother, the Lord Jesus hath sent me; He Who appeared to thee in the way as thou camest, that thou mayest receive thy sight and be filled with the Holy Ghost."

27. And at once there fell from the eyes of Saul, as it were, scales, and he recovered his sight. He was baptized and took the name of Paul, and began to preach Jesus Crucified with such ardor as to win many souls.

---

21. What did Saul answer? 22. What did Saul do? 23. Whom did the Lord then send to him? 24. What did Ananias answer? 25. What did the Lord reply? 26. What did Ananias say to Saul? 27. What happened?

CONVERSION OF SAUL.

CHAPTER III.

ST. PETER CURES THE SICK MAN.—RESTORES TABITHA TO LIFE.
—VISION OF THE UPRIGHT PAGAN, CORNELIUS.—VISION
OF PETER, ENJOINING HIM TO PREACH THE GOSPEL TO
THE GENTILES.—IMPRISONMENT AND MIRACULOUS DELIV-
ERANCE OF PETER.—PUNISHMENT OF HEROD.

1. AFTER the conversion of Saul, the Church enjoyed peace for a time, and St. Peter went through Judea and Samaria encouraging the faithful, and confirming them in the faith.

2. When he reached Lyd'-da, he found there a man who had kept his bed for eight years, on account of a palsy. The apostle said to him, "E-nē'-as, the Lord Jesus Christ healeth thee. Arise, and take thy bed." And at once he arose, cured.

3. The sight of this miracle converted all the inhabitants of Lydda. Peter was still preaching the faith to them, when he was sent for in haste by some of his disciples in Jop-pa, because a certain holy woman named Tabitha had just died there.

4. Peter hastened thither and entered the upper chamber where Tabitha lay, with many poor widows gathered about her, who showed him the garments she had made for them.

5. Peter was deeply moved. Bidding all to leave the room, he prayed. Then turning to the dead woman, he said: "Tabitha, arise." She immediately opened her eyes, and when she saw Peter, sat up. The fame of this miracle converted many to Christ.

6. There lived at this time in the city of Cesarea, a Roman centurion, named Cornelius. Although a pagan, he was a devout man, and very charitable to the poor.

7. One day, when he was at prayer, an angel appeared to him, and said: "Thy prayers and thy alms have ascended for a memorial in the sight of God. Send to Joppa, and call hither Simon,

---

1. What did Peter do during the time of peace? 2. What miracle did he perform at Lydda? 3. What was the effect of this miracle? 4. Whom did he find with Tabitha? 5. Did he restore her to life? 6.

who is surnamed Peter. He will tell thee what thou must do."

8. Cornelius therefore sent messengers to Peter. As they were drawing near Joppa, Peter went up to the house-top to pray, and was rapt in ecstasy. He saw Heaven opened, and a great net let down in which were all kinds of beasts and birds and creeping things.

9. At the same time a Voice said: "Arise, Peter, kill and eat." Now, as the net contained many animals which the Law of Moses forbade to be used as food, Peter answered that he could not eat what was common and unclean.

10. The Voice replied: "Call not that common which God hath purified." This was done three times, after which the vision disappeared. And while Peter was pondering upon its meaning, the Spirit of God directed him to go below and meet Cornelius's messengers.

11. The next day, he returned with them to Cesarea, and was met by Cornelius, who bowed down before him, and told him of his vision, and what the angel had said.

12. Peter then understood his own vision of clean and unclean animals. It signified that there was to be no difference between Jew and Gentile in the Church of Christ, because He had died for all mankind.

13. Peter therefore announced to Cornelius and his household the doctrine of Christ. And while he was still speaking, he and his disciples were astonished to hear these Gentiles speak in divers tongues, even as the apostles had done on the Day of Pentecost. And Peter commanded them all to be baptized.

14. From that time forth, the gospel was preached to the Gentiles. Paul and Barnabas preached it to them, especially at Antioch, where great numbers embraced the faith. Here,

---

8. What vision had Peter at this time? 9. What did a Voice command? 10. What did the Voice reply? 11. What did Cornelius tell Peter? 12. What did Peter understand from this? 13. What did Peter announce to Cornelius? 14. Did the apostles now preach to the Gentiles?

MIRACULOUS DELIVERANCE OF PETER.

for the first time the believers in Christ were called Christians after their Divine Founder.

15. Peter now returned to Jerusalem. The province of Judea was no longer under a Roman governor, but was ruled by Herod Agrippa, a grandson of Herod the Great, whom the Emperor Claudius had made its king in the year 43 A. D.

16. Desirous of winning the favor of the Jews, Herod had begun to persecute the Christians, and having put James, the brother of John, to death, caused Peter to be imprisoned, during the Jewish Passover, intending to put him to death after the festival was past.

17. But prayer was made unceasingly in the infant Church for its head, and on the night preceding the day fixed for his execution, an angel awakened Peter as he slept between two guards, and said to him: "Arise quickly."

18. Peter obeyed, and the chains fell from his limbs. Then the angel, having bade him gird himself and put on his sandals, led the way past the guards, into the street, where he disappeared.

19. Then Peter realized that God had indeed delivered him from the hands of Herod, and hastened to the house of Mark, a Christian, where he was received with the deepest joy.

20. In the morning, when the guards awoke, and did not find Peter, they were filled with consternation, for which there was good cause, for when Herod heard of the apostle's escape, he had them all put to death.

21. But Herod was soon punished for his impiety and cruelty. Shortly after, he received some foreign embassadors in his palace at Cesarea, and delivered an oration which drew forth the wildest plaudits from his courtiers, who declared he spoke, not as a man, but as a god.

---

15. Under whose rule was Judea when Peter returned to Jerusalem? 16. What did Herod do? 17. How were the prayers of the infant Church for Peter, answered? 18. Whither did the angel lead him? 19. Whither did Peter go? 20. What happened in the morning? 21. What of Herod?

22. This gross flattery was delightful to the vain king. But even in that hour, he was stricken with a loathsome disease, and expired, not long after, in the most awful torments—a terrible example of the pride of man, and the wrath of God.

CHAPTER IV.

FIRST MISSION OF ST. PAUL. (A. D. 45 TO 48.)—THE COUNCIL OF JERUSALEM.

1. THE Holy Ghost commanded the chief men of the Christians of Antioch to set apart Paul and Barnabas for the work to which they were called.

2. So, after they had prayed and fasted, they imposed hands upon both of them, and sent them forth to preach the gospel. Paul first preached to the Jews, but they refused the Word of Life.

3. Paul therefore turned to the Gentiles, whose special apostle he became. After preaching in different cities of Asia with great fruits, he and Barnabas went to Cyprus, an island in the Mediterranean Sea, off the coast of Asia Minor, and the birthplace of Barnabas.

4. After they had preached throughout the whole island, the Roman pro-consul or governor, Ser-gi-us Pau-lus, sent for them that he too might hear the Word of Life.

5. Now there was with Sergius a false prophet named Bar-Jesus, who put forth every effort to prevent the former from becoming a Christian. Paul, seeing this, declared to Bar-Jesus that God would punish him with blindness.

6. At once the false prophet was stricken with loss of sight. And Sergius, seeing this miracle, believed, and was baptized.

7. From Cyprus, Paul and Barnabas sailed for Asia Minor.

---

22. How was he punished?
1. What did the Holy Ghost command the chief men of Antioch to do? 2. Did they do so? 3. To whom did Paul turn? 4. Who asked to be instructed in the faith? 5. Who was with Sergius? 6. What happened? 7. Whither did they go from Cyprus?

Here, at another city called Antioch, they preached in the Jewish synagogue on the Sabbath, and pleased the people so much that they asked them to return on the following Sabbath.

8. But when that time came, the chief men among the Jews stood up and contradicted all the apostles said. Then Paul said: "To you it behooved us to speak first the Word of God, but seeing that you reject it, and judge yourselves unworthy of eternal life, behold, we turn to the Gentiles."

9. They therefore proclaimed the Gospel through the whole land to the Gentiles, who rejoiced greatly. The Jews, however, raised a persecution against the apostles, and finally expelled them from the country.

10. They therefore passed to I-cō-ni-um, where Paul cured a cripple from his birth. This miracle caused the inhabitants to view them as gods; they called Barnabas, Jupiter, on account of his height, and Paul, Mercury, on account of his eloquence.

11. Presently, the priest of Jupiter arrived at the gate of of their dwelling, with oxen, garlanded with flowers, to sacrifice in their honor.

12. At the sight, the apostles rent their garments, and hastening out among the people, cried out: "O men, why do ye these things? We also are mortals, like unto you, preaching to you to be converted from these vain things to the living God.

13. "Who made heaven, and earth, and the sea, and all things that are in them. Who, in past generations, suffered all nations to walk in their own way. Nevertheless, He left not Himself without testimony, giving rain and fruitful seasons, filling our hearts with food and gladness."

14. Hearing this, many believed in the word of God. But some Jews who had come from Antioch, stirred up those in

---

8. What did the chief men of the Jews do? 9. How was their ministry brought to a close in Antioch? 10. How were they regarded in Iconium? 11. What did the priest of Jupiter do? 12. What did the apostles say to the people? 13. What else did St. Paul say? 14. What effect had his words?

Iconium to rouse the people against Paul, so that they stoned him till they thought he was dead, and cast him out of the city.

15. But while his weeping disciples stood about him, Paul suddenly revived, and rising up, went back with them to the city. Then he and Barnabas departed to Der'be, and preached the gospel there.

16. They then made a visitation of all the cities wherein they had preached, exhorting the faithful to persevere, and ordaining priests for them in every church, and with fasting and prayer, commended them to the Lord.

17. After this was done, the two apostles returned to Antioch in Syria, and related the great things which God had done for them, and how He had opened the door of faith to the Gentiles.

18. About this time, some Christians of Antioch, who had been converted from the Jewish faith, declared that circumcision was necessary to salvation. Paul and Barnabas were opposed to this doctrine, but went up to Jerusalem to consider the matter in council with Peter and the other apostles.

19. This First General Council of the Church is known as the Council of Jerusalem, and took place about A. D. 50. After a long discussion, Peter arose and declared that circumcision was not necessary to salvation.

20. The voice of Peter finished the dispute and silenced all doubt. The Church recognized as infallible the doctrine of him whom Christ had appointed to guard the sacred deposit of faith, just as throughout the ages, she has recognized that of Peter's successors.

---

15. Did Paul revive? 16. What visitation did Paul and Barnabas make? 17. Whither did they then return? 18. What question now arose in the Church? 19. As what is this council known? 20. What effect had Peter's words?

CHAPTER V.

SECOND MISSION OF ST. PAUL.—THIRD MISSION OF ST. PAUL.
(A. D. 51 TO 54.)

1. SOME time after, St. Paul started on a second mission. After preaching with great zeal in many countries of Asia, and nearly all of Asia Minor, God directed him in a vision to pass over into Greece.

2. Paul at once set sail for the shores of Europe, in company with Silas, Luke, and Timothy, and landed safe in Philippi, the capital of Macedonia.

3. Here, on the Sabbath-day, Paul preached the gospel. Among his hearers was a pious woman named Lydia, a seller of purple, who was converted, with all her family.

4. They were not long permitted to preach in peace. One day, Paul and Silas were going, as usual, to the place of prayer, when a girl, possessed by a divining spirit, insisted on following them, crying out: "These men are servants of the Most High God, who show to you the way of salvation."

5. St. Paul, turning round, said to the spirit that possessed her: "I command thee, in the name of Jesus Christ, to go out of her." The spirit left her, whereupon her masters, to whom, when possessed, she had been a great source of gain, had the apostles arrested, beaten with rods, and imprisoned.

6. At midnight, Paul and Silas were praying, when suddenly an earthquake shook the walls of the prison to the foundations, the doors flew open, and their bonds were rent asunder.

7. The keeper of the prison was roused from sleep, and seeing the doors open, thought they had fled, and drew his sword to kill himself. But Paul cried out: "Do thyself no harm, for we are all here."

8. Then the jailer called for a light, and went in trembling,

---

1. What places did St. Paul visit on his second mission? 2. Did he go? 3. What woman was converted? 4. Who followed the apostle one day? 5. What did St. Paul do? 6. What took place at midnight? 7. What did the keeper do? 8. Was he converted?

and fell down at the apostles' feet. Then he brought them out and asked: "Masters, what must I do to be saved?" They answered: "Believe in the Lord Jesus Christ, and thou shalt be saved."

9. The jailer then dressed their wounds, and he and all his family were baptized. The next morning the magistrates released the apostles, and when they learned they were Roman citizens, begged their pardon for having ill-treated them.

10. After visiting many cities of Macedonia, St. Paul went to Athens, in Greece, where he disputed publicly in the synagogues with the Jews, and in the market-place with the pagans.

11. One day some philosophers conducted him to the Ar-e-op'-a-gus, or sovereign tribunal of Athens, and invited him to set forth his doctrine to its members.

12. St. Paul, therefore, stood up in the midst of this illustrious assemblage, and said: "Ye men of Athens, passing, and seeing your idols, I found an altar on which was written: *To The Unknown God*. What, therefore, you worship without knowing it, this I preach to you."

13. He then disclosed to them the doctrine of Jesus Christ, but only a few believed. Of them was Dī'-o-nys'-i-us, one of the most learned men of his time. He is known in the Church as Dionysius the Areopagite.

14. St. Paul then went to Corinth. Here he preached first to the Jews, but as they blasphemed God, and contradicted all he said, he was filled with just anger and said to them, "Your blood be upon your own heads; I am clean. From henceforth I will go to the Gentiles."

15. He then preached to the pagans of Corinth, many of whom were converted. After spending a year and a half in Corinth, preaching and instructing, St. Paul returned to Antioch.

---

9. Continue. 10. To what city of Greece did St. Paul go? 11. Before what learned assembly was St. Paul invited to preach? 12. How did St. Paul begin his discourse? 13. What did he disclose to them? 14. To what city did he go next? 15. How long did he stay here?

16. After spending some time in this city, St. Paul set out on a third mission. He passed through the greater part of Asia Minor, and finally came to Ephesus (ef' e-sus), the capital of the Roman province of Asia.

17. There he met some twelve disciples whom he asked: "Have you received the Holy Ghost?" They answered: "We have not so much as heard whether there be a Holy Ghost."

18. Then St. Paul asked: "In what, then, were you baptized?" They replied: "In John's baptism," meaning John the Baptist. Then Paul answered: "John baptized the people with the baptism of penance, saying that they should believe in Him who was to come after him: that is to say, Jesus."

19. Upon hearing this, they were baptized in the name of the Lord Jesus Christ. Then Paul laid his hands on them, and they received the Holy Spirit. The apostle remained for two years at Ephesus, preaching the Word of God.

20. During this time, God was pleased to work many wonderful miracles by the hand of this apostle, so that even handkerchiefs or aprons which had touched his body, cured the sick when applied to them. And the people were filled with fear, and glorified the name of Jesus.

21. Many of those who had dwelt in the magic art, brought their books, which were very valuable, and burned them before the apostle, and all the people.

22. But a certain silversmith named Demetrius, who along with his fellow-craftsmen, had been used to earn a good living by making miniature copies of the famous temple of the heathen goddess, Diana, which stood in Ephesus, denounced St. Paul for turning the people from her worship.

23. All the silversmiths joined him, crying out: "Great is Diana of the Ephesians!" A wild tumult followed, and had it

---

16. Did St. Paul undertake a third mission? 17. Whom did he meet at Ephesus? 18. What did St. Paul then ask? 19. Were they baptized again? 20. What was God pleased to do? 21. What did many do? 22. Who roused the silversmiths? 23. What followed?

not been for the persuasions of the town-clerk, the populace would have killed Paul and his disciples.

24. After peace had been restored, Paul exhorted the assembled Christians of Ephesus to persevere in the faith, and then, bidding them farewell, sailed for Macedonia. There he went to Troas, where he assembled all the faithful in an upper chamber, and preached to them till midnight.

25. During this long discourse, a young man named Eutychus, who was seated in a window, grew weary, and having fallen asleep, fell from the third story to the ground, and was taken up dead. St. Paul, hearing of the accident, went down and restored him to life.

26. After leaving Troas, the apostle visited the other principal cities of Macedonia. Thence he went to Miletus, where he sent for the clergy of Ephesus, and bade them a last tender farewell, telling them he was going to Jerusalem, not knowing what might befall him there.

27. He bade the bishops take heed how they ruled the flock over which the Holy Ghost had placed them, in the church, which He had purchased with His Blood. Then, kneeling down, he prayed with them all. Then they embraced him and accompanied him to the ship, sorrowing that they should see his face no more.

28. When St. Paul returned to Jerusalem, the Jews of that city, who hated him more than they did any other Christian, rose against him, and in order to save him from their fury, the Roman Governor of Judea imprisoned him.

29. After two years, he was sent, by his own request, to Rome, to be judged by the emperor. On the voyage, he was shipwrecked at Malta, but was saved by a miracle.

30. After his arrival in Rome, he was kept for two years in prison, but having then obtained his freedom, he began to preach the gospel as before, passing from city to city.

---

24. Whither did Paul go afterward? 25. What miracle did the apostle perform afterwards? 26. What did St. Paul do after leaving Troas? 27. What did he charge the bishops? 28. How was St. Paul treated in Jerusalem? 29. Whither was he sent after two years? 30. Did he

CHAPTER VI.

THE OTHER APOSTLES.

1. DURING these years, the other apostles had labored unceasingly to spread the gospel, and had worked many miracles, in proof of their divine mission. St. Peter, in his capacity of head of the church, visited the different churches, confirming their members in the faith.

2. St. Peter and the other apostles everywhere established bishops as their successors, who were to govern the faithful, and teach them the same doctrine that they had received from the apostles.

3. We must bear in mind that the apostles had no written books with which to convert the world. There was as yet no Bible; the apostles preached what they had heard and seen, and their successors preached what they had learnt from them.

4. Some of Our Lord's disciples, inspired of Him, wrote His life. These histories are called Gospels and were written by St. Matthew, Mark, Luke, and John the Evangelist.

5. St. Luke also wrote the Acts of the Apostles, and St. John wrote the Revelations, that is, all that God made known to him of the things that are to come.

6. Sts. Peter, Paul, James and Jude wrote several Epistles (ē-pis'ls), or Letters to the faithful of different cities, to instruct or advise them in matters relating to their faith or conduct. Portions of these are read in the Mass of each day.

7. By degrees, all these writings were gathered together, and along with much of the preaching of the apostles, form the New Testament. The unwritten preaching of the apostles has also come down to us, and is called Tradition.

8. After preaching at Jerusalem, St. Peter made Antioch the

---

1. What had the other apostles done? 2. Whom did they establish? 3. How did the apostles spread the Gospel? 4. Who wrote the Life of Our Lord? 5. What did St. Luke and St. John write? 6. What are the Epistles? 7. What do all these writings form? 8. Where did St. Peter finally fix his see?

THE HEAVENS OPENED TO ST. JOHN.

centre of his labors. Later, he fixed his Episcopal see at Rome, and from that capital of the ancient world, as the first Pope, he governed the Church for twenty-five years.

9. At length in the year A. D. 67, St. Peter gloriously suffered martyrdom under the Roman emperor Nero. He was crucified with his head downward, in which position he had begged in his humility, to suffer. On the same day, St. Paul, who had returned to Rome, also suffered martyrdom, but being a Roman citizen, was beheaded.

10. After Our Lord's death, St. John, the Beloved Disciple, took His Blessed Mother, and by his tender love, strove to supply as far as he could, for the loss of her Divine Son.

11. After her death, he was seized during a time of persecution and thrown into a caldron of boiling oil, but was saved from all harm by a miracle. He was then banished to the isle of Patmos, where He wrote His Revelations.

12. After a long period, he was allowed to come to Ephesus, where he wrote his Gospel. For many years before his death, this great saint whom Our Lord had loved so tenderly, preached but one sermon: "My children, love one another."

13. St. John died about the year A. D. 100, the only one of the apostles who died a natural death. All the others shed their blood for Christ. But the Church of Christ for which they labored with such zeal and utter devotion, continued to grow.

14. The faithful obeyed their bishops, and the bishops were obedient to St. Peter and his successors. Thus the bond of unity was maintained between the faithful and their priests, between the priests and their bishops, and between all the bishops and the Pope.

15. The Jews, who had rejected Christ, and persecuted His apostles soon experienced the Divine wrath. In the year 69, the Jews of Jerusalem revolted against Rome, and were

---

9. When did he suffer death? 10. What of St. John? 11. How was he saved from death? 12. What of the closing year of his life? 13. When did he die? 14. What was maintained in the Church? 15 What befell the Jews?

soon besieged by the Roman emperor, Titus, with a great army.

16. Within the doomed city, first famine and then pestilence raged, while one party fought against another. At last the walls fell; the city was taken, the temple burned, and the people killed or sold into slavery.

17. Ever since that time the Jews have remained scattered among different nations, without a country or a king, while Jerusalem, their Holy City, is held by infidels.

18. But the Church of Christ has flourished throughout all these ages. Time has proved the wisdom of Rabbi Gamaliel's views to the Sanhedrin, when they sought to stop it spreading.

19. "If it be the work of God, you cannot destroy it," said the Jewish Doctor. The Church is indeed, the conception and the work of God, who sealed it with His Precious Blood, and has promised that the infernal powers shall not prevail against It. TO HIS NAME BE GLORY FOR EVER AND EVER.

---

16. What took place within the city. 17. What of the Jews since that time? 18. What of the Church? 19. What were his words, and what is the Church?

www.ingramcontent.com/pod-product-compliance
Lightning Source LLC
Chambersburg PA
CBHW030408230426
43664CB00007BB/793